The Eastern
Junior League Cookbook

THE PARTICIPATING JUNIOR LEAGUES INCLUDE:

The Junior League of Albany, New York

The Junior League of Bangor, Maine

The Junior League of Bergen County, New Jersey

The Junior League of Binghamton, New York

The Junior League of Boston, Massachusetts

The Junior League of Bronxville, New York

The Junior League of Brooklyn, New York

The Junior League of Buffalo, New York

The Junior League of the Central Delaware Valley, New Jersey

The Junior League of the City of New York, New York

The Junior League of Elizabeth-Plainfield, New Jersey

The Junior League of Elmira, New York

The Junior League of Erie, Pennsylvania

The Junior League of Fall River, Massachusetts

The Junior League of Greater Bridgeport, Connecticut

The Junior League of Greater New Haven, Connecticut

The Junior League of Greater Utica, New York

The Junior League of Greater Waterbury, Connecticut

The Junior League of Greenwich, Connecticut

The Junior League of Hamilton-Burlington, Ontario

The Junior League of Harrisburg, Pennsylvania

The Junior League of Hartford, Connecticut

The Junior League of Kingston, New York

The Junior League of Lancaster, Pennsylvania

The Junior League of Lehigh Valley, Pennsylvania

Illustrations by Lauren Jarrett

The Eastern Junior League Cookbook

· ·

Edited by Ann Seranne

· ·

David McKay Company, Inc.
New York

THE EASTERN JUNIOR LEAGUE COOKBOOK

Copyright © 1980 by The Junior League of Albany, New York, Inc.; copyright © 1980 by the Junior League of Bangor, Maine, Inc.; copyright © 1980 by the Junior League of Bergen County; copyright © 1980 by The Junior League of Binghamton, Inc.; copyright © 1976 by The Junior League of Boston, Inc.; copyright © 1980 by the Bronxville Junior League; copyright © 1980 by the Junior League of Brooklyn, Inc.; copyright © 1980 by the Junior League of Buffalo, Inc.; copyright © 1973 by The Junior League of Trenton, N.J., Inc.; Recipes from New York Entertains *by The Junior League of New York City, Inc. Copyright © 1974 by The Junior League of New York, Inc. Reprinted by permission of Doubleday & Company, Inc.; copyright © 1979 by The Junior League of Elizabeth-Plainfield, New Jersey, Inc.; copyright © 1980 by The Junior League of Elmira, New York, Inc.; copyright © 1980 by the Junior League of Erie, Pennsylvania; copyright © 1980 by The Junior League of Fall River, Massachusetts; copyright © 1980 by the Junior League of Greater Bridgeport, Inc.; copyright © 1980 by The Junior League of Greater New Haven, Inc.; copyright © 1980 by the Junior League of Greater Utica; copyright © 1980 by the Junior League of Greater Waterbury, Inc.; copyright © 1976 United Publishing & Printing Corp.; copyright © 1980 by The Junior League of Hamilton-Burlington, Inc.; copyright © 1980 by The Junior League of Harrisburg, Inc.; copyright © 1979 by The Junior League of Hartford, Inc.; copyright © 1980 by The Junior League of Kingston, N.Y., Inc.; copyright © 1980 by the Junior League of Lancaster, Penna., Inc.; copyright © 1980 by the Junior League of the Lehigh Valley; copyright © 1980 by the Junior League of Monmouth County, Inc.; copyright © 1968 by The Junior League of Montclair, Inc.; copyright © by The Junior League of Montreal, Quebec, Canada; copyright © 1980 by the Junior League of Morristown, New Jersey, Inc.; copyright © 1980 by The Junior League of New Britain, Inc.; copyright © 1980 by the Junior League of the North Shore; copyright © 1980 by The Junior League of Northern Westchester, Bedford Hills, New York; copyright © by The Junior League of Orange County, New York; copyright © 1980 by The Junior League of the Oranges and Short Hills, Inc.; Recipes from* Bicentennial Cookbook *by The Junior League of Philadelphia, Inc., copyright © 1975, by The Junior League of Philadelphia, Inc., reprinted by permission of Chilton Book Company; copyright © 1974 by The Junior League of Pittsburgh, Inc.; copyright © 1976 Dutchess County Historical Society, Inc.; copyright © 1977, 1966 by The Junior League of Reading, Pa., Inc.; copyright © 1980 by the Junior League of Rochester, New York, Inc.; copyright © 1980 by the Junior League of Schenectady, Inc.; copyright © 1980 by the Junior League of Scranton; copyright © 1980 by the Junior League of Springfield, Massachusetts, Inc.; copyright © 1980 by the Junior League of Stamford-Norwalk, Inc.; copyright © 1980 by The Junior League of Summit, Inc.; copyright © 1980 by the Junior League of Syracuse, Inc.; copyright © 1980 by The Junior League of Troy, New York; copyright © 1980 by the Junior League of Westchester-on-Hudson, Inc.; copyright © 1980 by the Junior League of Wilkes-Barre, inc.; copyright © 1980 by the Junior League of Williamsport, Pennsylvania; copyright © 1980 the Junior League of Wilmington, Inc.; copyright © 1980 The Junior League of Worcester; copyright © 1980 by the Junior League of York; Illustrations copyright © 1977, 1978, 1979, 1980 by David McKay Company, Inc.*

Library of Congress Cataloging in Publication Data

Main entry under title:

The Eastern Junior League cookbook.

    Includes index.
    1. Cookery, American–Middle Atlantic States.
2. Cookery, American–Northwestern States. I. Seranne, Ann, 1914–
TX715.E169   641.5   80-18107
ISBN 0-679-51003-6

Manufactured in the United States of America

1 2 3 4 5 6 7 8 9 10

Preface

The purposes of the Junior League:

- To promote voluntarism
- To develop the potential of its members for voluntary participation in community affairs
- To demonstrate the effectiveness of trained volunteers

Proceeds from the sale of Junior League cookbooks go into the Community Trust Funds, which finance the League's community programs.

To find out how to obtain a particular League's own book of recipes, turn to pages 409–13.

Contents

Metric Equivalent Chart

LENGTH

1 inch (in)	=	2.5 centimeters (cm)
1 foot (ft)	=	30 centimeters (cm)
1 millimeter (mm)	=	.04 inches (in)
1 centimeter (cm)	=	.4 inches (in)
1 meter (m)	=	3.3 feet (ft)

MASS WEIGHT

1 ounce (oz)	=	28 grams (g)
1 pound (lb)	=	450 grams (g)
1 gram (g)	=	.035 ounces (oz)
1 kilogram (kg) or 1000 g	=	2.2 pounds (lbs)

LIQUID VOLUME

1 fluid ounce (fl. oz.)	=	30 milliliters (ml)
1 fluid cup (c)	=	240 milliliters (ml)
1 pint (pt)	=	470 milliliters (ml)
1 quart (qt)	=	950 milliliters (ml)
1 gallon (gal)	=	3.8 liters (l)
1 milliliter (ml)	=	.03 fluid ounces (fl. oz)
1 liter (l) or 1000 ml	=	2.1 fluid pints or 1.06 fluid quarts
1 liter (l)	=	.26 gallons (gal)

Appetizers

Delightful Ham Rolls

12 thin slices boiled ham
1 8-ounce package cream cheese
1 cup finely chopped nuts
1 garlic clove, chopped
Mayonnaise

Have butcher slice boiled ham paper-thin. Combine cream cheese, nuts, and garlic; add a small amount of mayonnaise. Do not get mixture too thin. Spread each slice of ham with mixture and roll as for jelly roll. Chill thoroughly; cut into three or four slices.

Serve each slice on round cracker.

YIELD: 12 SERVINGS

5 O'Clock Sustainers
THE JUNIOR LEAGUE OF SCRANTON, PENNSYLVANIA

. . . .

Bourbon Hot Dogs

1 pound hot dogs
½ cup brown sugar
2 ounces bourbon
2 tablespoons catsup
½ teaspoon dry mustard
1 tablespoon Worcestershire sauce

Broil hot dogs on both sides. If not using cocktail hot dogs, cut regular hot dogs into five pieces each. Mix hot dogs with remaining ingredients and cook slowly until syrupy. If there is not enough sauce, add a little more brown sugar, bourbon, and catsup. Heat before serving in chafing dish or ramekin.

YIELD: 12 SERVINGS

5 O'Clock Sustainers
THE JUNIOR LEAGUE OF SCRANTON, PENNSYLVANIA

· · · · · · · · · · · · · · · · · ·

Sweet-n-Sour Meat Balls

2 pounds ground round
3 slices bread
1 onion, chopped
2 teaspoons Worcestershire sauce
Garlic salt and pepper
Salad oil

Mix all ingredients and shape into 60 tiny meat balls. Brown on all sides in frying pan in a little salad oil. Drain and set aside.

YIELD: ABOUT 60 MEATBALLS

SAUCE:
1 8-ounce can tomato sauce
1 8-ounce jar grape jelly

Combine ingredients in saucepan and heat through, stirring.

Add meat balls to hot sauce in a fondue or chafing dish. No one will guess grape jelly is an ingredient.

YIELD: 2 CUPS

THE JUNIOR LEAGUE OF SCHENECTADY, NEW YORK

· · · · · · · · · · · · · · · · · ·

Mushroom-Cheese Rolls

1 long loaf thin-sliced, fine-textured white bread
1 large onion, finely chopped
½ pound fresh mushrooms, finely chopped
¾ stick butter (6 tablespoons), melted
1 8-ounce package cream cheese, softened
Salt and pepper to taste

Cut off crusts and roll bread out thinly with rolling pin.

Sauté onion and mushrooms in half the butter until onions are soft. Mash the onion-mushroom mixture into the cream cheese and add salt and pepper.

Spread about 1 tablespoon of the mixture on each piece of bread and roll. Cut each roll in half, brush with rest of melted butter, and brown at 350° for 15 minutes.

YIELD: 52 HORS D'OEUVRES

THE JUNIOR LEAGUE OF NEW BRITAIN, CONNECTICUT

· · · · · · · · · · · · · · · · · · · ·

Marvelous Mussels

5 dozen large mussels
3 tablespoons tomato purée
2 tablespoons lemon juice
1 tablespoon sherry
1 tablespoon cognac
1 clove garlic, minced
½ onion, minced
½ cup water
2 cups mayonnaise
1½ tablespoons sour cream
1 tablespoon horseradish
Salt to taste
Chives or red caviar for garnish

Steam mussels in covered kettle in 2 cups of water until shells open.

In a saucepan, put the next seven ingredients and simmer until mixture is reduced by two-thirds. Remove from heat and stir in remaining ingredients except garnish. Chill sauce.

Leave bottom shells on mussels and top each with sauce. Garnish with chopped chives or a dab of red caviar.

YIELD: 10 SERVINGS

Entirely Entertaining
THE JUNIOR LEAGUE OF MONTCLAIR-NEWARK, NEW JERSEY

Super Shrimp Elegant

MUST BE MADE 24 HOURS IN ADVANCE.
¾ cup olive oil
3 cloves garlic, minced
2 white onions, minced
3 pounds large shrimp, cooked, shelled, and deveined
½ cup vinegar
1 teaspoon salt
½ teaspoon pepper
1 teaspoon dry mustard
½ teaspoon celery salt

Heat ¼ cup oil in heavy skillet; add garlic and onions. Sauté lightly. Add shrimp and sauté for 5 minutes, *stirring constantly.*

Make marinade in bowl from remaining oil, vinegar, and seasonings. Add shrimp and toss thoroughly. Chill up to 24 hours.

Serve cold and use wooden picks to pluck them out of the sauce. Small crusts of French bread are good to use to dip in the sauce.

YIELD: 12 SERVINGS

Before and After Thoughts
THE JUNIOR LEAGUE OF PITTSBURGH, PENNSYLVANIA

Shrimp Puffs

12 shrimp, cooked
1 egg white
¼ cup grated Parmesan cheese
⅛ teaspoon salt
⅛ teaspoon paprika
Dash red pepper
½ cup mayonnaise
Crackers or rounds of toast

Preheat broiler. Cut shrimp in half lengthwise.

Beat egg white until stiff. Fold in cheese, spices, and mayonnaise. Spread mixture on crackers or toast. Top each with a shrimp. Broil until light brown, about 2 minutes. Serve hot.

YIELD: 24 APPETIZERS

THE JUNIOR LEAGUE OF BRONXVILLE, NEW YORK

. . . .

Bite-Size Spinach Egg Foo Yong

CAN BE PREPARED AHEAD AND CHILLED.
3 eggs, lightly beaten
½ 10-ounce package frozen chopped spinach, cooked and drained (½ cup)
½ cup finely chopped water chestnuts
¼ cup finely chopped green pepper
¼ cup finely chopped onion
¼ teaspoon salt
⅛ teaspoon pepper
Brown Sauce

Combine all ingredients except Brown Sauce. Drop 1 teaspoon of mixture at a time into a well-greased frying pan. Brown on both sides over medium-high heat.

Before serving, place on baking sheet, cover, and bake at 300° for 20–25 minutes. Serve with the Brown Sauce.

BROWN SAUCE:
2 tablespoons melted butter
4 teaspoons cornstarch
2 teaspoons sugar
1 cup water
3 tablespoons soy sauce

Blend all ingredients together until smooth.

YIELD: 3 DOZEN APPETIZERS

Hors D'Oeuvres Cookbook
THE JUNIOR LEAGUE OF READING, PENNSYLVANIA

. . . .

Spinach Squares

1 cup milk
1 cup flour
3 eggs, beaten
½ teaspoon baking powder
1 clove garlic, finely chopped
1 pound white Monterey Jack cheese, shredded
4 10-ounce packages frozen spinach, thawed and drained
¼ cup butter

In large bowl, combine milk, flour, eggs, baking powder, and garlic. Mix well. Add cheese and spinach. Melt butter in bottom of 9 x 12-inch baking pan. Pour spinach mixture into pan; pat down and into corners.

Recipe continues . . .

Bake at 350° for 30 minutes, or until edges are brown. Cool completely; cut into 1-inch squares. If desired, quick-freeze, then drop into plastic bags and store in freezer. Heat in 350° oven for 15 minutes without defrosting.

YIELD: 108 1- INCH SQUARES

THE JUNIOR LEAGUE OF GREATER BRIDGEPORT, CONNECTICUT

. . . .

Carol Lee's Sauerkraut Balls

1 pound bulk sausage, crumbled
¼ cup finely chopped onion
1 14-ounce can sauerkraut, drained and chopped
2 tablespoons dry bread crumbs
1 3-ounce package cream cheese, softened
2 tablespoons parsley
1 teaspoon prepared mustard
Garlic salt or minced fresh garlic to taste
¼ teaspoon pepper
¼ cup flour
¼ cup milk
2 eggs, well beaten
Additional bread crumbs for coating

In skillet, cook sausage and onion until onion is brown. Drain. Add sauerkraut and the 2 tablespoons bread crumbs. Combine cream cheese, parsley, mustard, garlic, and pepper. Stir into sauerkraut mixture. Chill.

Shape mixture into 24 balls. Coat with flour.

Add milk to beaten eggs. Dip floured balls into egg mixture and roll in bread crumbs. Fry in deep fat heated to 365°. Freeze. When ready to serve, bake frozen balls at 375° for 20 minutes.

YIELD: 24 SERVINGS

THE JUNIOR LEAGUE OF ERIE, PENNSYLVANIA

. . . .

Sauerkraut Balls

1 medium onion
2 tablespoons butter
1 cup minced ham
1 cup minced corned beef
¼ teaspoon garlic salt
1 tablespoon prepared mustard
3 tablespoons fresh chopped parsley
⅛ teaspoon pepper
½ teaspoon Worcestershire sauce
2 cups sauerkraut, very well drained and chopped
½ cup flour
2 eggs, well beaten
½ cup cracker crumbs
Cooking oil

Sauté onion in butter until wilted. Add ham and beef and cook for 5 minutes. Mix with next six ingredients. Cook for 10 minutes. Refrigerate for at least 1 hour. Shape into balls and refrigerate 1 hour more.

Roll in flour, then egg, then cracker crumbs. Fry at 370° until brown. Serve hot on warming tray.

YIELD: 5 DOZEN BALLS

Before and After Thoughts
THE JUNIOR LEAGUE OF PITTSBURGH, PENNSYLVANIA

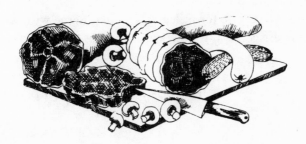

Marinated Antipasto

1 cup catsup
1 cup chili sauce
1 cup water
½ cup olive oil
½ cup tarragon vinegar
½ cup lemon juice
1 clove garlic, minced
2 tablespoons brown sugar
1 tablespoon Worcestershire sauce
1 teaspoon horseradish
Dash cayenne
Salt to taste
½ head cauliflower, cut into bite-size pieces
3 medium carrots, thinly sliced
2 stalks celery, diced
½ pound small mushrooms, trimmed
1 8-ounce jar pepperoncini, drained and diced
1 6-ounce can artichoke hearts, quartered
3 7½-ounce cans tuna, drained
1 6½-ounce can shrimp, drained
1 1-pound can cut green beans, drained

Combine first twelve ingredients in a saucepan and simmer for 3 minutes. Add cauliflower, carrots, celery, mushrooms, pepperoncini, and artichoke hearts to the marinade and simmer for 20 minutes, or until vegetables are tender but crunchy. Add tuna, shrimp, and green beans. Simmer for 5 more minutes.

Cool and refrigerate for at least 24 hours. Serve with wheat crackers. Keeps in refrigerator for at least 2 weeks.

YIELD: 8 SERVINGS

THE JUNIOR LEAGUE OF SCHENECTADY, NEW YORK

Asparagus Tart

2 pounds asparagus, cut into 3-inch lengths
¼ cup butter
¼ cup flour
½ cup milk
¾ cup cream
1 cup shredded Gruyère cheese
Salt and white pepper to taste
1 9-inch baked pastry shell

Cook asparagus in small amount of water until barely tender. Drain and dry.

In a saucepan, melt butter, add flour, and cook for 3 minutes, stirring. Stir in milk and cream; cook, stirring constantly, until thick and smooth. Stir in ½ cup of the cheese, salt, and pepper.

Arrange asparagus in pastry shell and spoon sauce over it. Sprinkle with remaining ½ cup cheese. Bake on upper shelf of oven at 400° for 12–15 minutes.

YIELD: 6–8 SERVINGS

THE JUNIOR LEAGUE OF LANCASTER, PENNSYLVANIA

Clam Lovers' Baked Clams

26 ounces minced clams or 4 6½-ounce cans, drained
1 large onion, chopped
3 cloves garlic, finely minced
8 tablespoons olive oil
1 cup chopped fresh parsley
2 teaspoons oregano
Salt and pepper to taste
6–8 slices soft white bread, trimmed and cubed
24 medium-size clam or scallop shells (real or ceramic)
Grated Parmesan cheese

Drain clams and reserve half the liquid.

Sauté onion and garlic in olive oil until onion is transparent. Add parsley, oregano, salt, and pepper; stir to mix. Add bread cubes and toss until oil is absorbed and all cubes are coated. Add clams and reserved liquid; stir gently to mix.

Fill shells with clam mixture and sprinkle with Parmesan cheese. Bake on a shallow pan at 350° for about ½ hour, or until slightly brown and bubbly.

YIELD: 24 SHELLS

THE JUNIOR LEAGUE OF BERGEN COUNTY, NEW JERSEY

. . . .

Clams Casino

½ stick butter
4 tablespoons olive oil
2 cloves garlic, minced
2 tablespoons chopped parsley
2 teaspoons lemon juice
1 teaspoon oregano
½ cup dry bread crumbs
30 cherrystone clams
10 slices bacon

Heat oven to 425°. Combine all ingredients except clams and bacon. Stir over low heat until butter is melted and ingredients are blended.

Open clams, discard top shells, and pour off some of the liquid. Top each with 1 teaspoon of the bread mixture and cover with 1/3 slice bacon. Arrange shells on baking sheet and bake for approximately 12–15 minutes, or until bacon is crisp.

YIELD: 5 SERVINGS

Entirely Entertaining
THE JUNIOR LEAGUE OF MONTCLAIR-NEWARK, NEW JERSEY

Deviled Clams

½ cup finely chopped onion
½ cup finely chopped celery
½ cup finely chopped green pepper
4 tablespoons butter
2 tablespoons flour
1 tablespoon grated Parmesan cheese
Salt and pepper to taste
½ teaspoon Worcestershire sauce
24 cocktail crackers, crushed
1 7½-ounce can minced clams
1 tablespoon melted butter
12 clam or scallop shells (real or ceramic)

In medium skillet, cook onion, celery, and green pepper in the 4 tablespoons of butter until tender. Stir in flour, cheese, salt, pepper and Worcestershire sauce. Add ½ cup cracker crumbs and mix well. Stir in undrained minced clams. Cook and stir until mixture thickens. Fill shells.

Combine remaining crumbs and the 1 tablespoon butter and sprinkle on top of shells. Bake at 350° for 15 minutes.

YIELD: 12 SHELLS

THE JUNIOR LEAGUE OF FALL RIVER, MASSACHUSETTS

Coquilles St. Jacques

1 cup dry sherry
2 pounds sea scallops, washed and drained
6 tablespoons butter
¼ cup finely chopped onion
¼ cup unsifted flour
½ cup milk
1 cup light cream
½ pound mushrooms, sliced
1 tablespoon Worcestershire sauce
⅛ teaspoon pepper
2 tablespoons melted butter
½ cup cornflake crumbs

Pour ½ cup sherry over scallops in saucepan. Mix well and bring to a slow boil. Remove from heat. Drain, reserving liquid. Cut scallops in halves or quarters and return to the sherry liquid.

Heat 4 tablespoons butter in medium-size saucepan and in it sauté onion for about 5 minutes, or until tender. Remove from heat; stir in flour. Gradually stir in milk and cream. Bring to a boil, stirring. Reduce heat; simmer, stirring frequently, for about 8–10 minutes, or until sauce is quite thick. Remove from heat.

Meanwhile, in remaining butter in medium skillet, sauté mushrooms for 5 minutes, or until golden brown.

Add Worcestershire sauce, pepper, and remaining ½ cup sherry to sauce; stir in scallops in sherry and the mushrooms. Turn into 8 scallop shells (real or ceramic) or a 1½-quart casserole.

Mix the 2 tablespoons melted butter with the cornflake crumbs. (If using casserole, use only 1 tablespoon butter and ¼ cup crumbs.) Sprinkle over scallops. Place shells on cookie sheet and bake for 20 minutes in oven preheated to 350°, or until mixture is bubbly and crumbs are lightly browned. (Bake casserole 25 minutes.)

YIELD: 8 SERVINGS

Hors D'Oeuvres Cookbook
THE JUNIOR LEAGUE OF READING, PENNSYLVANIA

Crabmeat Stuffed Eggs

12 hard-boiled eggs
¾ cup cooked crabmeat
½ cup chopped celery
1 teaspoon dry mustard
½ teaspoon salt
1/3 cup mayonnaise
Paprika

Cut eggs in half lengthwise; remove yolks and mash. Remove any cartilage from crabmeat; break meat into small pieces. Combine crabmeat, egg yolks, celery, mustard, salt, and mayonnaise. Mix well. Stuff egg whites with mixture; sprinkle with paprika.

YIELD: 12 SERVINGS

5 O'Clock Sustainers
THE JUNIOR LEAGUE OF SCRANTON, PENNSYLVANIA

Cheddar Beer Dip

12 ounces cream cheese
1½ cups beer
16 ounces cheddar cheese, cubed
2 cloves garlic
24 small gherkins

Put cream cheese and 1¼ cups of beer into blender. Cover and blend on high speed for 8 seconds. Add remaining beer, cheddar cheese, and garlic. Cover and blend on high speed about 30 seconds, or until smooth. Add gherkins and blend 2 or 3 seconds more, or until chopped.

Recipe continues . . .

Pour into chilled bowl and serve with carrot sticks or garlic-flavored crackers.

YIELD: 36 SERVINGS

5 O'Clock Sustainers
THE JUNIOR LEAGUE OF SCRANTON, PENNSYLVANIA

· · · · · · · · · · · · · · · · · · · ·

Pimento Cheese Dip

2 cups shredded pimento cheese,
1/2 cup sour cream
1 3-ounce package cream cheese, softened
1/2 cup tomato juice cocktail
2 green chili peppers, seeded and chopped
3 slices bacon, crisply cooked, drained, and crumbled

In small mixing bowl, combine pimento cheese, sour cream, cream cheese, tomato juice, and chilies. Beat with electric beater until light and fluffy. Stir in crumbled bacon. Chill.

Serve with vegetables and/or crackers.

YIELD: 2 CUPS

Hors D'Oeuvres Cookbook
THE JUNIOR LEAGUE OF READING, PENNSYLVANIA

· · · · · · · · · · · · · · · · · · · ·

Sesame Bar

1/2 stick butter
2 tablespoons sesame seeds
1 8-ounce package cream cheese
Assorted crackers
Parsley for garnish

In a medium skillet, melt the butter. When very lightly browned, add sesame seeds and brown over medium heat. When seeds are brown, remove from stove.

Place cream cheese in the center of the pan and, using a spatula and knife, frost it with all of the sesame seeds and butter, covering all sides. Transfer to a plate and put in freezer for 15 minutes.

Serve on a cheese tray surrounded with assorted crackers. Garnish with parsley.

YIELD: 6 SERVINGS

Cooks Book
THE JUNIOR LEAGUE OF GREATER NEW HAVEN, CONNECTICUT

· · · · · · · · · · · · · · ·

Chicken Liver Paté

½ pound chicken livers, cleaned and chopped
½ cup butter
1 onion, chopped
1–2 cloves garlic
1 bay leaf
1–2 tablespoons sherry

Cook all ingredients except sherry for 1 hour in covered pot over low heat. Cool. Discard bay leaf and purée in blender. Stir in sherry. Empty into serving dish and refrigerate.

Serve with toast triangles.

YIELD: 1 CUP

THE JUNIOR LEAGUE OF MONTREAL, QUEBEC

· · · · · · · · · · · · · · ·

Hot Clam Cracker Spread

2 8-ounce cans minced clams and liquid
1 cup bread crumbs
Garlic powder to taste
2 tablespoons parsley flakes
1 tablespoon oregano
¼ pound butter or margarine, melted
1 tablespoon lemon juice
Salt and pepper to taste

Mix all ingredients. Spoon into 9-inch pie pan or small baking dish. Bake for 15 minutes at 350°.

Serve with crackers.

YIELD: 8 SERVINGS

THE JUNIOR LEAGUE OF WILKES-BARRE, PENNSYLVANIA

Cranlilli

1 cup fresh cranberries
1 medium onion, quartered
1 medium green pepper, quartered
½ cup sugar
½ cup vinegar
¾ teaspoon salt

Put cranberries, onion, and pepper through food grinder. Combine all ingredients in saucepan, cover, and simmer for 10 minutes. Uncover and simmer for 10 more minutes.

Chill or seal in sterile jars.

Pour over a brick of cream cheese for a festive spread on crackers. Makes a nice gift.

YIELD: 1 PINT

THE JUNIOR LEAGUE OF BERGEN COUNTY, NEW JERSEY

Hot Crab

6-7 ounces frozen king crab, thawed and partially drained
Lemon juice
1 8-ounce package cream cheese at room temperature
1 teaspoon grated onion
1/4 teaspoon Worcestershire sauce
1/8-1/4 teaspoon curry
Slivered almonds

Break up crabmeat, sprinkle with lemon juice, and mix thoroughly with cream cheese, grated onion, and Worcestershire sauce. Season with curry to taste.

Spoon into heat-and-serve dish and bake at 350° for about 20 minutes, or until bubbly. Sprinkle with almonds and broil until almonds are browned. Serve with crackers.

YIELD: 1 PINT

THE JUNIOR LEAGUE OF BERGEN COUNTY, NEW JERSEY

Douglas's Curry Spread

½ pound cheddar cheese, coarsely shredded
1 cup chopped ripe olives
2 bunches green onion, chopped
1 cup mayonnaise
1 teaspoon curry (or to taste)

Mix all ingredients well. Spread on buttered plain melba toast rounds. Broil until bubbly, about 4 minutes. Serve immediately.

This spread will last for weeks if covered tightly and refrigerated.

YIELD: 20 SERVINGS

Before and After Thoughts
THE JUNIOR LEAGUE OF PITTSBURGH, PENNSYLVANIA

. . . .

Eggplant Caviar

2 large eggplants
2 large onions, chopped
2 green peppers, chopped
1 cup olive oil
2 large cloves garlic, minced
4 fresh tomatoes, peeled and chopped
Salt and pepper to taste
4 tablespoons dry white wine

Bake eggplants in 400° oven until soft, about 1 hour.

Sauté onions and peppers in oil until soft. Add garlic and cook a few more minutes. *Do not brown.* Peel and chop eggplants; add with tomatoes to the sauté mixture. Salt and pepper to taste. Add wine, mix thoroughly, and cook until fairly thick. Cool, then chill overnight.

Serve with *thinly* sliced pumpernickel or rye bread.

YIELD: 50 SERVINGS

THE JUNIOR LEAGUE OF WORCESTER, MASSACHUSETTS

Eggplant Spread

1 large eggplant, peeled and cut into small pieces
3-4 tablespoons olive oil
1 cup chopped onion
1 cup diced celery
1 10-ounce can stewed tomatoes
1 tablespoon capers
¼ cup cider vinegar
2 tablespoons sugar
Salt and pepper to taste

Sauté eggplant in oil until soft and lightly browned. Remove eggplant. Sauté onion and celery until tender in oil remaining in pan. Add tomatoes and simmer, covered, for 15 minutes. Return eggplant to pan; add capers, vinegar, sugar, salt, and pepper. Cover and simmer 20 minutes. Cool, then refrigerate.

Serve in a bowl surrounded by toast rounds or crackers.

This spread will keep well for several days in the refrigerator. It can also be frozen.

YIELD: 1 QUART

THE JUNIOR LEAGUE OF MONTREAL, QUEBEC

Curried Egg Spread

3 hard-boiled eggs, minced
2 tablespoons mayonnaise
1 tablespoon anchovy paste
1 teaspoon lemon juice
1 tablespoon finely shredded cheddar cheese
1 teaspoon minced onion
½ teaspoon curry powder

Combine all ingredients. Refrigerate until needed. Serve with bland crackers or party rye bread.

YIELD: 12 SERVINGS

Before and After Thoughts
THE JUNIOR LEAGUE OF PITTSBURGH, PENNSYLVANIA

Tapenade
(Provençal Dip)

1 cup chopped Italian or Greek black olives
15–16 flat anchovy filets, chopped
¼–1/3 cup chopped parsley
1/3 cup capers
1 7-ounce can tuna in water, drained and finely flaked
2 tablespoons cognac
1 teaspoon dry mustard
1½ cups mayonnaise
Hard-boiled eggs, quartered, and tomato wedges for garnish

Combine all ingredients except garnishes and blend thoroughly. Let "ripen" at room temperature for several hours.

Mound on a plate; garnish with egg and tomato wedges. Serve as a dip with raw vegetables, sesame crackers, or French bread.

YIELD: 3 CUPS

Greenwich Recommends
THE JUNIOR LEAGUE OF GREENWICH, CONNECTICUT

Watercress Dip

¼ cup sour cream
12 ounces cream cheese, cut into chunks
⅛ teaspoon garlic salt
½ teaspoon salt
¼ teaspoon pepper
1½ teaspoons horseradish
2 tablespoons lemon juice
1 small onion, sliced and separated into rings
1 bunch watercress leaves

Place all ingredients and one-quarter of the watercress into blender. Blend, covered, at high speed until mixture is partially blended. Remove cover and add remaining watercress, a little at a time. Blend until mixture is smooth. Total blending time—2 minutes.

Serve with chips.

YIELD: 2 CUPS

Hors D'Oeuvres Cookbook
THE JUNIOR LEAGUE OF READING, PENNSYLVANIA

Beignets Soufflés aux Fromages with Mustard Hollandaise

½ cup water
2 tablespoons butter
Dash cayenne
1/3 teaspoon salt
½ cup flour
2 eggs
1 teaspoon prepared mustard
2 small sections Camembert cheese, at room temperature
1 tablespoon grated Parmesan cheese

Bring first four ingredients to a boil slowly, then add the flour all at once. Cook, stirring, until mixture forms a ball in center of pan. Remove from heat. Beat in eggs, one at a time. Beat in mustard and Camembert cheese. Chill in refrigerator at least 1 hour.

When ready to cook, drop mixture by the ½ teaspoonful into oil heated to 365° and fry until golden. Drain on paper toweling. Roll in Parmesan cheese.

Serve hot on toothpicks with Mustard Hollandaise for dipping.

YIELD: ABOUT 24 BEIGNETS SOUFFLÉS

MUSTARD HOLLANDAISE:
2 egg yolks
1 teaspoon tarragon vinegar
4 teaspoons light cream
Dash cayenne
2 teaspoons prepared mustard
1 tablespoon soft butter

Mix all ingredients in top of double boiler. Be sure water in lower part of double boiler doesn't touch bottom of top part. Stir with whisk over hot water until thick. May be made ahead of time and refrigerated, but before reheating bring to room temperature for at least 1 hour.

YIELD: ABOUT ½ CUP

THE JUNIOR LEAGUE OF THE NORTH SHORE, LONG ISLAND, NEW YORK

Cheese Fondue

1 pound Swiss cheese, shredded
3 tablespoons flour
1 clove garlic
2 cups dry white wine
1 tablespoon lemon juice
3 tablespoons kirsch
Nutmeg and pepper to taste
2 loaves Italian or French bread, untrimmed and cut into cubes

Dredge the cheese lightly with flour. Rub the cooking pot with garlic. Pour in wine and set over moderate heat. When air bubbles rise to surface, add lemon juice, then add cheese by handfuls, stirring constantly with wooden fork or spoon until cheese is melted. Add kirsch and spices, stirring until blended.

Serve and keep bubbling hot over burner. Spear bread cubes through the soft side into crust, dunk, and swirl in fondue.

YIELD: 16 SERVINGS

5 O'Clock Sustainers
THE JUNIOR LEAGUE OF SCRANTON, PENNSYLVANIA

Cheese Pennies

¹/₂ pound shredded sharp cheddar cheese
¹/₄ pound sweet butter, softened
1¹/₂ cups sifted unbleached flour
¹/₂ teaspoon salt
Dash cayenne

Cream cheese and butter thoroughly. Blend in flour, salt, and cayenne and work into a smooth dough. Form dough into rolls about 1 inch in diameter and wrap in wax paper. Refrigerate for at least 2 hours.

Slice rolls into wafers about 1/3 inch thick. Arrange on ungreased cookie sheet. Bake in a 400° oven until golden, about 12–15 minutes.

YIELD: 2 DOZEN PENNIES

THE JUNIOR LEAGUE OF BROOKLYN, NEW YORK

· · · · · · · · · · · · · · · · · ·

Brooklyn Cheese Puffs

¹/₄ pound butter (¹/₂ cup), softened
3 ounces cheddar cheese at room temperature
2/3 cup flour
1 pound fresh ricotta cheese
1 teaspoon salt
¹/₄ teaspoon pepper
2 tablespoons chopped parsley
1 egg

Blend butter and cheese. Add remaining ingredients and combine thoroughly. Drop by teaspoonfuls onto a baking sheet and freeze. *These must be frozen.* Remove from sheet to plastic bags and store in freezer.

When ready to serve, bake in preheated 450° oven for 10 minutes, or until browned. Lightly salt. Serve hot!

YIELD: 50 PUFFS

THE JUNIOR LEAGUE OF BROOKLYN, NEW YORK

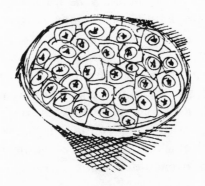

Reading Cheese Puffs

1 loaf firm unsliced white bread
1 3-ounce package cream cheese
¼ pound sharp cheddar cheese, diced
½ cup butter or margarine
2 egg whites, stiffly beaten

Trim crusts from bread and cut bread into 1-inch cubes.

Melt cheeses and butter in top of double boiler over hot water until of rarebit consistency. Remove from heat and fold in beaten egg whites.

Dip bread cubes into cheese mixture until well coated. Place on cookie sheet and refrigerate overnight. Bake at 400° for 12–15 minutes, or until puffy and golden brown.

YIELD: 4 DOZEN PUFFS

Hors D'Oeuvres Cookbook
THE JUNIOR LEAGUE OF READING, PENNSYLVANIA

Sesame Cheese Straws

1 cup flour
½ teaspoon salt
¼ teaspoon dry mustard
⅛ teaspoon cayenne
1/3 cup butter
1½ cups shredded cheddar cheese
1½ tablespoons water
1 teaspoon sesame seeds

Preheat oven to 350°.

Sift flour, salt, mustard, and cayenne into a bowl. Add butter and ½ cup of the cheese. Cut mixture to a coarse consistency. Add water. Toss mixture into a ball. Roll to ⅛-inch thickness on lightly floured board. Sprinkle with ½ cup cheese, fold over, and repeat with remaining cheese. Again roll to ⅛-inch thickness and cut into strips 4 x ½ inch. Sprinkle with sesame seeds and bake on a cookie sheet 12–15 minutes.

YIELD: 5–6 DOZEN PIECES

Hors D'Oeuvres Cookbook
THE JUNIOR LEAGUE OF READING, PENNSYLVANIA

. . . .

Cheese Mousse

1 envelope unflavored gelatin
½ cup cold water
2 cups commercial sour cream
2 teaspoons Italian salad dressing mix
½ cup crumbled blue cheese
1 cup small-curd cream-style cottage cheese
Parsley for garnish

Soften gelatin in cold water. Place over boiling water, stirring until gelatin dissolves. Stir into sour cream mixed with salad dressing mix, blue cheese, and cottage cheese. Beat until well blended. Pour into 3½-cup ring mold or small loaf pan. Chill until firm.

Unmold onto platter, garnish with parsley, and serve with assorted crackers.

YIELD: 12 SERVINGS

Hors D'Oeuvres Cookbook
THE JUNIOR LEAGUE OF READING, PENNSYLVANIA

. . . .

Chicken Nuggets

2 cups Italian-style seasoned bread crumbs
¼ cup grated Parmesan cheese
¼ cup chopped parsley
⅛ teaspoon salt
⅛ teaspoon pepper
4 chicken breasts, boned and cut into small bite-size pieces
1 stick butter (½ cup), melted

Combine bread crumbs, cheese, parsley, salt, and pepper. Dip chicken first into melted butter, then into bread crumb mixture. Bake at 400° for 15 minutes.

Can be frozen all prepared and baked when needed.

YIELD: 60 NUGGETS

Hors D'Oeuvres Cookbook
THE JUNIOR LEAGUE OF READING, PENNSYLVANIA

. . . .

Varm Krabbsmorgas

½ pound crabmeat
1 tablespoon dry sherry
1 teaspoon salt
⅛ teaspoon white pepper
1 tablespoon chopped fresh dill
1 tablespoon butter
2 tablespoons flour
1 egg yolk
1 cup light cream
1 loaf party-size bread

In large mixing bowl, combine crabmeat, sherry, salt, pepper, and dill. Set aside.

In saucepan, melt butter; remove from heat and stir in flour. In a small bowl, beat egg yolk with cream, then briskly stir into butter/flour roux with a wire whisk. Return pan to heat and cook slowly, whisking constantly, for 1–2 minutes, or until mixture thickens; do not let it boil. Pour sauce over crabmeat and stir until well combined.

Toast bread on one side only. Spread untoasted side generously with crabmeat mixture, mounding it slightly. May be prepared in advance up to this point and refrigerated.

Just before serving, place under a hot broiler for a minute or so until hot and lightly browned.

YIELD: APPROXIMATELY 24 PIECES

The Melting Pot
THE JUNIOR LEAGUE OF THE CENTRAL DELAWARE VALLEY, NEW JERSEY

Cucumber Rings

2 cucumbers
1 large chicken breast, cooked, boned, and minced
1 hard-boiled egg, finely chopped
2 tablespoons chopped fresh parsley
Salt and pepper to taste
Mayonnaise
Fresh bread
Parsley for garnish

Slice off ends of cucumbers and remove seeds with an apple corer. Remove strips of skin for striped effect.

Combine chicken, egg, parsley, salt, pepper, and 1 tablespoon mayonnaise. Fill hollowed cucumbers with mixture. Wrap and chill for 2–3 hours.

Cut 26 bread rounds from fresh bread with cookie cutter. Spread rounds with mayonnaise. Slice cucumbers in ¼-inch slices and place on bread rounds. Decorate with parsley.

Can be assembled a couple of hours ahead and refrigerated.

YIELD: **26** PIECES

Before and After Thoughts
THE JUNIOR LEAGUE OF PITTSBURGH, PENNSYLVANIA

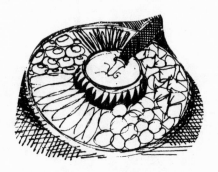

Ham Puffs

1 8-ounce package cream cheese, softened
1 egg yolk
1 teaspoon baking powder
Dash salt
4½ ounces deviled ham
10–15 thin slices bread
Mayonnaise
Paprika

Combine cream cheese with egg yolk, baking powder, salt, and deviled ham. Mix until blended and smooth.

Cut each bread slice into four triangles. Spread each triangle lightly with mayonnaise and then a generous amount of ham mixture. Sprinkle with paprika. This much can be done ahead and the appetizers frozen.

To serve, put in a moderately hot 375° oven for 12–15 minutes, or until puffed and browned.

YIELD: 45 SERVINGS

Before and After Thoughts
THE JUNIOR LEAGUE OF PITTSBURGH, PENNSYLVANIA

Egg Rolls

SKINS:

3 eggs

½ cup milk

½ cup pancake mix

FILLING:

¼ pound ground pork

1 tablespoon soy sauce

1 tablespoon dry sherry

¼ teaspoon sugar

¼ pound shrimp, cooked, cleaned, and chopped

¼ pound mushrooms, chopped

2 cups chopped celery

1 tablespoon peanut oil

1 teaspoon salt

1 16-ounce can bean sprouts, drained

3 teaspoons cornstarch

4 tablespoons chicken broth

Prepare skins. Beat together eggs, milk, and pancake mix. Pour small amount into a hot, lightly buttered 6-inch frying pan. Coat pan with a thin layer by rotating pan gently. Fry until light brown on the bottom and dry on the top. Do not turn. Remove and cool on wax paper.

Prepare filling. In skillet, fry pork until meat loses its color. Add soy sauce, sherry, sugar, shrimp, and mushrooms. Cook 1 minute and empty into bowl. Sauté celery in oil for 5 minutes and add salt and bean sprouts. Add to pork, mix, and cook over medium heat for 5 minutes. Combine cornstarch and chicken broth and stir into filling. Cook until slightly thickened. Cool.

To assemble, place 1 tablespoon filling in center of each skin; roll one edge over filling, fold in sides, then finish rolling skin. When all are rolled, fry in deep fat heated to 365° for 2 minutes. Drain and serve with hot Chinese mustard.

YIELD: 16–20 EGG ROLLS

THE JUNIOR LEAGUE OF HARRISBURG, PENNSYLVANIA

Fried Mozzarella

6 ounces mozzarella cheese
1 egg, beaten
½ cup bread crumbs
¼ cup olive oil
2 tablespoons butter

Slice mozzarella about ¼ inch thick. Dip slices in beaten egg, then in bread crumbs.

Heat oil and butter together in a skillet. Fry slices of mozzarella a few at a time, turning once, until all are fried. Serve hot.

YIELD: 4 SERVINGS

THE JUNIOR LEAGUE OF SCRANTON, PENNSYLVANIA

Mushrooms Supreme

½ pound butter
3 pounds mushrooms, thinly sliced
10 medium onions, sliced
2½ teaspoons salt
¼ teaspoon pepper
1½ teaspoons paprika
1 cup sour cream

Melt butter in large pan and add mushrooms, onions, and seasonings. Simmer, uncovered, until all the liquid is absorbed, about 2 hours, stirring mixture occasionally. Cool and freeze.*

On serving day, heat in double boiler over low heat until hot. Stir in sour cream and cook uncovered, without boiling, for about 30 minutes, or until thick and creamy.

*To serve without freezing, stir in sour cream and heat for 30 minutes.

Serve on plates with or without toast points or in patty shells.

YIELD: **50** SERVINGS

Hors D'Oeuvres Cookbook
THE JUNIOR LEAGUE OF READING, PENNSYLVANIA

.   .   .   .

Marinated Vegetables

1 10-ounce can jumbo pitted ripe olives, drained
1 small head cauliflower, broken into flowerets
3 small white onions, quartered
1 pound small fresh mushrooms
2 green peppers, cut into pieces
2-3 carrots, cut into sticks
½ pint cherry tomatoes

MARINADE:
½ cup olive oil
½ cup salad oil
1½ cups red wine vinegar
¼ cup sugar
¾ teaspoon black pepper
2 teaspoons salt
1 clove garlic

Wash and prepare vegetables. Set aside, keeping cherry tomatoes separate.

Combine marinade ingredients and bring to boil, then cool slightly. Pour over vegetables; add tomatoes when mixture is completely cool. Refrigerate 24 hours, turning frequently.

YIELD: **8-10** SERVINGS
THE JUNIOR LEAGUE OF BERGEN COUNTY, NEW JERSEY

.   .   .   .

Soups, Stews, Chowders

Curried Apple Soup

2 tablespoons butter
1 cup chopped celery
½ cup chopped onion
2 tablespoons flour
1 tablespoon curry powder
½ teaspoon salt
2 cups apple sauce
4 cubes beef bouillon
1½ cups water
½ cup light cream
3 tablespoons sherry (optional)
Apple slices or mint for garnish

Melt butter in saucepan. Add celery and onion. Sauté until the vegetables are limp, about 5 minutes. Blend in flour, curry powder, and salt. Cool 1 minute, then transfer to a blender. Add apple sauce and bouillon cubes. Blend until smooth.

Return mixture to saucepan, add water, and bring to boil. Remove from heat. Stir in cream and sherry. Garnish with slices of apple or mint.

YIELD: 4–5 SERVINGS

THE JUNIOR LEAGUE OF THE ORANGES AND SHORT HILLS, NEW JERSEY

Black Bean Soup

1 pound dried black beans
1 cup chopped onion
1 cup chopped green pepper
1 clove garlic, minced
½ cup olive oil
1 smoked ham bone
2 bay leaves
2 teaspoons salt
¼ teaspoon pepper
1 slice bacon or lean pork, minced
¼ cup wine vinegar
Cooked rice
Chopped sweet onion for garnish

Wash and soak black beans overnight in water to cover. Next morning, drain and add 6 cups water.

Cook onion, pepper, and garlic in olive oil for 5 minutes. Add to beans with ham bone, bay leaves, salt, pepper, and bacon. Cover and cook slowly for 2–3 hours, or until beans begin to fall apart, adding more water if necessary. Add vinegar.

Serve with a mound of rice in center of each soup plate and top with sweet onion.

YIELD: 3 QUARTS

Cooks Book
THE JUNIOR LEAGUE OF GREATER NEW HAVEN, CONNECTICUT

Black Bean Soup with Kielbasa

1 1-pound package black beans
3–4 cups beef broth
¾ cup white wine
2 cloves garlic, minced (optional)
1½ teaspoons crushed cumin
1½ teaspoons crushed coriander
1 teaspoon salt
1 kielbasa Polish sausage, about 1 foot long
Sour cream or lemon slices for garnish

Cover beans with water and soak overnight.

Cook beans in soaking liquid, adding more water if necessary, for 2 hours. Blend beans until smooth in blender or food processor. Add the beef broth, wine, garlic, and spices; simmer for 30 minutes.

Cook sausage separately in water, simmering for approximately 30 minutes. Drain, slice thinly, and add to the soup.

Serve with sour cream or lemon slices.

YIELD: 8 SERVINGS

Hudson River Hospitality
THE JUNIOR LEAGUE OF WESTCHESTER-ON-HUDSON, NEW YORK

Beef Barley Stew

3 pounds beef round or chuck, diced
2 tablespoons oil
2 medium onions, diced
½ teaspoon pepper
2 cloves garlic, minced
1 2-pound can tomatoes with juice
3 10½-ounce cans beef bouillon
1 cup red wine
⅛ teaspoon thyme
2 bay leaves
¾ cup barley
1 cup diced carrots
1 cup peas
1 cup sliced mushrooms
Salt to taste

Brown meat in the oil in a large casserole. Pour off any remaining oil. Add remaining ingredients. Cover and bake at 325° for 2½–3 hours, stirring occasionally. Remove cover for last hour of cooking.

If too thick, thin with a little water and bouillon. Correct seasoning before serving.

YIELD: 8 SERVINGS

THE JUNIOR LEAGUE OF BUFFALO, NEW YORK

Winter Beef Vegetable Soup

1½ pounds stewing beef
1 teaspoon pepper
2 bay leaves
1 cup chopped celery
½ cup chopped onion
4–5 medium carrots, sliced
1 cup chopped cabbage
8 ounces tomato sauce
1 tablespoon Worcestershire sauce
1 beef bouillon cube
1 teaspoon oregano
½ cup dry red wine

In heavy 6-quart pot, cover meat with cold water. Add pepper and bay leaves. Bring to a boil and skim lightly while preparing vegetables.

Turn heat low and add celery, onion, carrots, and cabbage. Simmer 2½ hours, or until meat is very tender.

Add tomato sauce. Worcestershire sauce, bouillon cube, and oregano. Simmer ½ hour. Stir in wine and serve with hot homemade bread, glass of wine, and salad.

YIELD: 6–8 SERVINGS

THE JUNIOR LEAGUE OF BERGEN COUNTY, NEW JERSEY

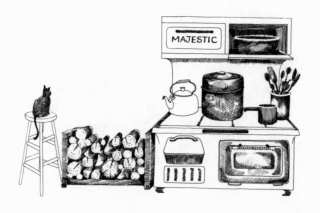

Beef Borscht with Sour Cream and Piroshki

1 4-pound shin of beef
1 large marrowbone
Salt
1 1-pound can tomatoes, undrained
1 medium onion, peeled and quartered
1 stalk celery, coarsely cut
3 sprigs parsley
6 whole black peppercorns
1 bay leaf
2 cups peeled, shredded beets (4 medium)
3 cups coarsely shredded cabbage (1 pound)
1½ cups peeled, thickly sliced carrots (4 medium)
1 cup chopped onion
2–3 tablespoons snipped fresh dill
¼ cup cider vinegar
2 tablespoons sugar
Sour cream
Piroshki

Day before serving: In a deep 8-quart kettle, put beef, marrowbone, 1 tablespoon salt, and 2 quarts water. Cover and bring to a boil; skim surface. Reduce heat and simmer, covered, for 1 hour. Add tomatoes, quartered onion, celery, parsley, peppercorns, and bay leaf; simmer, covered, 2 hours longer. Remove from heat.

Lift out beef and set aside. Remove marrowbone and discard. Strain soup; skim off fat. (You should have about 9 cups liquid.) Return soup and beef to kettle. Add beets, cabbage, carrots, chopped onion, 2 tablespoons dill, vinegar, sugar, and 1 teaspoon salt and bring to a boil. Reduce heat and simmer, covered, for 30 minutes, or until beef and vegetables are tender. Remove from heat. Refrigerate overnight.

Next day, remove beef from soup. Chop enough to measure 1 cup and reserve for Piroshki. Return remaining beef to soup. Heat gently to

Recipe continues . . .

boiling. Turn into soup tureen. Top with spoonfuls of sour cream. If desired, garnish with snipped dill. Serve with Piroshki.

YIELD: 8 LARGE SERVINGS

PIROSHKI:

2 tablespoons butter or margarine
2 tablespoons finely chopped onion
2 tablespoons sour cream
1 cup finely chopped cooked beef
½ teaspoon seasoned salt
1 14-ounce package refrigerated turnover pastries
1 egg yolk

Preheat oven to 400°.

Heat butter in small skillet and in it sauté onion until tender, 2–3 minutes. Add sour cream, chopped beef, and seasoned salt, and mix well. Set aside.

Unroll pastry from package of turnover pastries; separate into eight squares. (Save fruit filling and icing to use another time.) Spread 2 tablespoons of meat filling diagonally over half of each square. Fold pastry over to form triangle and press edges together to seal; cut slit in top of each. Beat egg yolk with 2 tablespoons water; brush over pastry triangles. Place pastries on lightly greased baking sheet and bake 12–15 minutes, or until puffed and brown. Serve warm.

YIELD: 8 PIROSHKI

THE JUNIOR LEAGUE OF BRONXVILLE, NEW YORK

Billi Bi Soup
(Mussel Soup)

2 pounds mussels
2 small onions, quartered
3 shallots, coarsely chopped
3 sprigs parsley
Dash cayenne
Salt and pepper
1 cup dry white wine (Chablis)
3 tablespoons butter
1 small bay leaf
½ teaspoon thyme
2¼ cups heavy cream

Scrub mussels well under cold running water and remove all exterior sand and dirt and the beards. Place mussels in a large pot. Add the onions, shallots, parsley, cayenne, salt and pepper, wine, butter, bay leaf, and thyme. Cover and bring to a boil. Simmer for about 10 minutes, or until all the mussels have opened. (Discard any mussels that do not open.)

Strain the liquid from the pot through a double thickness of cheesecloth. Remove the mussels from the shells and use as a garnish for the soup (or serve without the garnish and reserve the mussels for another use).

In a saucepan, bring the liquid to a boil and add the heavy cream. Heat the soup long enough for it to thicken slightly. Serve hot or cold.

YIELD: **4** SERVINGS

THE JUNIOR LEAGUE OF THE CITY OF NEW YORK, NEW YORK

Vegetable Soup

48 ounces canned chicken broth
29 ounces canned tomato purée
1 20-ounce can white kidney beans, undrained
2 parsnips, peeled and chopped
1 large potato, peeled and diced
½ pound fresh green beans, cut to 1-inch lengths
1 large onion, chopped
2 zucchini, chopped
2 stalks celery, chopped
1 wedge cabbage (½ pound), chopped
1 clove garlic, minced
¾ cup uncooked rice
Salt and pepper to taste

In large soup pot, combine chicken broth and tomato purée. In blender, purée undrained beans. Add beans to broth mixture, then add remaining ingredients. Simmer over low heat 1¼ hours, or until vegetables are fork-tender. Season with salt and pepper.

YIELD: 6 SERVINGS

Hudson River Hospitality
THE JUNIOR LEAGUE OF WESTCHESTER-ON-HUDSON, NEW YORK

Broccoli Soup

1 large bunch fresh broccoli *good quality*
2–3 tablespoons butter
1 medium onion, chopped
1 clove garlic, finely chopped
1 medium potato, peeled and diced
4 cups chicken or vegetable broth *save broc. cook. liq*
2 cups milk
½ teaspoon salt *could do with*
¼ teaspoon pepper *cream or butter*
1 small lemon, very thinly sliced *for richness*

Cut off flowerets from broccoli stalks, then boil the flowerets until tender in a small amount of water. Drain and set aside. Peel the stalks if tough. Slice and dice the stalks.

Heat butter in a large, heavy saucepan. Add the broccoli stalks, onion, and garlic. Cook slowly, stirring frequently. After 10 minutes, add the potato and broth. Bring to a boil and simmer for 15 minutes, or until the potato is tender. Add the milk, salt, and pepper.

Purée 1 cup at a time in the blender until very smooth. Return to saucepan and add flowerets. Reheat and garnish with lemon slices.

This is thick and creamy but not terribly fattening.

YIELD: 6 SERVINGS

The Everyday Gourmet
THE JUNIOR LEAGUE OF NORTHERN WESTCHESTER, BEDFORD HILLS, NEW YORK

Cream of Carrot Soup

4 cups sliced carrot
2 tablespoons chopped onion
½ teaspoon sugar
½ teaspoon marjoram
¼ teaspoon thyme
2 tablespoons butter
2 tablespoons flour
2 cups milk
2 teaspoons dill weed
1 tablespoon chicken stock base
2 cups half and half or light cream
1 cup heavy cream
Salt and white pepper to taste
1 carrot, grated

Braise first five ingredients in the butter until carrots are tender. Sprinkle with flour and cook, stirring, until flour is slightly brown. Gradually add milk and 1 teaspoon of the dill, stirring until smooth. Simmer for 30 minutes, stirring occasionally. Purée in blender. Add chicken stock base and creams.

At serving time, reheat but do not boil. Adjust seasonings. Stir in grated carrot and ladle into soup bowls. Sprinkle with remaining dill.

Can be served chilled as well.

YIELD: 8 SERVINGS

THE JUNIOR LEAGUE OF ROCHESTER, NEW YORK

Carrot Vichyssoise

2 cups peeled, diced potatoes
1¼ cups peeled, sliced carrots
3 leeks, white part only, sliced
3 cups chicken stock (or 4 chicken bouillon cubes
combined with 3 cups water)
White pepper and salt to taste
1 cup heavy cream
Shredded carrot for garnish

Combine vegetables in stock, bring liquid to a boil, then simmer for about 25 minutes. Pour mixture into blender or food processor and purée. Add white pepper and salt to taste. Chill

Before serving, add 1 cup heavy cream. Garnish with shredded raw carrot.

YIELD: 4 SERVINGS

THE JUNIOR LEAGUE OF BROOKLYN, NEW YORK

Chelmsford Cauliflower Soup

1 stalk celery, chopped
2 carrots, peeled and chopped
1 medium cauliflower
1 thick slice lemon
2 tablespoons butter
1 medium onion, chopped
4 fresh mushrooms, diced
A few celery leaves, chopped
2 tablespoons flour
4 cups chicken stock
1 teaspoon salt
¼ teaspoon white pepper
¼ cup medium pearl barley
½ cup heavy cream
½ cup milk

Put celery, carrots, cauliflower, and lemon slice in a large pot and add enough water to cover. Bring to a boil and simmer until vegetables are tender, about 15 minutes. Discard lemon. Strain vegetables, reserving 1 cup of the liquid. Break cauliflower into flowerets. Set vegetables aside.

In same pot, melt butter. Sauté onion, mushrooms, and celery leaves. Stir in flour. Slowly add the reserved cup of liquid, stirring constantly, until well blended. Add the chicken stock, salt, pepper, barley, and reserved vegetables. Bring mixture to a boil and simmer for 20 minutes, or until barley is tender. Add cream and milk and heat thoroughly.

YIELD: 6 SERVINGS

THE JUNIOR LEAGUE OF ROCHESTER, NEW YORK

Chicken Bisque Normande

½ cup small julienne carrot strips
¼ cup chopped green onion
3 tablespoons butter
3 tablespoons flour
Dash nutmeg
Dash white pepper
1 10½-ounce can chicken broth
¼ cup apple brandy (Calvados or applejack)
1 cup half and half (or heavy cream for a really thick bisque)
¼ cup milk
1 cup finely chopped cooked chicken
Chopped chives for garnish

Sauté carrot and onion slowly in butter just until tender. Stir in flour, nutmeg, and pepper. Slowly add chicken broth and brandy and heat until boiling. Lower heat and simmer, stirring constantly, until thickened. Add half and half, milk, and chicken. Return just to simmering. Serve garnished with chopped chives.

YIELD: **4** SERVINGS

THE JUNIOR LEAGUE OF MONMOUTH COUNTY, NEW JERSEY

Chicken Cheese Chowder

1 cup shredded carrot
¼ cup chopped onion
4 tablespoons butter
¼ cup flour
2 cups milk
1¾ cups chicken broth
1 cup diced cooked chicken
1 tablespoon dry white wine or vermouth
½ teaspoon Worcestershire sauce
½ teaspoon celery seed
1 cup shredded cheddar cheese

Cook carrot and onion in butter until tender but not brown. Blend in flour. Add milk and broth. Cook and stir until liquid is thick and bubbly. Stir in chicken, wine, Worcestershire sauce, and celery seed. Heat through. Just before serving add cheese and heat until melted.

YIELD: 6 SERVINGS

THE JUNIOR LEAGUE OF WILLIAMSPORT, PENNSYLVANIA

. . . .

Fran's Crab-Corn Chowder

2 cups fresh or frozen white corn
1/3 cup thinly sliced carrots
1/3 cup thinly sliced celery
½ small onion, chopped
1 10½-ounce can chicken broth
2 cups crab claw meat
1 teaspoon Old Bay seasoning
1-1½ cups half and half or light cream
Parsley and paprika for garnish

Heat vegetables in broth to boiling and simmer for 10 minutes, or until vegetables are tender. Add crabmeat and seasoning and simmer about 5 minutes longer. Stir in enough cream to cover, correct seasoning, and heat to serving temperature.

Garnish with parsley and a dash of paprika.

YIELD: 6 SERVINGS

Something Special
THE JUNIOR LEAGUE OF YORK, PENNSYLVANIA

Cold Cucumber Soup

2 tablespoons butter
¼ cup chopped onion or 1 leek, cubed
2 cups diced, unpeeled cucumber
1 cup watercress leaves
½ cup diced raw potato
2 cups chicken broth
2 sprigs parsley
½ teaspoon salt
¼ teaspoon freshly ground black pepper
1 teaspoon dry mustard
1 cup heavy cream
Chopped chives and cucumber for garnish

In a saucepan, melt butter and in it cook onion until transparent. Add rest of ingredients, except cream and garnish, and bring to a boil. Simmer for 15 minutes, or until potato is tender. Purée a little at a time in a blender. Correct seasonings and chill.

Recipe continues . . .

Before serving, stir in cream and garnish with chopped chives and cucumber.

YIELD: 4–6 SERVINGS

The Melting Pot
THE JUNIOR LEAGUE OF THE CENTRAL DELAWARE VALLEY, NEW JERSEY

· ·

Egg and Lemon Soup

1½ quarts chicken stock
½ cup uncooked rice
6 eggs
6 tablespoons fresh lemon juice
Salt to taste
3 tablespoons finely chopped fresh mint (optional)

In large pot or kettle, bring chicken stock to a boil. Pour in rice and reduce heat to low. Simmer partially covered for about 15 minutes, or until grains of rice are tender.

Beat eggs with a wire whisk until frothy. Beat in lemon juice and ¼ cup of the hot chicken broth. Slowly pour the egg-lemon mixture into the broth, stirring rapidly. Cook for about 5 minutes, or until soup thickens enough to lightly coat a spoon. Do not let the soup boil; you don't want scrambled eggs. Add salt to taste and sprinkle with mint leaves, if desired.

YIELD: 6 SERVINGS

THE JUNIOR LEAGUE OF MONMOUTH COUNTY, NEW JERSEY

· ·

Fish Chowder

2 pounds boneless white fish
A few chopped celery leaves
2½ teaspoons salt
1 clove garlic, minced
½ cup butter
¼ teaspoon pepper
2 cups boiling water
4 potatoes, peeled and sliced
1 bay leaf
4 whole cloves
3 large onions, sliced
½ teaspoon dill seed
½ cup dry vermouth
2 cups light cream
Chopped fresh dill or parsley for garnish

Put all ingredients except cream and garnish into a casserole. Cover and bake at 375° for 1 hour. Heat cream to scalding and add to chowder. Stir to break up fish.

Serve with a garnish of chopped fresh dill or parsley.

YIELD: **4** SERVINGS

THE JUNIOR LEAGUE OF WORCESTER, MASSACHUSETTS

Chilled Garden Soup

1 pint chicken broth or bouillon
1 teaspoon salt
1 medium potato, peeled and diced
1 medium cucumber, chopped
1 medium onion, chopped
1 large stalk celery with leaves, chopped
1 tart apple, peeled and diced
1 cup light cream
1 tablespoon butter
1½ teaspoons curry powder
Freshly ground pepper
Chopped parsley or chives for garnish

To the broth, add salt, vegetables, and apple. Simmer until the vegetables are tender. Put through food mill or mix in blender until smooth. Stir in cream, butter, curry powder, and pepper. Chill thoroughly. Garnish with parsley or chives.

YIELD: **6** SERVINGS

THE JUNIOR LEAGUE OF WILLIAMSPORT, PENNSYLVANIA

Garden Summer Soup

1 medium onion, sliced
1 medium carrot, sliced
2 stalks celery with leaves, sliced
1 clove garlic, minced
½ cup water
1 large potato, peeled and sliced
1 bunch broccoli, chopped
1 cucumber, peeled and sliced
2 zucchini, peeled and diced
5 cups chicken broth
½ cup sour cream

Simmer onion, carrot, celery, and garlic in water for 10 minutes in covered saucepan. Add remaining vegetables and chicken broth and simmer until all vegetables are tender, about 20 minutes. Cool. Blend until smooth in a blender, then chill.

Add sour cream before serving and stir in thoroughly.

YIELD: 10 SERVINGS

THE JUNIOR LEAGUE OF SPRINGFIELD, MASSACHUSETTS

Potage Jardin

½ cup parsley sprigs
½ head Boston lettuce, cut
into pieces
2 cups chicken broth
1 17-ounce can small peas, undrained
½ cup heavy cream
Salt to taste
Freshly ground white pepper to taste
Toasted croutons for garnish

Recipe continues . . .

Put parsley, lettuce, ½ cup broth, and undrained peas into blender. Purée 15 seconds at high speed. Pour into a saucepan and add remaining broth. Simmer 5 minutes. Add cream and season with salt and pepper. Garnish with croutons.

Can be served hot or cold, but it is better cold.

YIELD: 4 SERVINGS

Simply Superb
THE JUNIOR LEAGUE OF ELIZABETH-PLAINFIELD, NEW JERSEY

. . . .

Thai Lemongrass Soup

1 quart clear chicken stock
3 tablespoons fish sauce (available
at Oriental grocery stores)
2 green onions, thinly sliced
Dash chili pepper
3 cloves garlic, minced
Fresh coriander or ground (also known as Chinese parsley)
Handful lemongrass (available
dried in spice shops)
3 shrimps, with tails on, per person
Fresh coriander, parsley, or chopped
green onion for garnish

Combine first seven ingredients and simmer gently for about an hour. Add shrimp and simmer 5 minutes longer.

Garnish each serving with a few sprigs of fresh coriander, parsley, or green onion.

YIELD: 4 SERVINGS

THE JUNIOR LEAGUE OF BROOKLYN, NEW YORK

. . . .

Lentil and Polish Sausage Stew

1 cup lentils
½ teaspoon salt
2 tablespoons oil
2 medium onions, chopped
3 cloves garlic, minced
2 cups drained and crushed
canned tomatoes
2 pounds Polish sausage, skinned
½ teaspoon pepper
1 bay leaf

Place lentils in a saucepan and cover with cold water. Add salt; bring to a boil. Simmer, covered, for 30–45 minutes, or until tender.

Heat oil in a casserole, and in it sauté onions and garlic until translucent. Add tomatoes and cook until most of liquid is evaporated.

Cut sausage in ½-inch pieces and add to casserole. Drain lentils, reserving liquid. Add lentils, pepper, bay leaf, and some lentil liquid. Simmer for 30 minutes. Correct seasoning with salt to taste and add more liquid for desired consistency.

Good served in bowls accompanied by hot corn bread and a green salad or coleslaw.

YIELD: **6** SERVINGS

THE JUNIOR LEAGUE OF ALBANY, NEW YORK

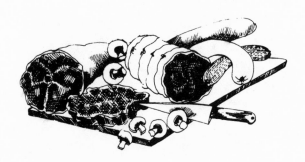

Lobster Stew

½ cup butter
Coral and tomalley from a
couple of lobsters
2 pounds lobster meat
1 quart light cream
1 pint milk

In a large saucepan, melt butter and simmer the coral and tomalley for 5–10 minutes. Add the lobster meat, left in fairly large chunks, and cook slowly for about 10 minutes. Remove from heat and cool slightly. Add the cream and milk very slowly, stirring constantly.

Refrigerate for 5–6 hours or overnight to develop the flavor. Reheat very slowly but *do not boil.*

YIELD: **6** SERVINGS

THE JUNIOR LEAGUE OF FALL RIVER, MASSACHUSETTS

Hearty Minestrone Soup

1/4 *cup salad oil*
1 clove garlic, minced
1 pound ground beef
2 cups chopped onion
1 cup chopped celery
2 tablespoons parsley
1 6-ounce can tomato paste
1 10½-ounce can beef broth
9 cups water
1 cup chopped cabbage
2 carrots, sliced
2 teaspoons salt
¼ teaspoon pepper
⅛ teaspoon sage
1 20-ounce can chick-peas, undrained
1 16-ounce can corn, undrained
1 cup uncooked macaroni
1 cup shredded cheddar cheese (optional)

Heat oil. Add garlic, beef, onion, celery, and parsley. Cook until meat loses its color.

Stir in tomato paste and next seven ingredients. Mix well. Bring to a boil, then simmer, covered, for 1 hour. Add remaining ingredients and cook 10 minutes more, or until macaroni is tender. Sprinkle with cheese when served, if desired.

YIELD: 16 SERVINGS

THE JUNIOR LEAGUE OF SPRINGFIELD, MASSACHUSETTS

Mystery Soup

2 13½-ounce cans beef broth
1 8-ounce package cream cheese

Heat, mixing well.
Very special hot or cold (but best hot).

YIELD: 4 SERVINGS

THE JUNIOR LEAGUE OF WORCESTER, MASSACHUSETTS

A Cold Winter's Day Potato Soup

6 slices bacon, cut into ½-inch pieces
2 cups chopped onion
2 large leeks (white part
only), thinly sliced
3 medium potatoes, peeled and cubed
1 large turnip, peeled and cubed
6 cups chicken broth
1 cup sour cream
Salt and pepper to taste
Snipped parsley for garnish

Fry bacon until crisp. Set aside.

Sauté onion and leeks in bacon fat until golden. Add potatoes, turnip, and chicken broth. Heat to boiling; lower heat and simmer for 15 minutes, or until potatoes and turnips are tender. Purée in food processor or blender. Return to heat and keep warm.

Just before serving, stir in sour cream with wire whisk. Add salt and pepper to taste. Add crisp bacon pieces. Garnish with parsley and serve immediately.

YIELD: 4–6 SERVINGS

THE JUNIOR LEAGUE OF THE NORTH SHORE, LONG ISLAND, NEW YORK

Oyster Bisque

1 pint oysters
4 cups light cream
1 slice onion
2 stalks celery
1 sprig parsley
Piece bay leaf
1/3 cup butter
1/3 cup flour
Salt and pepper to taste

Drain oysters and chop. Heat slowly to the boiling point and press through a coarse sieve.

Scald cream with onion, celery, parsley and, bay leaf. Melt butter, stir in flour, and strain cream into butter-flour mixture. Stir over a low fire or over hot water until mixture thickens. Add the strained oysters and season with salt and pepper to taste.

If a thinner soup is desired, milk may be substituted for the light cream.

Serve hot with fried croutons.

YIELD: 4 SERVINGS

THE JUNIOR LEAGUE OF STAMFORD-NORWALK, CONNECTICUT

New England Quahog Chowder

1½ quarts little-neck clams or small quahogs
1½ tablespoons minced green onion or
1 small onion, finely chopped
4 small potatoes, diced
3 cups milk
3 tablespoons butter
⅛ teaspoon pepper

Recipe continues . . .

Scrub and wash clams and put into saucepan with 1 cup water. Cover pan and steam over low heat until clams are fully opened. Remove clams, discard shells, and cut clams into small pieces with scissors; set aside.

Pour liquid carefully off any sand in bottom of saucepan into another saucepan. Add onion and potatoes to liquid in second saucepan and simmer until potatoes are tender. Add clams, milk, butter, and pepper. Heat and stir, but do not let boil or curdling could occur.

Serve with oyster crackers.

YIELD: 6 SERVINGS

THE JUNIOR LEAGUE OF FALL RIVER, MASSACHUSETTS

Pumpkin Soup

3 tablespoons butter
½ cup chopped celery
½ cup chopped green pepper
½ small onion, chopped
¼ teaspoon thyme
1 bay leaf
1 cup canned tomatoes
1 1-pound can pumpkin or 2 cups
mashed cooked fresh pumpkin
2 cups chicken stock
2 tablespoons flour
1 cup milk
1 teaspoon salt
¼ teaspoon white pepper
Toasted croutons

Melt butter in large saucepan. Add the celery, green pepper, onion, thyme, and bay leaf. Cook for 5 minutes. Add tomatoes, pumpkin, and chicken stock. Cover and simmer for 30 minutes. Purée mixture 1 cup at a time in blender and return to saucepan.

Blend together flour and milk. Stir mixture into soup. Add salt and pepper and cook until mixture comes to a boil, stirring frequently. Serve hot with croutons.

YIELD: 6 SERVINGS

THE JUNIOR LEAGUE OF HARRISBURG, PENNSYLVANIA

Green Onion Soup

¼ pound sweet butter
5 bunches green onions, finely chopped
1 teaspoon salt
½ teaspoon pepper
2 tablespoons flour
3 cups hot chicken broth
¾ pound fresh mushrooms, sliced
1¼ cups cream

Put the stick of butter in a large saucepan. Add green onions, salt, and pepper. Mix thoroughly and cook slowly without browning for about 10 minutes, stirring all the while. Remove from heat and stir in flour. Add the chicken broth and stir until mixture boils. Simmer for 10 minutes, uncovered.

Remove from heat and add ½ pound mushrooms. Blend 2 cups at a time in blender and return to saucepan. Add the cream and heat without boiling.

Garnish with remaining mushrooms before serving.

YIELD: 6 SERVINGS

THE JUNIOR LEAGUE OF WORCESTER, MASSACHUSETTS

Scallop and Artichoke Soup

A subtle soup from Lacy's in London.

1 10-ounce package frozen artichoke
hearts, defrosted
4 tablespoons butter
2 tablespoons flour
2 cups chicken broth
½ pound fresh scallops, chopped
Salt to taste
1 cup heavy cream
⅛ teaspoon lemon juice

Sauté artichokes in butter for a few minutes. Add flour and blend well. Add chicken broth and simmer until artichokes are tender.

Purée mixture in blender. Return to low heat and add the chopped scallops. Heat for a few minutes, or until scallops are no longer opaque. Add cream and lemon juice. Heat to serving temperature; do not boil.

YIELD: 4–6 SERVINGS

Presenting Boston . . . A Cookbook
THE JUNIOR LEAGUE OF BOSTON, MASSACHUSETTS

Seafood Chowder

1/2 cup minced onion
1/4 cup butter
2 cups fish stock or water
1/2 cup white wine
1/2 cup thinly sliced celery
1 cup thinly sliced carrot
1 cup diced potato
1 bay leaf
1/2 teaspoon thyme
2 teaspoons salt
Pepper to taste
1 pound haddock or cod filet, diced
3 cups milk
1/4 cup flour
1 cup half and half
6 ounces flaked crabmeat
Parsley

Sauté onion in butter. Add the liquid, vegetables, seasoning, and fish; simmer for 20 minutes. Gradually add 1 cup milk to the flour to make a thin paste. Add to hot mixture, stirring and cooking until thick. Gradually add remaining milk, half and half, crabmeat, and parsley. Heat thoroughly before serving.

YIELD: 6–8 SERVINGS

THE JUNIOR LEAGUE OF STAMFORD-NORWALK, CONNECTICUT

Chilled Shrimp Soup

¾ pound shrimp, cooked and chopped
1 medium cucumber
1 tablespoon chopped fresh dill
or 1 teaspoon dried
1 tablespoon prepared mustard
1 teaspoon salt
1 teaspoon sugar
4 cups buttermilk

Peel cucumber and slice in half lengthwise; scoop out seeds and discard. Finely dice the cucumber. Combine all the ingredients and chill for 2 hours or longer.

Don't let the buttermilk scare you off. Even buttermilk haters love this soup—just don't tell them it's buttermilk!

YIELD: 6 SERVINGS

Hudson River Hospitality
THE JUNIOR LEAGUE OF WESTCHESTER-ON-HUDSON, NEW YORK

Chilled Cream of Tomato Soup

½ cup minced onion
½ cup minced leek
2 cloves garlic, minced
2 tablespoons butter
2 pounds ripe tomatoes, peeled,
seeded, and chopped
3¼ cups chicken broth or stock
2 tablespoons tomato paste
2 tablespoons cornstarch
½ cup heavy cream
½ cup light cream
¼ cup snipped dill
Salt
White pepper

In a saucepan, sauté the onion, leek, and garlic in the butter until tender. Add the tomatoes and 1 cup chicken broth and simmer for 20 minutes, or until the tomatoes are soft.

Add 2 cups more broth, tomato paste, and cornstarch mixed with remaining cold chicken broth and bring mixture to a boil over high heat. Reduce heat and simmer, stirring occasionally, for 10 minutes, or until thickened.

Let the soup cool; force it through a sieve into a soup tureen and chill, covered, overnight.

Just before serving, stir in heavy cream, light cream, and dill. Then salt and pepper to taste.

YIELD: **6** SERVINGS

THE JUNIOR LEAGUE OF SPRINGFIELD, MASSACHUSETTS

Vichyssoise

1 pound leeks
½ cup chopped onion
¼ cup butter
1 pound potatoes, peeled and
diced to make 2 cups
½ teaspoon salt
White pepper to taste
2 13¾-ounce cans chicken broth
2 cups milk
1 cup light cream
½ cup chives

Trim and wash leeks. Slice ¼ inch thick, using a small amount of the green part. Combine with onion and sauté in butter for 5 minutes. Add potatoes, salt, pepper, and broth. Simmer 45 minutes, or until potatoes are mushy. Purée in blender. Heat milk and whisk into mixture. Chill at least 6 hours.

Just before serving stir in cream and sprinkle with chives.

YIELD: 6 SERVINGS

Simply Superb
THE JUNIOR LEAGUE OF ELIZABETH-PLAINFIELD, NEW JERSEY

. . . .

Cream of Zucchini

1½ pounds unpeeled zucchini, diced
2/3 cup chopped onion or leek
(white part only)
¼ cup butter
½ cup chopped fresh parsley
2 cups chicken broth
1 cup heavy cream
Salt, pepper, and curry powder to taste

Cook zucchini and onion in butter over low heat in covered pan until onion is transparent, about 10 minutes. Empty into blender container. Add parsley and chicken broth and blend until smooth. Add cream and seasonings. Chill thoroughly.

This freezes well and is excellent hot or cold.

YIELD: 8 SERVINGS

THE JUNIOR LEAGUE OF MONTREAL, QUEBEC

Sour Cream Zucchini Soup

1 zucchini, sliced
1 onion, finely chopped
1 teaspoon curry powder
1 13¾-ounce can chicken broth
1 cup sour cream

Cook zucchini, onion, and curry in chicken broth until zucchini is soft. Cool and empty into blender container. Add sour cream and blend until smooth. Chill to allow it to thicken.

Delicious served hot or cold.

YIELD: 3–4 SERVINGS

THE JUNIOR LEAGUE OF SCHENECTADY, NEW YORK

Curried Zucchini and Potato Soup

4 large zucchini (about 2 pounds),
chopped or sliced
2 onions, chopped
½ teaspoon curry powder
½ cup chopped parsley
4 cups chicken broth
1 cup cooked potatoes
½ cup light cream
Salt to taste
½ cup sour cream
Chopped watercress or parsley for garnish

Cook zucchini, onions, curry, and parsley in chicken broth until vegetables are tender. Purée with potatoes in electric blender, 1 cup at a time. Stir in cream and salt to taste.

Serve hot or cold. Top with dollop of sour cream and sprinkle with parsley or watercress.

May be frozen before cream is added. Defrost and serve cold with cream added, or heat, then add cream.

YIELD: 8 SERVINGS

THE JUNIOR LEAGUE OF GREATER BRIDGEPORT, CONNECTICUT

Meats

Great Roast

6-8 pounds boneless beef roast (not standing rib)
Salt and pepper

Anytime from 9 AM to mid-afternoon, salt and pepper the roast. Put in shallow open roaster and roast at 350° for 1 hour. Turn oven off. *Do not open.* Turn oven back to 350° for ½ hour at dinnertime. The roast will be rosy rare all the way through.

YIELD: 6–8 SERVINGS

Recipes by Request
THE JUNIOR LEAGUE OF GREATER WATERBURY, CONNECTICUT

Bavarian Pot Roast

5-6 pounds boneless chuck roast
2 tablespoons fat
2 cups water
1½ cups beer
1 cup canned tomatoes or tomato sauce
1 tablespoon vinegar
2/3 cup chopped onion
2 tablespoons sugar
1 teaspoon salt
1 teaspoon cinnamon
½ teaspoon ginger
1 large bay leaf

Heat the fat in a heavy skillet or Dutch oven and in it brown the meat evenly on all sides.

Mix together remaining ingredients and pour over meat. Cover and simmer gently 3–3½ hours, or until very tender. Strain broth and thicken if desired.

YIELD: 8 SERVINGS

Entirely Entertaining
THE JUNIOR LEAGUE OF MONTCLAIR-NEWARK, NEW JERSEY

·   ·   ·   ·   ·   ·   ·   ·   ·   ·   ·   ·   ·   ·   ·   ·

Pot Roast à la Danieli

4–5 pounds sirloin or rump roast
Flour
Salt and pepper
6 tablespoons shortening
4 slices bacon
1 onion, minced
2 cloves garlic, minced
½ cup tomato purée
1 small bay leaf
Dash rosemary
2 cups white wine
1 tablespoon minced parsley
2 cups water
2 teaspoons flour
½ cup cognac

Coat meat in flour, and sprinkle with salt and pepper.

Heat shortening in roasting pan and sear roast on all sides. Cover meat with bacon. Add onion, garlic, tomato purée, bay leaf, rosemary, wine, parsley, and 1 cup water. Cover and bake at 350° for 3–4 hours, basting frequently. When meat is tender, remove it to make pan gravy. Keep meat in warm oven. Scrape sides of pan and add the 2 teaspoons flour mixed with remaining water. Simmer, stirring, on top of stove until

Recipe continues . . .

gravy is reduced by half. Put gravy and vegetables through a sieve into a saucepan. Add cognac and simmer to heat through.

Slice meat diagonally across grain. Pour hot gravy over it and serve at once.

YIELD: 5–6 SERVINGS

Hudson River Hospitality
THE JUNIOR LEAGUE OF WESTCHESTER-ON-HUDSON, NEW YORK

· · · · · · · · · · · · · · · · · · ·

Spicy Pot Roast

3 pounds beef pot roast
1 tablespoon fat
1½ teaspoons salt
¼ teaspoon pepper
¼ cup flour
¼ teaspoon each cinnamon, cloves, and allspice
1 cup uncooked dried apricots
2 tablespoons brown sugar
2 tablespoons vinegar
3 cups beef broth

Brown meat in fat. Mix the rest of the ingredients and bring to a boil. Pour over the meat. Cover and simmer for 2½ hours.

YIELD: 6 SERVINGS

THE JUNIOR LEAGUE OF MONTREAL, QUEBEC

· · · · · · · · · · · · · · · · · · ·

Poppie's Pot Roast

3-4 pounds beef pot roast
2 medium onions, chopped
3 stalks celery with leaves, chopped
1 bay leaf (optional)
4 carrots, quartered
4 potatoes, peeled and quartered
Salt and pepper to taste

In a large Dutch oven, brown pot roast on all sides. Put onions and celery on top of roast. Add 2–3 cups water and bay leaf. Cover tightly and simmer for 1½ hours, or until tender. Add carrots, potatoes, salt, and pepper to taste. Continue cooking until vegetables are tender, about 20 minutes.

YIELD: 6 SERVINGS

THE JUNIOR LEAGUE OF STAMFORD-NORWALK, CONNECTICUT

•   •   •   •   •   •   •   •   •   •   •   •   •   •   •   •   •

Roast Barbecue

3 pounds chuck roast
2 tablespoons shortening
1 large onion, chopped
2 tablespoons vinegar
2 tablespoons lemon juice
¾ cup water
½ cup chopped celery
2 cups catsup
3 tablespoons Worcestershire sauce
2 tablespoons brown sugar
1 tablespoon yellow mustard
2 tablespoons chili powder
1 teaspoon salt
¼ teaspoon pepper

Recipe continues . . .

Brown meat in shortening. Pour off excess fat and add all other ingredients. Bring to a boil; reduce heat to low. As soon as meat is tender enough to shred, approximately 2–3 hours, use two forks and shred meat. Continue cooking until shreds are very tender, from 1 to 3 hours longer. Serve on buns.

YIELD: 12 SERVINGS

THE JUNIOR LEAGUE OF ROCHESTER, NEW YORK

. . . .

Marinated London Broil

2½–3 pounds London broil

MARINADE:
1 can beer
½ cup peanut or vegetable oil
1 teaspoon dry mustard
½ teaspoon ginger
½ teaspoon Worcestershire sauce
1 tablespoon sugar
2 tablespoons orange or ginger marmalade
1 teaspoon minced garlic
Salt and freshly ground pepper to taste

Mix marinade ingredients together and pour into oblong *glass* casserole. Place meat in mixture and spoon over top and sides. Cover and place in refrigerator for 24 hours; turn meat at least twice for even marinating.

When ready to serve, reserve some marinade for brushing on meat at cooking time. Barbecue to personal taste.

YIELD: 6 SERVINGS

Bicentennial Cookbook
THE JUNIOR LEAGUE OF PHILADELPHIA, PENNSYLVANIA

. . . .

Filets Madeira

6 tablespoons butter
½ pound mushrooms, sliced
2 tablespoons flour
2 teaspoons salt
½ teaspoon freshly ground black pepper
1 cup heavy cream
6 beef filets, ¾ inch thick
1/3 cup Madeira wine

In a skillet, melt 3 tablespoons butter, add mushrooms and sauté for 5 minutes. Stir in flour, 1 teaspoon salt, and ¼ teaspoon pepper. Add cream and cook, stirring, until liquid boils. Cook over low heat for 5 minutes. Stir in the wine. Keep warm over low heat.

In another skillet, melt remaining butter and sauté filets for about 4 minutes on each side. Season with remaining salt and pepper.

Put filets on serving platter and pour sauce over.

YIELD: **6** SERVINGS

THE JUNIOR LEAGUE OF BUFFALO, NEW YORK

Tournedos with Shallot Butter and Pâté

2–3 pounds filet of beef
2 tablespoons melted butter or margarine
2 cloves garlic, minced
1 teaspoon pepper
6 slices white bread
1 4¾-ounce can liver pâté, chilled
Shallot Butter

Recipe continues . . .

With a sharp knife, cut filet crosswise into 6 steaks, each about ½ inch thick. Brush all over with a mixture of the melted butter or margarine and garlic. Sprinkle with pepper. Set aside.

Toast bread slices and trim to same size as steaks. Slice liver pâté into 6 round slices. (It must be well chilled first or it won't be easy to slice.) Place steaks on rack of broiler pan. Broil 4 inches from heat for 4 minutes; turn and broil 3–4 minutes longer for rare. Place each steak on a toast round, then top with a slice of liver pâté and a generous spoonful of Shallot Butter. Serve at once.

SHALLOT BUTTER:

¼ cup dry white or red wine
2 tablespoons chopped shallot
½ teaspoon chopped garlic
8 tablespoons butter (1 stick)
1 tablespoon chopped parsley
¼ teaspoon salt
⅛ teaspoon white pepper

In saucepan, combine wine and chopped shallot and garlic. Bring to a boil over high heat and boil until almost all liquid is evaporated. Remove from heat. Beat in the butter, a little at a time, until creamy. Then beat in chopped parsley, salt, and pepper until well blended. Keep butter in warm place but do not let it melt.

YIELD: 6 SERVINGS

Bicentennial Cookbook
THE JUNIOR LEAGUE OF PHILADELPHIA, PENNSYLVANIA

Stuffed Filet of Beef

3 large onions, thinly sliced
6 tablespoons olive oil
4 tablespoons butter
2 cloves garlic, minced
18–20 pitted black olives, coarsely chopped
½ cup chopped cooked Virginia ham
1 teaspoon freshly ground black pepper
1 teaspoon thyme
1 teaspoon salt
2 egg yolks, beaten
2 tablespoons chopped parsley
2-pound filet of beef
Cooking oil

Sauté onions in oil and butter until limp. Add garlic, olives, ham, pepper, thyme, and salt and cook until well blended. Stir in beaten egg yolks and parsley and cook about 3 minutes.

Cut filet not quite through in rather thick slices (about 1 inch) and spoon stuffing between slices. Place on rack in roasting pan, brush with oil, and roast at 300° for about 50 minutes, or until internal temperature is 125°. Let rest 10 minutes out of oven before serving.

YIELD: 8–10 SERVINGS

The Everyday Gourmet
THE JUNIOR LEAGUE OF NORTHERN WESTCHESTER, BEDFORD HILLS, NEW YORK

Steak au Poivre Vert

1 tablespoon corn oil
4 club steaks, 1 inch thick
3 tablespoons cognac
1½ tablespoons crushed green peppercorns
½ cup heavy cream
1 teaspoon Dijon mustard
Salt to taste

Heat the oil in a heavy skillet and in it fry the steaks until cooked to taste. Transfer to heated platter and keep warm.

Deglaze pan with the cognac. Add the crushed peppercorns and cream. Bring to a simmer, stirring, and stir in the mustard. Pour sauce over the steaks and season with salt.

YIELD: 4 SERVINGS

THE JUNIOR LEAGUE OF THE NORTH SHORE, LONG ISLAND, NEW YORK

. . . .

Yugoslavian Barbecue

1-2 pounds round steak, pounded
1½ cups cooking oil
4 cloves garlic, minced
2 teaspoons rosemary
1½ teaspoons salt
½ teaspoon pepper
3 tablespoons prepared mustard

Cover beef with marinade of oil, garlic, 1 teaspoon rosemary, salt, and pepper. Marinate in refrigerator for 3-5 days. Just before grilling, spread meat with a mixture of mustard and 1 teaspoon rosemary. Best grilled over charcoal to desired doneness.

Serve with freshly baked bread and a salad of tomatoes, cucumbers, and onions.

YIELD: 4–6 SERVINGS

Something Special
THE JUNIOR LEAGUE OF YORK, PENNSYLVANIA

. . . .

Beef Stroganoff

1 pound boneless sirloin
Flour
2 tablespoons butter
2 tablespoons olive oil
½ cup diced onion
1 clove garlic, minced
½ pound fresh mushrooms, sliced
1 tablespoon tomato paste
¾ cup beef broth
1 cup sour cream
2 tablespoons dry sherry

Cut sirloin into ¼ x 2-inch strips, then dredge in flour. Brown quickly in butter and olive oil, leaving steak pink in center. Transfer to small casserole.

Sauté onion and garlic, then add mushrooms and sauté for 8 minutes. Add mushroom mixture to casserole with steak.

Combine tomato paste and broth in a saucepan. Boil until reduced by half, then add to steak.

Just before serving, preheat beef mixture and stir in sour cream and sherry. Serve over rice or noodles.

YIELD: 4 SERVINGS

THE JUNIOR LEAGUE OF WILKES-BARRE, PENNSYLVANIA

. . . .

Quick-Fry Chinese Dish

1 pound boneless beef
4 teaspoons cornstarch
½ teaspoon sugar
3 tablespoons soy sauce
2 tablespoons water
3 tablespoons vegetable oil
2–3 medium onions, thinly sliced
2 carrots, thinly sliced on the diagonal
1 stalk celery, thinly sliced on the diagonal
½ cup bean sprouts
Any of the following: sliced green beans,
shredded spinach leaves, sliced broccoli,
sliced cauliflower, sliced cabbage,
snow peas, thinly sliced green pepper,
sliced mushrooms
1 teaspoon shredded fresh ginger

Slice beef against the grain into 2 x 1 x ¼-inch pieces. Combine the cornstarch with sugar, soy sauce, and water and add to the beef. Mix well and set aside to marinate.

Heat wok or frying pan and add 1 tablespoon oil. Add vegetables and stir-fry for about 4 minutes, or until crispy-tender. Remove vegetables from pan.

Pour remaining 2 tablespoons oil into pan and heat. Add beef and ginger and stir-fry for 1 minute. Add cooked vegetables to pan and stir to blend with the meat. Serve immediately over hot rice.

YIELD: **4** SERVINGS

THE JUNIOR LEAGUE OF NEW BRITAIN, CONNECTICUT

Chinese Pepper Steak

2 pounds round steak, thinly sliced
3 tablespoons butter
1 10½-ounce can consommé
10½ ounces water
Salt and pepper to taste
1 tablespoon soy sauce
2 tablespoons chopped fresh ginger root
½ pound fresh mushrooms, sliced
3 large green peppers, thinly sliced

Brown steak in butter. Add consommé and water. Season with salt, pepper, and soy sauce. Add chopped ginger and simmer on low heat for 1 hour, or until meat is tender.

Add mushrooms and sliced green peppers; cover and cook for 10 minutes longer. Peppers should still be crisp. Serve with cooked rice.

YIELD: **4** SERVINGS

THE JUNIOR LEAGUE OF ALBANY, NEW YORK

• • • • • • • • • • • • • • • • •

Lemon Beef Teriyaki

1/3 cup saki
1/3 cup soy sauce
2 tablespoons sugar
½ teaspoon ground ginger
Dash garlic salt
½ lemon, thinly sliced
1 pound lean beef (preferably shell steak)
2 tablespoons vegetable oil

Recipe continues . . .

Combine first six ingredients and stir until sugar dissolves. Cut meat into thin strips. Marinate meat for at least ½ hour in mixture. Pan-fry quickly in hot oil in skillet until brown on both sides.

Serve rare with rice and Japanese-style stir-fried vegetables.

YIELD: **4** SERVINGS

THE JUNIOR LEAGUE OF MONMOUTH COUNTY, NEW JERSEY

Marinated Flank Steak

1 pound flank steak
3 tablespoons minced onion
1½ tablespoons soy sauce
2 tablespoons salad oil
½ tablespoon Italian seasoning
1 tablespoon lemon juice
Few drops Tabasco

Score steak in a diamond pattern on each side. Combine remaining ingredients, add meat, and marinate steak overnight, turning occasionally.

Broil steak 6 minutes on each side, for medium-rare. Slice very thinly, across the grain. Serve with pan juices.

YIELD: **4** SERVINGS

THE JUNIOR LEAGUE OF GREATER UTICA, NEW YORK

Beef with Broccoli

1 pound flank steak, partially frozen
½ bunch fresh broccoli
4 tablespoons soy sauce
1 tablespoon cornstarch
1 tablespoon dry sherry
1 teaspoon sugar
5 tablespoons vegetable oil
½ teaspoon salt
¼ cup sliced onion
1 teaspoon grated fresh ginger

While partially frozen, cut beef across the grain into ¼-inch slices 2 inches long. Cut the broccoli into flowerets and cut peeled stalks into ½-inch-thick slices. Wash broccoli and dry thoroughly.

Mix soy sauce, cornstarch, sherry, and sugar together. Add the beef. Set aside.

Heat 2 tablespoons of oil in a skillet over high heat and add the salt and broccoli. Stir and turn constantly until broccoli turns dark green, but not over 2 minutes. Remove from skillet.

Add remaining oil to skillet. When hot, add the onion, ginger, and beef mixture and cook, stirring, for 2 minutes or less. Add broccoli and heat thoroughly. Serve immediately.

Excellent with rice.

YIELD: 4 SERVINGS

Simply Superb
THE JUNIOR LEAGUE OF ELIZABETH-PLAINFIELD, NEW JERSEY

Carbonnade à la Flamande

4 pounds lean beef, cut in ½-inch cubes
½ cup flour
½ cup oil
2 pounds large onions, thickly sliced
6 cloves garlic, minced
3 tablespoons brown sugar
¼ cup red wine vinegar
½ cup chopped parsley
2 small bay leaves
2 teaspoons thyme
1 teaspoon salt, or to taste
Pepper
2 10½-ounce cans beef broth
24 ounces beer
Bisquick for dumplings

Dust beef lightly with flour and brown, a few cubes at a time, in hot oil. When brown, transfer to a deep 6-8-quart ovenproof casserole. Add onions and garlic to oil and brown lightly, using more oil if necessary. Add to casserole. Add sugar, 2 tablespoons vinegar, parsley, bay leaves, thyme, salt, and pepper; stir once or twice. Add the beef broth and beer. Cover and bake at 325° for 2 hours.

This recipe can be made a day ahead and refrigerated at this point. To finish, place casserole on top of stove, add the remaining vinegar, and cook over medium heat until the sauce bubbles. Drop baking powder biscuit batter by the teaspoonful on the hot stew. Cover, reduce heat, and cook for 15 minutes. Do not remove cover while dumplings are cooking.

YIELD: 8 SERVINGS

Greenwich Recommends
THE JUNIOR LEAGUE OF GREENWICH, CONNECTICUT

Braised Beef with Beer

2½ pounds beef chuck, cubed
2 tablespoons butter
2 tablespoons oil
3 tablespoons flour
3 large onions, sliced
2 cups beer
½ teaspoon thyme
1 teaspoon sugar
⅛ teaspoon nutmeg
1 teaspoon salt
1 small loaf French bread, sliced
Dijon mustard

Sauté beef in butter and oil. Transfer to casserole with tight cover and sprinkle with flour. Add onions, beer, and seasonings. Cover and cook for 2 hours at 350°.

Coat one side of bread heavily with mustard. Place mustard side of the bread down on the stew, uncover, and cook for 20 minutes more.

YIELD: **4** SERVINGS

THE JUNIOR LEAGUE OF MORRISTOWN, NEW JERSEY

Juicy Meat Loaf

1 large egg
1 12-ounce bottle chili sauce
½ green pepper, chopped
1 large onion, chopped
2 teaspoons Worcestershire sauce
1 tablespoon prepared mustard
2 tablespoons chopped fresh parsley or 1 tablespoon dried parsley
Freshly ground pepper
1 cup bread crumbs (optional)
1½ pounds equal parts ground beef, pork, and veal
Bacon

Mix first ten ingredients together, adding meat last. Put in ovenproof casserole and cover top with bacon slices. Bake in preheated oven at 350° for 1 hour.

YIELD: 4 SERVINGS

THE JUNIOR LEAGUE OF SUMMIT, NEW JERSEY

. . . .

Reuben Meat Loaf

1½ pounds ground beef
1½ cups rye bread crumbs
1 egg
½ cup chopped onion
¼ cup pickle relish
¼ cup Russian dressing
1 tablespoon Worcestershire sauce
1½ cups shredded Swiss cheese
1 14-ounce can sauerkraut

Mix the first seven ingredients and spread on wax paper. Sprinkle with the cheese and sauerkraut. Roll like a jelly roll. Place in a baking dish and bake at 350° for 1 hour.

YIELD: 4–6 SERVINGS

THE JUNIOR LEAGUE OF WILLIAMSPORT, PENNSYLVANIA

Yankee Red Flannel Hash

1–2 cups cooked corned beef
6 potatoes, peeled and cooked
8 carrots, peeled and cooked
1 small head cabbage, cooked and quartered
2 15-ounce cans beets, drained
4 turnips, peeled and cooked
4 onions, peeled and cooked
¼ cup milk
1 teaspoon salt
3–4 drops hot pepper sauce

In a meat grinder, cut the corned beef, potatoes, carrots, cabbage, beets, turnips, and onions. Then mix together and add the milk, salt, and hot pepper sauce.

The hash can be fried in ½ cup oil until crusty or baked at 350° for 30–40 minutes.

YIELD: 6–8 SERVINGS

THE JUNIOR LEAGUE OF SPRINGFIELD, MASSACHUSETTS

Lamb Korma Curry

This is a true Indian curry. The creation of your own curry powder makes all the difference in taste. May be prepared early in the day and reheated.

2 tablespoons ground coriander
1 teaspoon cumin
1 tablespoon poppy seed
1 teaspoon turmeric
4 cloves garlic
1" piece fresh ginger
¼ teaspoon cayenne
1 fresh or pickled green chili
3 tablespoons unsweetened coconut
1 teaspoon paprika
6 cloves
¼ teaspoon ground cardamon
2 medium onions
3 tablespoons vegetable oil
2" stick cinnamon
2 pounds lamb, cubed
1 teaspoon salt
1 cup yogurt

Put first 12 ingredients and 1 of the onions in a blender, and blend until a paste is formed. Chop the other onion and brown in the vegetable oil. Add the spice paste and cinnamon stick and sauté for 3 minutes. Add meat and sauté for 5 minutes. Add salt and yogurt. Cover and simmer for 20–30 minutes, or until meat is tender, stirring occasionally. Add only enough water to prevent burning. The sauce should be thick.

YIELD: 5–6 SERVINGS

Presenting Boston . . . A Cookbook
THE JUNIOR LEAGUE OF BOSTON, MASSACHUSETTS

Steak Teriyaki

1¹/₂–2 pounds lean beef, preferably flank steak
1 tablespoon salad oil
¹/₂ cup soy sauce
¹/₄ cup brown sugar
1 teaspoon ground ginger
2 tablespoons dry sherry
1 clove garlic, minced
¹/₂ teaspoon salt

Score steak in diamond pattern or cut into strips and roll pinwheel style. Fasten pinwheels with toothpicks. Combine remaining ingredients, pour over meat, and marinate 1½ hours or more. Broil until done to taste.

YIELD: **4–6** SERVINGS

THE JUNIOR LEAGUE OF ROCHESTER, NEW YORK

Stuffed Leg of Lamb

1 6–7-pound leg of lamb
Olive oil
1 teaspoon crushed oregano
1 teaspoon crushed basil
1 teaspoon crushed rosemary
½ cup dry bread crumbs
3 tablespoons minced parsley
2 tablespoons softened margarine
2 teaspoons grated lemon peel
1 clove garlic, minced
1 teaspoon salt
⅛ teaspoon pepper

Bone lamb, leaving only the shank bone. Remove fat. Combine remaining ingredients and spread the mixture as evenly as possible over the inside cut surface of the meat. Close up and tie with string. For well-done lamb, roast at 400° for 2 hours.

YIELD: 10 SERVINGS

Greenwich Recommends
THE JUNIOR LEAGUE OF GREENWICH, CONNECTICUT

Lamb Chasseur

1 6-pound leg of lamb, boned and butterflied
2 tablespoons oil
2 onions, chopped
2 carrots, sliced
3 stalks celery, sliced
1 bouquet garni
1½ cups white wine
1½ cups consommé
2 tablespoons tomato paste
1½ cups cherry tomatoes
1½ cups quartered mushrooms

Brown lamb on smooth side in oil. Spread stuffing on boned side of lamb, roll, and tie. Put in casserole with all remaining ingredients except tomatoes and mushrooms; cover and braise for 1½ hours at 350°. Add tomatoes and mushrooms 15 minutes before end of braising time.

YIELD: 8 SERVINGS

STUFFING:
1 cup fresh bread crumbs
2 tablespoons chopped walnuts
Grated rind of 1 lemon
1 tablespoon chopped parsley
2 tablespoons melted butter
1 onion, chopped
1 egg, lightly beaten
Salt and pepper to taste

Mix all ingredients for stuffing.

THE JUNIOR LEAGUE OF THE NORTH SHORE, LONG ISLAND, NEW YORK

Agneau à la Moutarde

1 8-ounce jar Dijon mustard
½ cup olive oil
2–3 cloves garlic, minced
1 teaspoon crushed rosemary
1 teaspoon thyme
1 teaspoon crushed bay leaves
Pepper
1 6-pound leg of lamb, boned and butterflied in one piece

Mix all marinade ingredients together. Slash lamb in several places and spread the marinade generously on all sides. Cover and marinate for several hours or overnight.

Next day, broil lamb on a charcoal grill or in oven broiler for 25–30 minutes for medium-rare, turning several times throughout the cooking. Do not overcook or meat will be dry.

YIELD: 8 SERVINGS

Bicentennial Cookbook
THE JUNIOR LEAGUE OF PHILADELPHIA, PENNSYLVANIA

Herb Basted Rack of Lamb

1 8-rib rack of lamb
1 tablespoon salt
1 tablespoon freshly ground pepper, or more to taste
2 tablespoons each minced chives, shallot, and marjoram
2 cloves garlic, minced
1 tablespoon olive oil
½ stick butter
½ cup bread crumbs
2 tablespoons chopped parsley

Preheat oven to 450°. Trim fat away from ends of chops, about 1½ inches down. Score fat with sharp knife. Sprinkle with salt and pepper. Make a paste with the herbs, half the garlic, and olive oil; rub scored side with the paste. Roast 25–30 minutes in the preheated oven.

While roasting, melt butter and combine it with bread crumbs, remaining garlic, and parsley. Remove roast and sprinkle with the bread crumb mixture. Return to oven for 5 minutes for rare; 10 minutes for medium, 15 minutes for well-done.

YIELD: **4** SERVINGS

Cooks Book
THE JUNIOR LEAGUE OF GREATER NEW HAVEN, CONNECTICUT

Lamb Curry

3 pounds lean lamb
½ cup oil
3–4 cloves garlic, minced
4 onions, chopped
1 bay leaf, crumbled
1 teaspoon cinnamon
5–6 whole cloves
1 teaspoon salt
2 tablespoons curry powder
1 tablespoon paprika
½ teaspoon pepper
1 teaspoon ground cumin
1 teaspoon coriander
3 ripe tomatoes, peeled and chopped
1–1½ cups water

Recipe continues . . .

Trim fat from lamb and chop into 1-inch pieces.

Heat oil in a 3-quart kettle and in it sauté garlic and onions until transparent but not brown. Add bay leaf, cinnamon, and cloves. Cover and simmer for 5 minutes. Add meat and cook uncovered over medium heat, stirring constantly, until most of the water from the meat has steamed off and liquid thickens. Stir in remaining ingredients and add enough water to just cover meat. Simmer for 1 hour.

Serve over rice.

YIELD: 6 SERVINGS

THE JUNIOR LEAGUE OF FALL RIVER, MASSACHUSETTS

· · · · · · · · · · · · · · · ·

Dolmas
(Stuffed Grape Leaves)

This is a basic recipe. If desired, ½–1 cup of pine nuts or raisins, or a flavoring of herbs, may be added. The grape leaves can be bought at or ordered from any food store carrying Near Eastern groceries. Gourmet stores also carry them.

1 pound ground lamb
1 cup finely chopped onion
¼ cup long-grain rice
¼ cup chopped parsley
1 teaspoon salt
Freshly ground pepper to taste
Juice of 1 lemon
1/3 cup tomato paste
1 pound grape leaves
Chicken broth or water
2 tablespoons olive oil
Lemon slices for garnish

Preheat oven to 350°.

In a large mixing bowl, combine the lamb, onion, rice, parsley, salt, pepper, lemon juice, and tomato paste.

Rinse the grape leaves in cold water. Place shiny side of grape leaves on a flat surface. Place 1 teaspoon of lamb mixture in center of each leaf and roll fairly tightly, tucking in the ends. If the leaves are torn, use a second leaf for each roll. Place in rows in 2-quart baking dish. Add enough broth or water to cover and the olive oil. Weight leaves down with a plate. Cover the baking dish and bake at 350° for 1 hour.

Serve hot or cold as a main dish, but do not chill or the flavor will be lost. Garnish with lemon slices.

YIELD: 6 SERVINGS

The Melting Pot
THE JUNIOR LEAGUE OF THE CENTRAL DELAWARE VALLEY, NEW JERSEY

. . . .

Lamb and Zucchini Casserole

6 medium or 3 large zucchini
Salt and pepper
1 cup bread crumbs
4 tablespoons butter
2 tablespoons olive oil
3/4 cup chopped onion
1 clove garlic, finely chopped
1½ pounds ground lamb
¼ cup converted rice
1 teaspoon grated lemon rind
2 tablespoons chopped fresh mint or 1 tablespoon dried mint
1 cup chicken broth

Recipe continues . . .

Preheat oven to 375°.

Wash zucchini and slice thinly. Arrange half the slices in bottom of a buttered medium-size casserole, and sprinkle with salt and pepper.

Sauté bread crumbs over low heat in 4 tablespoons butter until browned.

Heat oil and in it sauté onion, garlic, lamb, and rice together until lamb is gray, not brown; stir often. Add salt and pepper to taste, lemon rind, and mint. Mix together and spoon into casserole over zucchini.

Cover lamb with remaining zucchini. Pour chicken broth over top layer of zucchini and sprinkle with bread crumbs.

Bake in oven for 35–40 minutes.

YIELD: 4 SERVINGS

THE JUNIOR LEAGUE OF BROOKLYN, NEW YORK

·   ·   ·   ·   ·   ·   ·   ·   ·   ·   ·   ·   ·   ·   ·   ·

Joanne's Lamb Curry

4 large apples, peeled, cored, and sliced
1½ large onions, sliced
1 clove garlic
3 tablespoons flour
1½ tablespoons curry powder
1 tablespoon freshly squeezed lemon juice
2 cups meat stock or bouillon
1 teaspoon gravy flavoring
Grated rind of ½ lemon
¾ cup raisins
3 whole cloves
2 cups cubed leftover cooked lamb

Sauté apples, onions, and garlic in butter until golden brown. Discard garlic. Blend in flour and curry powder.

Combine lemon juice, stock, and gravy flavoring; stir in gradually.

Stir in lemon rind, raisins, and cloves. Cover and simmer for 30 minutes. Add lamb. Heat thoroughly.

Serve with cooked rice.

YIELD: **4** SERVINGS

Show House Recipes
THE JUNIOR LEAGUE OF BINGHAMTON, NEW YORK

• • • • • • • • • • • • • • • • • • • •

Roast Veal with Parsley Sauce

2 small cloves garlic
4½ pounds roast veal (leg portion)
1½ teaspoons thyme
Salt and pepper
8 slices bacon
3 tablespoons melted butter
6 tablespoons dry Madeira

Peel the garlic, cut in half, and rub over the entire roast. Sprinkle thyme on the meat. Add salt and pepper. Cover the veal roast with the bacon and arrange on a rack in open roasting pan. Pour melted butter and Madeira over meat.

Preheat oven to 325° and roast meat for about 2 hours, or until meat thermometer reaches 160°. Baste the meat often with the accumulated pan juices. Cool meat for about 3 hours, then discard the bacon. Slice meat very thinly and serve with Parsley Sauce.

YIELD: **6** SERVINGS

Recipe continues . . .

PARSLEY SAUCE:

3 cups heavy cream
Salt
Dash pepper
1 tablespoon dry mustard
2½ tablespoons tomato paste
3 tablespoons very finely chopped fresh parsley

In a saucepan, simmer the heavy cream, salt, and pepper for about 10 minutes, or until cream is reduced to about 2 cups. Mix mustard and tomato paste together and slowly beat into the hot cream. Cool the sauce; it will thicken as it cooks.

Stir in the parsley and correct the seasoning.

THE JUNIOR LEAGUE OF THE CITY OF NEW YORK, NEW YORK

. . . .

Stuffed Breast of Veal

2 tablespoons oil or fat
½ pound sausage meat
½ pound ground chuck
1 large onion, minced
¼ teaspoon each garlic salt, salt, paprika, pepper, and nutmeg
2 eggs
2 cups bread crumbs
1 4-ounce can mushrooms with 1 teaspoon mushroom juice
¼–½ cup water
1 2-pound breast of veal with pocket
Bacon slices

In hot fat or oil, cook sausage and beef until all color is gone from the beef. Add onion and seasonings and cook, stirring occasionally, for 10 minutes. Cool.

In large bowl, mix eggs, bread crumbs, mushrooms and juice, and water. Add meat and onions and combine. Stuff pocket in the veal and skewer closed. Arrange bacon slices on top.

Roast in shallow roasting pan, uncovered, for 3 hours at 325°.

YIELD: 6 SERVINGS

Recipes by Request
THE JUNIOR LEAGUE OF GREATER WATERBURY, CONNECTICUT

. . . .

Veal Mozzarella

½ cup olive oil or vegetable oil
1 large onion, chopped
2 cloves garlic, minced
3 tablespoons chopped green pepper
¼ pound fresh mushrooms, sliced
3 8-ounce cans tomato sauce
1 bay leaf
¼–½ teaspoon oregano
1 egg
½ cup milk
1 teaspoon salt
⅛ teaspoon pepper
1½ pounds veal cutlets, thinly sliced
1 cup fine dry bread crumbs
6 ounces mozzarella cheese, shredded

Heat half the oil in large skillet, and in it sauté onion, garlic, green pepper, and mushrooms until limp. Add tomato sauce, bay leaf, and oregano. Cover and simmer for 20 minutes; discard bay leaf.

Beat together egg, milk, salt, and pepper. Dip veal cutlets, one at a time, into egg and milk mixture, coat with bread crumbs, then brown on both sides in remaining oil.

Arrange cutlets in shallow baking dish, cover with tomato sauce

Recipe continues . . .

mixture, and bake in a preheated 350° oven for 30 minutes. Sprinkle cheese on top and bake 5–10 minutes longer, or until cheese is bubbly and golden.

Serve with a tossed green salad and egg noodles.

YIELD: 6 GENEROUS SERVINGS

THE JUNIOR LEAGUE OF MONTREAL, QUEBEC

· · · · · · · · · · · · · · · ·

Veal Vermouth

2 pounds veal cutlets, cut into serving pieces
Salt and pepper to taste
Butter
Parmesan cheese, finely grated
2 large onions, chopped
4–5 carrots, sliced not too thin
½ pound mushrooms, sliced
3 chicken bouillon cubes
1½ cups boiling water
½ cup vermouth or white wine

Sprinkle cutlets with salt and pepper and cheese. Brown in butter in heavy skillet. Arrange in 3-quart casserole.

Sauté the onions, carrots, and mushrooms in skillet, adding more butter if necessary. Dissolve bouillon cubes in water and add wine. Pour over semicooked vegetables; pour vegetables over veal. Refrigerate casserole.

When ready to serve, bake, covered, at 325° for 1 hour. Juice is good served over noodles, rice, or mashed potatoes.

YIELD: 6 SERVINGS

Recipes by Request
THE JUNIOR LEAGUE OF GREATER WATERBURY, CONNECTICUT

· · · · · · · · · · · · · · · ·

Swiss Veal Dish

1½ pounds veal, thinly sliced
1 medium onion, chopped
2 tablespoons butter
1 pint light cream
1 teaspoon salt
Freshly ground pepper
2 tablespoons chopped parsley

Sauté onion in butter until soft. Add veal, cut into very small pieces. Cook 3–4 minutes, or until veal is done. Reduce heat. Add cream, salt and pepper, and most of the parsley. Stir constantly until cream is heated through. Add remaining parsley.

Serve on rice or with hashed brown potatoes.

YIELD: 6 SERVINGS

THE JUNIOR LEAGUE OF SUMMIT, NEW JERSEY

Mahieux's Escalopes de Veau

6 thinly sliced veal cutlets
6 tablespoons butter
2 tablespoons oil
Salt and pepper to taste
1 lemon, halved
1 pound fresh mushrooms, sliced
1 tablespoon cornstarch
1 cup heavy cream
½ cup dry white wine or ¼ cup dry vermouth
Parsley for garnish

Recipe continues . . .

Dry the cutlets on paper toweling. Heat 2 tablespoons butter and 1 tablespoon oil in a large skillet. As soon as the butter foam has almost subsided, arrange half the veal in the skillet. Sprinkle with pepper and some juice from one of the lemon halves. Sauté on one side for 3–4 minutes; turn, sprinkle more pepper and lemon juice on the veal, and sauté on the other side until lightly browned (4–5 minutes). Remove to a separate ovenproof dish and repeat with remaining veal cutlets, using more butter and remaining oil.

Using the same skillet, melt remaining 2 tablespoons butter and in it sauté the mushrooms lightly, sprinkling with pepper and juice from the other lemon half. Stir in 1 tablespoon cornstarch mixed with 2 tablespoons of the cream. Reduce heat and stir in remaining cream and wine. Season to taste with salt and pepper and simmer for 1 minute.

Spoon cream and mushrooms over the veal. May be covered with aluminum foil and kept in warm oven until serving time. To serve, surround veal with cooked rice and garnish with parsley.

YIELD: 4 SERVINGS

THE JUNIOR LEAGUE OF FALL RIVER, MASSACHUSETTS

. . . .

Veal Scallops in Cream

2 small, thin slices veal
Salt and pepper to taste
2 tablespoons butter
2–3 large mushrooms, sliced
¼ cup port wine
1 teaspoon butter
1 teaspoon flour
½ cup heavy cream
Pinch cayenne

Sprinkle the veal slices with salt and pepper. In skillet, heat butter and in it sauté the veal until lightly brown on both sides. Remove meat to heated serving dish and add mushrooms to butter and juices remaining in pan. Sauté for 3–4 minutes.

Stir in port and cook until wine is reduced a little. Blend in butter mixed with flour bit by bit. Add cream and cayenne to taste. Heat to simmering. Pour over veal and serve.

YIELD: 1 SERVING

THE JUNIOR LEAGUE OF WORCESTER, MASSACHUSETTS

Leone's Saltimbocca

6 very thin veal slices, cut into 3-inch squares
6 very thin 3-inch squares prosciutto
Fresh sage leaves, dried if fresh aren't available
2 tablespoons butter
2 tablespoons olive oil
½ teaspoon salt
⅛ teaspoon pepper
¼ cup dry white wine

Pound each slice of veal. Place sage leaf on each piece, top with prosciutto, and pin together with 2 toothpicks. Brown and cook in hot butter and oil. Season with salt and pepper.

Remove meat from pan. Stir wine into drippings, scraping bottom and sides of pan. Simmer about 1 minute, then pour over veal.

Serve with cooked fettucine and green vegetable for a delicious dinner.

YIELD: 4 SERVINGS

THE JUNIOR LEAGUE OF ORANGE COUNTY, NEW YORK

Veal Scallopini with Cheese

2 pounds veal, cut into thin, even slices
½ cup butter (8 tablespoons)
3 tablespoons sherry
1 tablespoon flour
½ cup water
½ cup milk
1 bouillon cube
Dash nutmeg
Freshly ground black pepper to taste
½ pound Swiss cheese, thinly sliced

Pound veal until very thin.

Heat 6 tablespoons of the butter in a frying pan; add veal and cook until brown on both sides.

Remove veal and arrange in a baking dish. Drain off any excess butter into saucepan. Add sherry to frying pan and simmer 1 minute, stirring to loosen particles. Pour over veal.

To make sauce, add remaining butter to butter in saucepan and melt. Add flour and stir until blended. Bring water and milk to a boil and dissolve bouillon cube in the mixture. Add all at once to flour mixture, stirring constantly until sauce is thickened and smooth. Season with nutmeg and pepper.

Arrange Swiss cheese over veal. Pour sauce over all.

May be refrigerated for several hours. Before serving, heat in 425° oven until cheese melts and is lightly browned, about 20 minutes.

YIELD: 6 SERVINGS

THE JUNIOR LEAGUE OF ORANGE COUNTY, NEW YORK

Veal Scallopini with Mustard Sauce

8 thin slices veal from leg (about ¾ pound)
1/3 cup flour
Salt and pepper
4 tablespoons butter
2 tablespoons minced shallots
¼ cup dry white wine
½ cup heavy cream
1 tablespoon imported Dijon mustard

Pound scallopini with a mallet until very thin. Blend flour, salt, and pepper and dredge meat on both sides.

Heat butter in heavy skillet; do not brown. Add scallopini. Cook quickly until golden, about 2 minutes on each side. Remove from skillet and keep on a warm dish covered with foil.

Add shallots to skillet and cook briefly. Add wine and cook until it is almost totally evaporated. Add cream and bring to a boil. Cook about 30 seconds; turn off the heat. Stir in the mustard but do not cook further.

Spoon sauce over the meat. Serve with fine buttered noodles.

YIELD: 4 SERVINGS

THE JUNIOR LEAGUE OF KINGSTON, NEW YORK

Blanquette de Veau

1½ *pounds shoulder or breast of veal*
1 stick butter
1 carrot, quartered
1 onion, halved
2 cloves
1 bay leaf
Salt and pepper to taste
Pinch thyme
Pinch parsley
2½ *cups chicken or veal broth or water*
½ *pound mushrooms, trimmed*
Juice of ½ *lemon*
2 tablespoons flour
20 small white onions, peeled
1 egg yolk
½ *cup heavy cream*

Cut meat into 1-inch cubes. Melt 2 tablespoons butter in a Dutch oven and in it brown the meat lightly. Add the carrot, halved onion, cloves, bay leaf, salt, pepper, thyme, parsley, and broth. Cover and simmer for 30 minutes. Drain, reserving the liquid.

In a separate pan, melt 1 tablespoon butter and in it sauté mushrooms. Add a few drops of lemon juice and cook gently.

In another pan, simmer the whole onions in 1 tablespoon butter and 3 tablespoons of the liquid from the meat for 5 minutes.

Remove meat from the Dutch oven. Discard the carrot, onion, and bay leaf. Melt remaining 4 tablespoons butter in the Dutch oven, add the flour, and stir with a wire whisk for 1-2 minutes. Gradually stir in liquid from the meat, the meat, mushrooms, and the whole onions. Simmer for 35 minutes.

Mix egg yolk, heavy cream, and lemon juice with 4 tablespoons of the sauce. Stir this into the sauce, heat, but do not boil. Serve with rice or steamed potatoes.

YIELD: 4 SERVINGS

Simply Superb
THE JUNIOR LEAGUE OF ELIZABETH-PLAINFIELD, NEW JERSEY

. . . .

Veal Marengo in Toast Boxes

4 pounds boneless leg of veal, cubed
½ cup olive oil
1 pound onions (about 6 medium), chopped
4 cloves garlic, minced
2/3 cup flour
3-4 cups dry white wine
1 bouquet garni (1 bay leaf, 1 teaspoon thyme,
10 sprigs fresh parsley in cheesecloth bag)
2 teaspoons salt
1 teaspoon black pepper
8 fresh ripe tomatoes, cored and quartered
(use canned if not ripe and flavorful)
1 pound small fresh button mushrooms, cleaned
¼ cup chopped fresh parsley
12 Toast Boxes

Dry veal cubes on paper toweling. Over high heat in a large kettle, quickly brown one-quarter of the veal in 1 tablespoon olive oil. Remove veal and set aside while browning remaining meat in same manner. Add remaining ¼ cup oil to kettle and lightly brown onions and garlic. Add the flour and a little wine to onions and cook for 3 minutes, stirring. Return the browned veal to the casserole and add remaining wine, bouquet garni, salt, and pepper.

Cover the casserole and gently simmer for 30 minutes. Stir

Recipe continues . . .

frequently to prevent burning. Add the tomatoes and mushrooms and simmer, covered, another 30 minutes. Check to make sure veal is tender. Discard the bouquet garni. Check for salt and pepper.

At this point stew may be refrigerated for 2–3 days or frozen. Bring to room temperature and reheat. Spoon into Toast Boxes, sprinkle with parsley, and serve.

YIELD: 12 SERVINGS

TOAST BOXES:

4 1-pound loaves unsliced firm white bread
1 pound butter, melted (do not substitute margarine)

Remove all crusts from the loaves. (Dry out all this excess bread and crusts for homemade bread crumbs.) Slice each loaf crosswise into approximately three equal cubes, each cube approximately 2½–3 inches square. To shape each box, place a single cube flat on a cutting surface. Cut around inside of cube ¼ inch from the sides and no deeper than ¼ inch up from the bottom. Then slip knife through only one side of box ¼ inch up from bottom and cut across that one side to release center piece of bread. Lift this center cube out and add to bread crumb reserve.

Dip bread boxes on all sides into melted butter. Let excess drain back into saucepan. Place dipped bread boxes on cookie sheet. Cover with plastic wrap and leave at room temperature or refrigerate overnight. When ready to serve, bake in a 350° oven for 10–15 minutes or until golden brown.

YIELD: 12 TOAST BOXES

From Our House
THE JUNIOR LEAGUE OF HARTFORD, CONNECTICUT

Veal Madelon

1 clove garlic, minced
2 tablespoons butter
2 pounds boneless veal, cut into bite-size chunks
2 tablespoons flour
1 teaspoon salt
½ teaspoon pepper
2 lemon peels
1 cup hot water
1 cup heavy cream

Sauté garlic in butter. Remove garlic and brown veal in the same butter. Sprinkle the browned veal with flour, salt, and pepper and let the flour brown. Add lemon peels and water, mix, and simmer, covered, until meat is tender, about 1 hour. Discard lemon peels, stir in cream, and heat through.

Serve with hot buttered noodles.

YIELD: **4** SERVINGS

THE JUNIOR LEAGUE OF ROCHESTER, NEW YORK

. . . .

Sautéed Calves' Liver with Vinegar Glaze

½ cup flour
Salt and freshly ground pepper
1 pound calves' liver, very thinly sliced
8 tablespoons butter
¼ cup chopped fresh parsley
¼ cup red wine vinegar

Recipe continues . . .

Blend flour with salt and pepper to taste and dredge the liver on all sides with the mixture.

Heat half of the butter in a heavy skillet and add the liver. Cook for 3–4 minutes, shaking pan and tossing liver frequently. Don't overcook. Transfer liver to a heated platter and sprinkle with parsley.

Add remaining butter to the skillet. Let it brown, then pour over liver. Add vinegar to the skillet and bring it to a boil, swirling it around in the skillet. Pour over the liver and serve.

YIELD: **4** SERVINGS

The Everyday Gourmet
THE JUNIOR LEAGUE OF NORTHERN WESTCHESTER, BEDFORD HILLS, NEW YORK

. . . .

The-Only-Way-My-Family-Will-Eat-Liver Casserole

4 slices bacon
¼ cup bacon fat and/or margarine
2 cups sliced onion
¾ teaspoon salt
¼ teaspoon pepper
2 tablespoons flour
1½ cups beef bouillon
1 pound calf, beef, lamb, pork, or chicken liver,
preferably frozen for easy cubing
4 medium potatoes, peeled and thinly sliced
Sprinkle rosemary and sweet basil
Chopped parsley

Fry bacon in large skillet; drain, crumble, and set aside.

Measure bacon fat and, if necessary, add margarine to make ¼ cup. Put in skillet, add onion slices, and sauté until onion is golden brown. Sprinkle with salt, pepper, and flour. Mix well, gradually adding bouillon, and bring to a boil, stirring.

Cut liver in ½-inch cubes. If liver is not frozen, it is easier to cut with kitchen scissors. Add liver and potatoes to skillet. Sprinkle potatoes lightly with rosemary and sweet basil. Stir once. Cover and simmer for 25 minutes, or until potatoes are tender and liquid is of gravy consistency. Sprinkle with parsley, salt and pepper, if needed, and reserved bacon. Serve in an attractive casserole.

YIELD: 4–6 SERVINGS

THE JUNIOR LEAGUE OF ERIE, PENNSYLVANIA

· ·

Baked Pork Tenderloin

3 whole pork tenderloins, all fat removed
Salt and pepper
Butter

SAUCE:
½ cup currant jelly
¼ cup Dijon mustard
Water

Dust pork with salt and pepper. Sauté in butter for about 5 minutes, or until brown on all sides. Place in shallow baking dish about 7 x 11 x 1½ inches.

Melt jelly and mustard in saucepan and blend well. Pour over pork and add ½ inch water to pan. Bake for 50 minutes at 325°. Add a little more sauce or water to pan if necessary to keep it from baking dry. Turn pork once or baste with the sauce.

Serve sliced on a warm platter with sauce on the side.

YIELD: 6 SERVINGS

THE JUNIOR LEAGUE OF THE ORANGES AND SHORT HILLS, NEW JERSEY

· ·

Elegant Pork Chop Broil

1¼–1½–inch loin or shoulder chop per person
Chopped parsley for garnish

SAUCE FOR 6 CHOPS:
½ cup brown sugar
¼ cup cider vinegar
3 teaspoons prepared brown mustard
1 teaspoon Worcestershire sauce
Dash powdered cloves (optional)

Mix ingredients for sauce. If time permits, marinate chops in sauce for 2–3 hours. However, if time is short, use marinade to baste chops without marinating first.

Broil about 4 inches from heat for 8–10 minutes, basting occasionally. Turn and continue to broil for 8–10 minutes longer.

Serve on bed of rice. Pour drippings over meat and rice. Sprinkle with chopped parsley.

YIELD: 6 OR MORE SERVINGS

THE JUNIOR LEAGUE OF ALBANY, NEW YORK

Pork Chops with Beer

4 rib or loin pork chops, about 1 inch thick
3 cloves garlic, minced
½ teaspoon caraway seeds
½ teaspoon salt
¼ teaspoon pepper
2 tablespoons flour
2 tablespoons vegetable oil
1 cup light beer
1 tablespoon prepared mustard
1 cup canned beef broth or brown stock
or 2 bouillon cubes dissolved in 1 cup water

Rub each pork chop on both sides with garlic, caraway seeds, salt, and pepper. Dredge in flour. Brown chops on both sides in oil in a large skillet. Remove and keep warm.

Drain off all fat in skillet, leaving brown bits in pan. Add beer and bring to a boil over high heat, stirring and scraping skillet to loosen brown bits; simmer liquid until reduced to ½ cup. Stir in mustard and beef broth. Simmer until sauce is reduced to 1 cup.

Arrange browned pork chops in skillet, cover, and simmer for 45 minutes, turning once. Serve with sauce.

YIELD: **4** SERVINGS

Show House Recipes
THE JUNIOR LEAGUE OF BINGHAMTON, NEW YORK

Pork Chops Senegalese

½ teaspoon salt
4 pork chops, 1 inch thick
2/3 cup raw long-grain rice
½ cup raisins
½ cup sliced almonds
2 green onions, minced
½ teaspoon curry powder
1 8-ounce can tomato sauce
1 cup dry white wine

Put salt in heavy frying pan large enough to hold the chops. Brown chops on both sides over moderate heat.

Combine the rice, raisins, almonds, onions, and curry powder. Spoon this mixture around browned chops. Pour tomato sauce and wine over chops. Cover pan, bring liquid to a boil, then simmer for about 30 minutes, or until rice is tender.

YIELD: 2–4 SERVINGS

THE JUNIOR LEAGUE OF BROOKLYN, NEW YORK

. . . .

Special Pork Chops

4 thick pork chops
1½ tablespoons olive oil
1½ tablespoons butter
Salt and freshly ground pepper
¼ pound Gruyère cheese, shredded
1–2 teaspoons dry mustard
Light cream

Sauté chops in oil and butter in heavy frying pan until browned on both sides. Season to taste with salt and pepper. Reduce heat and continue to cook for about 20 minutes, or until cooked through.

Remove chops from pan and spread with a thick paste made from Gruyère, mustard, and enough cream to give a spreading consistency. Arrange chops in a small pan and put under broiler until sauce is hot and bubbling.

YIELD: **4** SERVINGS

THE JUNIOR LEAGUE OF ELMIRA, NEW YORK

Pork and Sauerkraut

2 27-ounce cans sauerkraut with liquid
2 tablespoons light brown sugar
1 tablespoon granulated sugar
1 cup water
6 pounds center-cut pork loin

Preheat oven to 450°. Spread sauerkraut in bottom of a large roasting pan. Add brown sugar, granulated sugar, and water; mix. Place pork roast on top. Salt and pepper meat to taste. Roast without lid until meat is nicely browned, about 35–40 minutes. Reduce heat to 250° and cover roaster. Bake slowly for 3 hours (or more if you like your meat falling apart). Cooking the meat longer won't hurt the sauerkraut; it gets better the longer it cooks, but you may have to add more water to the meat juices to keep it from burning.

Serve with mashed potatoes.

YIELD: **6–8** SERVINGS

THE JUNIOR LEAGUE OF THE LEHIGH VALLEY, PENNSYLVANIA

Smothered Pork

1 tablespoon lard
4 pork chops
2 cups drained and rinsed sauerkraut
¼ cup chopped onion
4 apples, peeled, cored, and sliced
4 tablespoons brown sugar
1 teaspoon caraway seeds

Melt lard in skillet and slowly brown pork chops on both sides. Remove chops from skillet, drain off fat.

Combine sauerkraut, onion, apples, sugar, and caraway seeds. Pour sauerkraut mixture into skillet and place pork chops on top. Cover and simmer 45 minutes, or until chops are tender.

YIELD: 4 SERVINGS

THE JUNIOR LEAGUE OF POUGHKEEPSIE, NEW YORK

. . . .

Skewered Pork de Brasília

¼ cup soy sauce
¼ cup lemon juice
2 tablespoons brown sugar
8 Brazil nuts, grated
1 cup minced onion
3 cloves garlic, minced
1½ tablespoons crushed coriander seeds
¼ teaspoon crushed red pepper
¼ cup olive oil
2 pounds lean pork, cut into cubes
Kumquats

Make marinade of all ingredients except pork and kumquats. Marinate pork in the marinade for at least ½ hour.

Put pork on skewers. Place in a shallow baking pan and pour marinade over them. Bake in preheated 450° oven for 25 minutes.

Garnish with kumquats and serve with remaining sauce and cooked rice.

YIELD: 6 SERVINGS

The Everyday Gourmet
THE JUNIOR LEAGUE OF NORTHERN WESTCHESTER, BEDFORD HILLS, NEW YORK

· ·

Pork Chop Bake

3 tablespoons oil
6 pork chops
1 large onion, sliced
2 teaspoons chili powder
1 cup uncooked rice
1 cup canned tomatoes
1 cup water
1 teaspoon salt

Heat oil in a skillet. Brown the pork chops on both sides in the oil. Remove the chops and brown the onion slices until soft and clear. Stir in the chili powder, rice, tomatoes, water, and salt. Heat to boiling.

Pour into a 9 x 13-inch baking dish and place the pork chops on top. Cover and bake at 375° for 1 hour, or until all the liquid is absorbed.

YIELD: 6 SERVINGS

THE JUNIOR LEAGUE OF SYRACUSE, NEW YORK

· ·

Sweet Ham and Pork Loaf

1 pound ground smoked ham
1½ pounds ground fresh pork
2 eggs, beaten
1 cup milk
1 cup bread or cracker crumbs
Salt and pepper
1½ cups brown sugar
¼ cup water
½ cup vinegar
1 tablespoon dry mustard

Mix ham, pork, eggs, milk, crumbs, and a little salt and pepper. Form into a loaf on an ovenproof container.

Boil brown sugar, water, vinegar, and mustard together for 5 minutes. Baste loaf with one-quarter of the sugar mixture. Bake loaf at 375° for 2 hours, basting with sugar mixture frequently.

Good served with raisin sauce.

YIELD: 8 SERVINGS

THE JUNIOR LEAGUE OF HARRISBURG, PENNSYLVANIA

. . . .

Hungarian Goulash

3 medium onions, chopped
2 tablespoons shortening
1½ pounds fresh pork shoulder, cubed
1½ teaspoons sweet paprika
Salt to taste
½ teaspoon caraway seeds
½ 6-ounce can tomato paste
1¼ cups water
2 medium raw potatoes, shredded
1 pound fresh sauerkraut
½ pint sour cream

In a heavy 2½-quart saucepan, cook onions in shortening until golden. Add and brown the pork over medium heat. Add the paprika, salt, caraway seeds, tomato paste, and water. Cover and cook slowly for 30 minutes. Add the potatoes and sauerkraut. Cover and cook slowly for 1 hour. At this point, you can cool and freeze the goulash if desired.

Before serving, add 2/3 cup of the sour cream and stir thoroughly. Serve remaining sour cream on top of the dish. Unlike most goulashes, liquid is all absorbed during the cooking time.

Serve with cucumber and onion rings marinated in vinaigrette.

YIELD: 5 SERVINGS

Cooks Book
THE JUNIOR LEAGUE OF GREATER NEW HAVEN, CONNECTICUT

· ·

Tourtière

This dish is traditional French Canadian Christmas Eve fare—served after midnight Mass with a glass of red wine and crusty bread.

1 pound pork, minced
1 small onion, minced
1 clove garlic, minced
1 teaspoon salt
½ teaspoon savory
¼ teaspoon celery salt
¼ teaspoon ground cloves
¼ teaspoon cinnamon
½ cup water
Dash sage
¾ cup soft bread crumbs
Pastry for a 2-crust pie

Recipe continues . . .

Put first ten ingredients into a large saucepan and cook for 20 minutes, uncovered, over medium heat. Add bread crumbs. Remove from heat and cool until tepid.

Fill a 9-inch pie plate lined with pastry with the pork mixture and cover with pastry. Trim and flute edge. (Freeze if desired).

Bake at 400° until golden brown, about 30 minutes. Serve with Spiced Applesauce.

YIELD: 6–8 SERVINGS

SPICED APPLESAUCE:
1 19-ounce can applesauce
½ cup brown sugar
½ teaspoon cinnamon
3 whole cloves

Simmer all ingredients for 1 hour. Serve with the Tourtière.

THE JUNIOR LEAGUE OF HAMILTON-BURLINGTON, ONTARIO

. . . .

Philadelphia Scrapple

2 cups diced lean pork
1½ teaspoons salt
⅛ teaspoon sage
⅛ teaspoon marjoram
½ teaspoon pepper
2 cups corn meal
2 cups whole wheat flour

Boil pork in 4 quarts water. Drain, reserving 3 quarts of the broth. Grind the meat.

Bring reserved broth to a boil and add the seasonings. Gradually stir corn meal and flour into the boiling broth. Add meat. Cook slowly for 30 minutes, stirring frequently. Pour into loaf pans and chill.

To serve, slice and fry until brown.

YIELD: 2 LOAF PANS

Bicentennial Cookbook
THE JUNIOR LEAGUE OF PHILADELPHIA, PENNSYLVANIA

. . . .

Barbecued Spareribs

1 cup molasses
1 cup catsup
1 cup chopped onion
Juice of 1 orange
3 tablespoons grated orange rind
2 tablespoons butter
2 tablespoons vinegar
2 tablespoons salad oil
2 tablespoons bottled steak sauce
2 cloves garlic, minced
5 whole cloves
1 teaspoon prepared mustard
1 teaspoon Worcestershire sauce
½ teaspoon hot pepper sauce
½ teaspoon salt
½ teaspoon pepper
4 pounds spareribs

Combine all ingredients except spareribs in a saucepan. Bring to a boil and cook for 5 minutes.

Sprinkle spareribs lightly with salt, place on rack in baking pan, and cover with foil. Bake in preheated 325° oven for 1 hour. Pour off fat.

Recipe continues . . .

Brush with barbecue sauce and bake at 400° for 45 minutes, basting with remaining sauce every 15 minutes until glazed.

YIELD: 6–8 SERVINGS

THE JUNIOR LEAGUE OF LANCASTER, PENNSYLVANIA

Peachy Spareribs

3 pounds country-style ribs
1 teaspoon salt
1 29-ounce can peach halves with syrup
1 cup catsup
2 tablespoons Worcestershire sauce
1 tablespoon instant onion or ¼ cup minced fresh onion
2 tablespoons flour
2 tablespoons prepared mustard
½–1 teaspoon ground cloves
1 teaspoon salt
½ teaspoon pepper

Arrange ribs meaty side up in 9 x 12-inch pan and sprinkle with salt.

Mix syrup from peaches with remaining ingredients and stir over low heat until slightly thickened. Pour mixture over ribs. Bake at 375° for 1½ hours, turning once. Put peaches in pan during the last 15 minutes.

YIELD: 4 SERVINGS

THE JUNIOR LEAGUE OF TROY, NEW YORK

Spanish Pisto

¼ cup olive oil
1 cup diced cooked ham
2 large Spanish onions, sliced
2 cloves garlic, minced
2 canned pimentos, diced
2 cups diced, unpeeled eggplant
1 9-ounce package frozen artichoke hearts
1 1-pound can whole peeled tomatoes
⅛ teaspoon pepper

Heat oil in saucepan; add ham and cook for 5 minutes. Add onions, garlic, pimentos, and eggplant, and cook for 5 minutes more, or until eggplant is tender, not brown. Add frozen artichokes, tomatoes, and pepper. Cook for 15 minutes, covered.

Serve hot as a main dish or as an accompaniment to meat or fish.

YIELD: 6–8 SERVINGS

THE JUNIOR LEAGUE OF LANCASTER, PENNSYLVANIA

Poultry

Enjoy
LONG ISLAND
DUCKLING
Famous for its
Succulent
Flavor

Chicken Stuffed under Its Skin

1 roasting chicken, about 3½ pounds
9 tablespoons butter
3 large cloves garlic, minced
5 shallots, minced
2 tablespoons parsley
½ teaspoon thyme
2 chicken livers, chopped
2 tablespoons cognac
½–1 cup bread crumbs
Salt and pepper
Additional butter
1 cup chicken stock for basting

With poultry shears, cut out the backbone of the chicken and remove it. Turn the chicken over and flatten it skin side up. With fingers and small knife, loosen the chicken's skin from neck, over breasts, to the thigh portion.

Cream butter in a mixing bowl. Add the garlic, shallots, parsley, thyme, chopped chicken livers, cognac, half of the bread crumbs, and salt and pepper to taste. Add more bread crumbs if needed.

Preheat oven to 375°. Gently stuff the chicken between the skin and the meat with the stuffing mix. Butter a roasting pan, add the chicken, dot with butter, and roast for about 1 hour, basting occasionally with 1 cup chicken stock.

Defat the pan juices and serve in a sauceboat on the side.

YIELD: 4 SERVINGS

THE JUNIOR LEAGUE OF THE CITY OF NEW YORK, NEW YORK

Chicken Oyster Stifle

Stifle is an early English culinary term meaning "smothered." This old English recipe was adapted by vineyardists long ago.

2 tablespoons butter
2 tablespoons vegetable oil
2 broiler chickens, quartered
1 teaspoon salt
Freshly ground pepper
1 tablespoon flour
1 cup milk
½ cup light cream
1 quart fresh oysters, drained

In a skillet, heat butter and oil until foaming subsides. Season chicken pieces with salt and pepper. Place chicken in skillet and cook over moderate heat until golden on both sides. Transfer chicken to a large casserole.

Add flour to fats in skillet and cook, stirring, until smooth. Add milk and continue to stir until sauce is smooth and thickened. Strain sauce over chicken pieces in casserole and bake, covered, at 350° for 1 hour, or until chicken is tender. Pour cream over chicken and top with oysters. Return casserole to oven for 15 minutes, or until edges of oysters curl.

Remove casserole from oven; place chicken and oysters on a heated serving platter and pour the sauce over all.

YIELD: 6 SERVINGS

From Our House
THE JUNIOR LEAGUE OF HARTFORD, CONNECTICUT

Chicken in Tarragon Cream Sauce

2 3-pound chickens, cut into serving pieces
2 cups dry white wine
2 cups chicken broth
1 tablespoon finely chopped fresh tarragon
or ½ tablespoon dried
1 cup heavy cream
Salt and freshly ground pepper
1 tablespoon butter
1 tablespoon flour

Bone the chicken breasts but leave the main wing bone intact.

Arrange chicken pieces skin side down in one layer in a heavy casserole. Add wine, broth, tarragon, and salt and pepper to taste. Cover and bring to a boil; cook for 15–20 minutes. Remove the chicken pieces and keep warm.

Cook the sauce over high heat until it is reduced by half. Add the heavy cream and cook 8–10 minutes longer over high heat. Add salt and pepper to taste.

Blend the butter and flour; add bit by bit to sauce, stirring. Do not boil. Pour hot sauce over the chicken and serve with buttered noodles.

YIELD: **6–8** SERVINGS

THE JUNIOR LEAGUE OF BROOKLYN, NEW YORK

Lemon Chicken with Raisins

1 3½-pound chicken
3 ounces white raisins
4 tablespoons cognac
2 tablespoons water
4 tablespoons butter
2 tablespoons oil
8 small white onions, sliced
Rind of 1 lemon
Juice of 3 lemons
Salt and pepper

HOLLANDAISE SAUCE:
2 egg yolks
5 tablespoons butter
Salt and pepper to taste

Cut the chicken into serving pieces. Soak the raisins in mixture of cognac and water for about 45 minutes.

Melt butter and oil in a heavy skillet and in it sauté chicken pieces until golden but not brown. Remove the chicken to a platter.

Sauté the onions until translucent. It may take 10–15 minutes. Discard any accumulated fat. Arrange the chicken pieces on top of the onions. Add the soaked raisins, cognac and water mixture, lemon rind, and lemon juice. Cover with a round piece of buttered parchment paper, then place lid tightly on top. Simmer for 45–50 minutes.

Prepare the Hollandaise: Over low heat whisk egg yolks until they start to thicken. Very slowly whisk in small pieces of the butter. Season with salt and pepper.

Remove chicken, onions, and raisins to a serving platter. Keep warm. Add the cooking liquids to the Hollandaise Sauce and taste for seasoning. Pour sauce over chicken and serve immediately.

YIELD: 4 SERVINGS

THE JUNIOR LEAGUE OF THE CITY OF NEW YORK, NEW YORK

Valley Chicken

1 3–3½-pound chicken, cut up
Dash each salt, pepper, and thyme
¼ pound bacon, diced
2 tablespoons oil
½ pound mushrooms, sliced
1 small onion, chopped
2 apples, peeled, cored, and sliced
¼ cup dark rum
½ cup apple juice
½ cup heavy cream
2 tablespoons finely chopped parsley

Season chicken with salt, pepper, and thyme. In skillet, fry bacon until crisp; set bacon aside. Add oil to bacon fat in pan and heat. Brown chicken pieces on all sides in the hot oil. Add bacon, mushrooms, onion, and apples.

Heat rum, ignite, and pour flaming over chicken. Add apple juice; cover and simmer about 40 minutes, or until chicken is tender.

Arrange chicken on a heated platter. Stir cream into sauce and heat to boiling point. Pour over chicken. Garnish with parsley. Serve with cooked rice.

YIELD: 4–6 SERVINGS

THE JUNIOR LEAGUE OF WILKES-BARRE, PENNSYLVANIA

Chicken Sauté au Parmesan

1 2½–3-pound chicken, cut into serving pieces
Salt and freshly ground pepper
4½ tablespoons butter
1½ tablespoons flour
¾ cup milk
¼ cup heavy cream
¼ teaspoon nutmeg
½ cup shredded Swiss or Gruyère cheese
½ cup grated Parmesan cheese
2 tablespoons bread crumbs

Sprinkle chicken with salt and pepper and brown on all sides in 3 tablespoons butter for about 20 minutes.

Preheat oven to 350°.

Melt remaining butter in a saucepan and stir in flour. When blended, add milk and cream, stirring rapidly with a whisk. When mixture is boiling, thickened, and smooth, remove from heat and stir in nutmeg and shredded cheese.

Sprinkle a baking dish with half the Parmesan cheese and arrange the chicken pieces over it. Spoon the sauce over the chicken, and sprinkle with remaining Parmesan cheese and bread crumbs. Bake until golden brown, about 20–30 minutes.

YIELD: 4 SERVINGS

THE JUNIOR LEAGUE OF WILMINGTON, DELAWARE

Baked Chicken and Potatoes

1 3-4-pound fryer, cut into serving pieces
6 potatoes, peeled and quartered
1 cup crushed tomatoes
2 tablespoons parsley
1 teaspoon basil
2 cloves garlic, minced
Salt and pepper to taste
¼ cup grated Parmesan cheese
3 tablespoons vegetable oil

Wash chicken and wipe dry with paper toweling. Put enough oil in a large roasting pan to cover bottom of the pan. Place chicken in pan and place potatoes between the chicken pieces.

Sprinkle tomatoes, parsley, basil, garlic, salt, and pepper over the chicken and potatoes. Lastly, sprinkle with the grated cheese and the oil.

Bake in 375° oven for 1-1¼ hours, or until chicken is done.

YIELD: 4 SERVINGS

THE JUNIOR LEAGUE OF ORANGE COUNTY, NEW YORK

. . . .

Brandied Chicken

2½ pounds chicken, cut for frying, or boned chicken breasts
2 cloves garlic, minced
½ stick butter
1 cup heavy cream
3 ounces brandy
1 tablespoon curry powder
Salt and pepper to taste
Parsley
Paprika

Sauté chicken and garlic in butter. Transfer to a casserole with juices from pan.

Mix cream, brandy, curry powder, salt, and pepper and pour over chicken. Cover and bake at 350° for 35–40 minutes. Sprinkle with finely chopped parsley and paprika.

YIELD: **4** SERVINGS

THE JUNIOR LEAGUE OF BRONXVILLE, NEW YORK

Garlic Chicken

1 2½–3-pound frying chicken, cut into serving pieces
Salt and pepper to taste
12 (yes, 12) cloves garlic, peeled
1 medium onion, thinly sliced
1 cup chopped celery
2 carrots, thinly sliced
¼ cup chopped parsley
1/3 cup sherry
1/3 cup sour cream

Pat chicken dry, then sprinkle with salt and pepper to taste. Place chicken in casserole dish. Sprinkle with garlic, onion, celery, carrots, and parsley. Pour sherry over chicken and vegetables. Cover tightly and bake in 350° oven for 1½ hours. Do not peek! Remove from oven and stir in sour cream.

Serve over rice or noodles.

Garlic becomes *very* mild—not at all overpowering, as one might expect. A truly tender chicken dish.

YIELD: **6** SERVINGS

THE JUNIOR LEAGUE OF FALL RIVER, MASSACHUSETTS

Chicken Überraschung

2 frying chickens, cut into pieces
Salt and pepper
¼ pound butter
1 large yellow onion, thinly sliced
1 green pepper, thinly sliced
½ teaspoon garlic powder or minced fresh garlic
1 teaspoon salt
½ teaspoon pepper
1 tablespoon chopped parsley
½ teaspoon powdered thyme
½ teaspoon oregano
1½ tablespoons curry powder
4 cups tomato juice

Sprinkle chicken with salt and pepper and sauté in butter until golden brown. Remove chicken. To butter remaining in pan, add the onion and pepper; sauté slowly until glossy. Mix remaining ingredients into tomato juice. Add this to onion and pepper and cook slowly for 5 minutes.

In a 3-quart casserole, arrange chicken, pour sauce over, and bake, covered, at 350° for 1 hour.

Serve with hot fluffy rice.

YIELD: 8 SERVINGS

THE JUNIOR LEAGUE OF NEW BRITAIN, CONNECTICUT

Cold Dodine of Chicken

A delicious cold dish, good for luncheon or dinner during the heat of summer.

2 3-pound chickens, cut up
Salt and pepper
½ teaspoon powdered thyme
3 onions, peeled and quartered
1 bay leaf
4 cups good red wine
4 slices bacon
½ cup brandy
½ pound mushrooms, peeled and sliced
Butter
Thin carrot strips, parsley, and truffles for decorations
Parsley for garnish

One day ahead, sprinkle chicken pieces with salt, pepper, and thyme and marinate with onions, bay leaf, and wine.

Next day, cook the bacon in a large pot, then discard. Brown the chicken pieces quickly in bacon fat until lightly browned, then add the marinade and brandy. Simmer for 1 hour, or until chicken is tender. Halfway through, correct seasoning. Ten minutes before cooking time is over, sauté the mushrooms in butter and add to the pot. Remove from stove and cool.

Grease a casserole or mold large enough to accommodate everything. Put carrot strips, parsley, and truffles in a nice pattern in bottom. Put pieces of chicken close together on top. Strain liquid carefully over all, so the liquid doesn't disturb decorations. Refrigerate for at least 6 hours, or until set.

When ready to serve, turn out on a platter and garnish with parsley.

YIELD: 6 SERVINGS

Cooks Book
THE JUNIOR LEAGUE OF GREATER NEW HAVEN, CONNECTICUT

Apricot Chicken

1 2½–3-pound chicken, cut up
3 tablespoons butter
Salt and pepper
1 cup chopped celery
1 6-ounce can water chestnuts, drained and sliced
½ teaspoon dried rosemary
½ teaspoon salt
2 cups cooked long-grain rice
¾ cup dry white wine
1 16-ounce can apricot halves
4 teaspoons cornstarch

Brown chicken in butter. Season with salt and pepper. Remove chicken and set aside. To pan, add celery, water chestnuts, rosemary, and ¼ teaspoon salt. Cook until celery is tender. Remove from heat. Add rice and ½ cup wine.

Turn mixture into baking dish. Top with chicken. Cover and bake at 375° for 1 hour.

Drain apricots, reserving syrup. Combine syrup, cornstarch, and remaining ¼ teaspoon salt. Cook until thickened. Add remaining ¼ cup wine. Arrange apricots around chicken. Pour glaze over all. Bake, uncovered, for 10 minutes longer.

YIELD: 4 SERVINGS

THE JUNIOR LEAGUE OF KINGSTON, NEW YORK

Mediterranean Chicken

2 3-3½-pound frying chickens, cut into serving pieces
2 tablespoons salad oil
Salt and pepper to taste
4 tablespoons butter
2 Bermuda onions, diced
1 clove garlic, minced
3 shallots, minced
1 5-ounce jar pitted green olives, undrained
2 1-pound cans peeled tomatoes, chopped
1 cup dry white wine
3 bay leaves
1 teaspoon crushed thyme
1 small bunch parsley, chopped

In a large skillet, brown chicken in salad oil. Sprinkle with salt and pepper. Transfer to a bake-and-serve dish.

Melt butter in skillet and sauté onions, garlic, and shallots until translucent. Add remaining ingredients except parsley. Reduce over medium heat for about 20 minutes, or until sauce is thick.

Pour sauce over chicken, cover, and bake at 350° for 1 hour. Garnish with chopped parsley.

YIELD: 8 SERVINGS

THE JUNIOR LEAGUE OF GREATER UTICA, NEW YORK

Chinese Chicken

2 3-3½-pound frying chickens, cut into serving pieces
½ cup soy sauce
1 cup dry sherry
1 large clove garlic, minced
1 teaspoon ginger root, minced
½ cup hoisin sauce
½ cup catsup
1/3 cup brown sugar
1 clove garlic, minced
1 tablespoon molasses

Marinate chickens overnight in mixture of soy sauce, ½ cup sherry, garlic, and ginger root. Turn occasionally.

Remove chicken from marinade and place in a buttered baking dish. Combine marinade with remaining ingredients, stirring until sugar is dissolved. Pour sauce over chicken and bake, uncovered, for 1 hour in a 350° oven. Baste with sauce every 10–15 minutes.

YIELD: 8 SERVINGS

THE JUNIOR LEAGUE OF GREATER UTICA, NEW YORK

. . . .

Chicken Breasts in Phyllo Pastry

6 whole chicken breasts, split, boned, and skinned
½ pound unsalted butter (2 sticks)
4 tablespoons olive oil
1/3 cup cognac
12 sheets phyllo pastry (strudel pastry may be substituted)
Duxelles
White Wine Sauce

Sauté chicken breasts in ¼ pound butter and the oil in a heavy skillet until lightly browned on each side, about 1–2 minutes. Remove to a plate (reserve butter and juices). Heat and ignite cognac and pour over chicken breasts. When flames are extinguished, pour liquid into skillet and set aside.

Melt remaining butter in a clean saucepan. Spread a sheet of pastry on a damp cloth, brush with butter, fold in half, and brush again with butter. Put half a chicken breast at narrow end, spread with Duxelles, and fold pastry to make a rectangular package.

Butter a jelly-roll pan and put chicken packages on it; brush tops with butter. The recipe may be prepared in advance up to this point, wrapped, and refrigerated.

When ready to serve, bake in a 400° oven 25–30 minutes, or until puffed and brown.

Serve with White Wine Sauce.

YIELD: 8 SERVINGS

DUXELLES:
1½ pounds mushrooms
6 shallots
¼ pound sweet butter
2 tablespoons cognac or Madeira
2 tablespoons minced parsley

Chop mushrooms very finely. Mince shallots. Sauté mushrooms and shallots in butter over moderate heat until most of the moisture is evaporated from the mushrooms. Moisten with cognac or Madeira and stir in parsley.

WHITE WINE SAUCE:
½–¾ cup white wine
2 cups chicken stock
1 carrot, peeled and sliced
2–3 shallots, coarsely chopped
2 sprigs parsley
1 bay leaf

Recipe continues . . .

Thyme
Chervil
2–3 truffles, chopped, with juice (optional)
1 teaspoon meat glaze available in specialty stores (optional)
Salt and freshly ground pepper to taste
1 tablespoon arrowroot
1 tablespoon unsalted butter

To make sauce, add wine to cognac and juices in pan in which chicken was browned and cook to reduce slightly, scraping up brown bits. Add chicken stock, carrot, shallots, parsley, bay leaf, and a good pinch of thyme and simmer 30 minutes. Strain. It is best to put it now in freezer for a while, or in the refrigerator overnight, so that fat rises to the top and solidifies.

Remove fat. Heat and add a good pinch of chervil, truffles, and juice if desired. Stir in meat glaze if desired and season to taste with salt and pepper. Make a paste of the arrowroot and a little hot sauce or water and add to sauce. Stir until thickened. Just before serving, beat in the butter.

New York Entertains
THE JUNIOR LEAGUE OF THE CITY OF NEW YORK, NEW YORK

Chicken Bianco

1 pound boned chicken breasts
Flour
4 eggs, beaten
¼ teaspoon salt
⅛ teaspoon pepper
Approximately 4 teaspoons butter
½ cup heavy cream
¼ cup sherry

Pound chicken breasts until thin. Coat both sides with flour. Dip into the egg beaten with salt and pepper.

Melt the butter in a heavy skillet. Brown the chicken breasts on both sides. (This will take no more than 6–8 minutes.) Add the heavy cream, then turn the chicken to coat on both sides. Add sherry. Simmer 1 minute.

Serve immediately. This dish is good served with long-grain and wild rice.

YIELD: 2–3 SERVINGS

THE JUNIOR LEAGUE OF ORANGE COUNTY, NEW YORK

. . . .

Chicken Momi

6 whole chicken breasts, split and boned
Salt
¼ cup butter
¼ cup honey
2 tablespoons soy sauce
4 tablespoons sesame seeds
Papaya and lime slices for garnish (optional)

Recipe continues . . .

Pound chicken breasts to flatten slightly. Sprinkle with salt. Top each with a scant ¼ cup of stuffing and fasten with skewers or toothpicks. Place skin side up in greased baking dish.

Melt butter with honey and beat in soy sauce. Spoon over chicken. Bake at 325° for about 45 minutes, basting with drippings frequently. Sprinkle with sesame seeds. Increase temperature to 450° and bake 10 minutes longer, or until well browned. Garnish with papaya and lime slices.

YIELD: 12 SERVINGS

STUFFING:
½ cup light cream
2 cups soft bread crumbs
2/3 cup finely chopped onion
2 3-ounce cans water chestnuts, drained and minced
¼ cup butter
½ pound ground veal
½ pound ground pork, cooked and drained
2 eggs
2 tablespoons soy sauce
2 teaspoons grated fresh ginger root
⅛ teaspoon cayenne

Pour cream over bread crumbs. Sauté onion and water chestnuts in butter. Mix cooked onion mixture with softened bread crumbs and remaining ingredients.

THE JUNIOR LEAGUE OF HAMILTON-BURLINGTON, ONTARIO

Opulent Chicken

6 whole chicken breasts, split and boned
Paprika, salt, and pepper
½ pound butter
2 15-ounce cans artichoke hearts, drained
1 pound fresh mushrooms, sliced
¼ teaspoon tarragon
6 tablespoons flour
1 cup dry or sweet sherry
3 cups chicken bouillon

Heat oven to 350°. Coat chicken breasts with paprika, salt, and pepper. Sauté chicken in 1 stick butter until brown. Transfer to casserole and add artichokes.

Put mushrooms and remaining butter in a skillet, season with tarragon, and sauté for 5 minutes. Sprinkle with flour; stir in sherry and bouillon. Simmer for 5 minutes and pour sauce over chicken and artichokes. Cover casserole and bake for 45 minutes.

YIELD: 12 SERVINGS

Entirely Entertaining
THE JUNIOR LEAGUE OF MONTCLAIR-NEWARK, NEW JERSEY

Chicken Breasts with Garlic Cream and Onions

1½ cups chicken broth
10 small white onions, peeled
3 cloves
¼ teaspoon tarragon or thyme
4 tablespoons butter
4 tablespoons oil
4 tablespoons flour
Salt and pepper
2 chicken breasts, split and skinned
½ pound mushrooms, sliced
2 cloves garlic, minced
1 cup light cream

Bring broth to a boil and add onions, one of which is stuck with cloves and tarragon. Simmer for 10 minutes, or until onions are soft.

Heat 2 tablespoons each butter and oil in a large skillet. Put 2 tablespoons flour, seasoned with salt and pepper, in a brown bag and shake the chicken in it. Brown chicken well on both sides in the skillet. Add the onions and broth, cover, and cook gently for 20 minutes.

In another pan, sauté the mushrooms and garlic in the remaining butter and oil. Add remaining flour, season, and stir to a smooth paste. Add cream and stir until sauce is smooth.

Remove chicken and onions to a platter and keep warm. Combine the chicken broth and cream sauce and heat, stirring constantly, until smooth. Correct seasoning and pour sauce over chicken.

NOTE: This can be made ahead of time and gently reheated, but keep the chicken and sauce separate. Before serving, reheat chicken, reheat sauce, then pour sauce over the chicken.

YIELD: 4 SERVINGS

Greenwich Recommends
THE JUNIOR LEAGUE OF GREENWICH, CONNECTICUT

Reunion Chicken

1 cup flour
¾ teaspoon salt, ⅛ teaspoon pepper, and 1¼ teaspoons savory
6 whole chicken breasts, boned and skinned
5 tablespoons butter
1 pound mushrooms, sliced
2 onions, chopped
1 clove garlic, minced
1 tablespoon chopped parsley
Additional salt, pepper, and savory to taste
½ cup each chicken broth, white wine, and orange juice
2 teaspoons brown sugar
1 10-ounce package each frozen snow peas, green peas,
and artichoke hearts

Combine flour, ¾ teaspoon salt, pepper, and savory and coat chicken breasts. Brown chicken in 3 tablespoons butter and transfer to a 2-quart casserole.

Melt remaining 2 tablespoons butter and sauté mushrooms, onions, garlic, and parsley. Add additional salt, pepper, and savory. Stir in the broth, wine, juice, and brown sugar. Pour sauce over the chicken.

Cover the casserole with foil and bake at 350° for 45 minutes. Remove from oven and add *frozen* snow peas, green peas, and artichokes. Return to oven and bake uncovered for 20 minutes.

YIELD: 6 SERVINGS

THE JUNIOR LEAGUE OF MORRISTOWN, NEW JERSEY

Mandarin Chicken Breasts

1½ cups cooked long-grain and wild rice
3 whole chicken breasts, split and boned
½ cup flour
½ teaspoon paprika
½ teaspoon salt
3 tablespoons butter
1¾ cups chicken broth
2 tablespoons lemon juice
1 bay leaf
1 tablespoon cornstarch
1 11-ounce can Mandarin oranges, drained
1 cup seedless green grapes

Spoon rice into hollows of chicken breasts. Roll edges of chicken over rice to cover completely. Fasten with toothpicks.

Mix flour, paprika, and salt together and dip chicken into mixture to coat well. Brown slowly in butter in large frying pan. Stir in chicken broth, lemon juice, and bay leaf. Heat to simmer, cover, and cook 25 minutes. Remove bay leaf. Place chicken on heated serving platter and keep warm.

Reheat liquid to boiling. In a cup, mix cornstarch with a little water to form a smooth paste. Stir paste into liquid in frying pan. Cook, stirring constantly, until sauce thickens. Boil 3 minutes. Stir in oranges and grapes. Heat until bubbly.

Spoon some of sauce over chicken and reserve the rest to serve separately. Serve immediately.

YIELD: **6** SERVINGS

Simply Superb
THE JUNIOR LEAGUE OF ELIZABETH-PLAINFIELD, NEW JERSEY

Chicken Breasts with Sour Cream

4 whole chicken breasts, split, boned, and skinned
7 tablespoons butter
3 tablespoons apple brandy (calvados)
3 tablespoons flour
1/2 teaspoon tomato paste
1/2 teaspoon meat glaze
1 cup chicken stock
2/3 pint sour cream
Salt
Freshly ground pepper
1/2–3/4 pound fresh mushrooms
Juice from 1/2 lemon
1/2 cup grated Parmesan cheese

Slowly brown chicken on both sides in 3 tablespoons foaming butter. Heat brandy in small pan, ignite, and pour flaming over chicken. Remove chicken from pan.

Add 1 tablespoon butter to pan and remove from heat. Stir in flour, tomato paste, and meat glaze. Add chicken stock; return to heat and stir constantly until mixture comes to a boil. Stir in sour cream a little at a time. Season with salt and pepper.

Return chicken to pan, cover pan with wax paper overhanging edge a bit, then put on the lid and cook slowly for 25 minutes, or until chicken is tender. Five minutes before chicken is done, add mushrooms which have been sautéed briefly in 2 tablespoons butter with lemon juice.

Arrange chicken on an ovenproof serving dish, sprinkle with Parmesan cheese, and dot with remaining 1 tablespoon butter. Brown under broiler.

YIELD: 4 SERVINGS

THE JUNIOR LEAGUE OF BRONXVILLE, NEW YORK

Wrapped Chicken Breasts

3 whole chicken breasts, split and boned
Water or chicken broth and white wine
6 slices baked ham
French mustard
Tarragon
6 slices Swiss cheese
1 package frozen patty shells, thawed

Poach breasts in water, or chicken broth, and wine until tender.

Wrap each breast in a slice of ham that has been brushed with mustard and sprinkled with tarragon. Then wrap in a slice of Swiss cheese.

Finally, wrap each breast, envelope-style, in a patty shell that has been rolled thinly into a rectangle. Seal with water.

Arrange on baking sheet and bake at 425° for about 20 minutes, or until golden brown and puffed.

YIELD: **4–6** SERVINGS

Show House Recipes
THE JUNIOR LEAGUE OF BINGHAMTON, NEW YORK

. . . .

Chicken Breasts in Sour Cream Lemon Sauce

4 half chicken breasts
4 tablespoons butter
3 tablespoons flour
2 cups sour cream
1 teaspoon salt or to taste
¼ teaspoon pepper
1 cup sliced fresh mushrooms
2 tablespoons chopped fresh parsley
4 green onions, chopped
Grated rind of 1 lemon
3–4 tablespoons fresh lemon juice

Brown chicken breasts lightly in butter. Remove breasts from skillet to a casserole dish.

Stir flour into butter remaining in skillet, cook 1 minute; add sour cream and seasonings and simmer for 4 minutes. Add mushrooms, parsley, and green onions; stir in lemon rind and 2 teaspoons lemon juice.

Pour sauce over chicken breasts, cover casserole, and bake for 45 minutes to 1 hour at 350°.

Before serving, skim butter from top of sauce and stir in remaining lemon juice to taste.

YIELD: 4 SERVINGS

THE JUNIOR LEAGUE OF BANGOR, MAINE

Orange Chicken

2 cups brown or white rice
3 large whole chicken breasts, split and boned
Salt and pepper to taste
4 tablespoons butter
1/3 cup finely chopped onion
1½ cups orange juice
1 8-ounce can sliced mushrooms
2–3 tablespoons flour
½ cup water

Prepare rice according to package directions.

Season chicken with salt and pepper. In large skillet, brown chicken slowly in butter. Add onion and orange juice, cover, and simmer over low heat about 15 minutes, or until chicken is done.

Spoon rice into a 9 x 13-inch casserole dish. Place chicken breasts on rice. Drain mushrooms and spoon over chicken. Put flour and water in shaker and mix well. Add to orange juice in skillet and cook over

Recipe continues . . .

medium heat until sauce is thick and bubbly. Pour orange sauce over chicken and rice. Cover and bake at 350° for 20–30 minutes.

Casserole may be made ahead of time, refrigerated, and heated for 45 minutes to 1 hour at 350° before serving.

YIELD: 6 SERVINGS

THE JUNIOR LEAGUE OF TROY, NEW YORK

Chicken Piccata

4 whole chicken breasts, split, skinned, and boned
½ cup flour
1 teaspoon salt
¼ teaspoon freshly ground pepper
¼ teaspoon paprika
¼ cup clarified butter
1 tablespoon olive oil
2–4 tablespoons dry Madeira or water
3 tablespoons lemon juice
1 lemon, thinly sliced
3–4 tablespoons capers
¼ cup minced parsley

Pound chicken breasts until ¼-inch thick. Combine flour, salt, pepper, and paprika in bag. Add breasts and coat well; shake off excess.

Heat butter and olive oil in large skillet until bubbling. Sauté chicken breasts in the hot butter mixture for 2–3 minutes on each side. Do not overcook. Drain on paper toweling and keep warm.

Stir wine or water into oil and butter remaining in pan and cook, stirring in all brown bits from bottom of skillet. Add lemon juice and heat sauce to boiling. Return chicken to skillet, cover with lemon slices, and cook until sauce is thickened. Add capers and sprinkle with parsley.

YIELD: 4–8 SERVINGS

THE JUNIOR LEAGUE OF BUFFALO, NEW YORK

·   ·   ·   ·   ·   ·   ·   ·   ·   ·   ·   ·   ·   ·   ·   ·   ·   ·

Chicken à l'Orange

4 whole chicken breasts, split and boned
½ cup flour
1 teaspoon salt
1 teaspoon garlic powder
½ teaspoon paprika
2 teaspoons grated orange peel
5 tablespoons butter
¼ cup white wine
1¼ cup orange juice
¼ teaspoon thyme
1 teaspoon marjoram
1 11-ounce can Mandarin oranges, drained
1/3 cup toasted sliced almonds

Pound chicken breasts between sheets of wax paper. Shake chicken in a bag with flour, salt, garlic powder, paprika, and orange peel. Brown in butter. When brown, transfer to a shallow baking dish.

To skillet, add wine, orange juice, thyme, and marjoram. Heat to a boil. Pour over the chicken.

Bake chicken at 350° for 15 minutes. Top with oranges and almonds and bake for another 15 minutes—for a total baking time of 30 minutes. Serve with a curried rice pilaf.

YIELD: 8 SERVINGS

THE JUNIOR LEAGUE OF ALBANY, NEW YORK

·   ·   ·   ·   ·   ·   ·   ·   ·   ·   ·   ·   ·   ·   ·   ·   ·   ·

Chicken Breasts Wellington

3 whole chicken breasts, split, skinned, and boned
Salt and pepper
1/4 pound mushrooms, sliced
2 tablespoons butter
1 6-ounce package long-grain and wild rice
1/4 cup grated orange peel
2 eggs, separated
1 10-ounce package frozen patty shells, rolled out to 6–7-inch rounds

Season breasts with salt and pepper; refrigerate.

Sauté sliced mushrooms in butter; set aside.

Cook rice according to instructions for drier rice, adding orange peel; cool.

Beat egg whites until soft peaks form. Fold into cooled rice; add mushrooms.

Place ½ chicken breast in center of each pastry circle. Spoon ⅓– ½ cup rice mixture under each breast; moisten edge with water, press to seal edges together. Repeat for each ½ breast. Place seam side down on large cookie sheet.

Beat egg yolks lightly with 1 tablespoon water; brush over dough. Bake uncovered for 45 minutes at 375°. Serve immediately with Berry Sauce.

YIELD: 6 SERVINGS

BERRY SAUCE:
1 16-ounce can whole-berry cranberry sauce
2 tablespoons Grand Marnier
⅛ cup lemon juice
Dash dry mustard

Heat above ingredients in saucepan; serve over and accompanying chicken.

JUNIOR LEAGUE OF SPRINGFIELD, MASSACHUSETTS

•   •   •   •   •   •   •   •   •   •   •   •   •   •   •   •

Chicken Breasts with Brandy

2 large chicken breasts, split, boned, and skinned
Flour for dredging
1/4 cup olive oil
2 tablespoons butter
1/2 cup dry white wine
3 cloves garlic, minced
Salt and pepper to taste
3 tablespoons finely chopped fresh parsley
1/4 cup brandy

Pound chicken breasts and dust lightly with flour. Heat oil and butter in a skillet. Sauté the chicken slowly in the oil. When the chicken is browned, add the white wine, garlic, and salt and pepper to taste. Cook slowly for about 15 minutes. Add chopped parsley.

Before serving, heat brandy; pour over chicken and ignite.

YIELD: 4 SERVINGS

THE JUNIOR LEAGUE OF SCRANTON, PENNSYLVANIA

. . . .

Herbed Chicken Breasts

1 cup fine bread crumbs
1/2 teaspoon salt
1/2 teaspoon ground thyme
1/2 teaspoon ground rosemary
1/2 teaspoon black pepper
Dash marjoram
2 boneless chicken breasts (approximately 6 ounces each),
skinned and boned
1 egg, beaten
2 tablespoons oil
1/2 cup white wine or cooking wine (optional)

Recipe continues . . .

Mix together bread crumbs and spices in pie pan. Dip chicken into egg, then in bread crumb mixture.

Heat oil and in it sauté chicken until lightly browned on each side. Add wine and bring to a boil. Cover, reduce heat, and simmer for 10–15 minutes.

YIELD: 2 SERVINGS

THE JUNIOR LEAGUE OF ALBANY, NEW YORK

Sour Cream Chicken

12 chicken breasts
2 cups sour cream
Juice of 1 lemon
2 teaspoons Worcestershire sauce
¼ teaspoon celery salt
½ teaspoon paprika
Freshly ground pepper to taste
¼ teaspoon onion salt
¼ teaspoon garlic salt
1½ cups fresh bread crumbs
½ cup melted butter

Butter a glass dish. Mix sour cream with the next seven ingredients. Coat chicken breasts and marinate, covered, in the glass dish overnight.

Next day, sprinkle with bread crumbs and drip half the butter on top. Bake for 45 minutes at 350°, covered. Then add remaining butter and bake uncovered 15 minutes longer.

YIELD: 12 SERVINGS

THE JUNIOR LEAGUE OF SCHENECTADY, NEW YORK

Pollo alla Florentine

4 chicken breasts, boned
8 ounces butter
Salt and pepper
2 bay leaves
½ cup white wine
1 pound spinach or 2 10-ounce packages frozen, semicooked and drained
4 tablespoons flour
1 pint cream or milk
8 slices mozzarella cheese
Dash nutmeg
8 slices prosciutto or other thinly sliced ham
4 ounces grated Parmesan cheese

Flatten the breasts and sauté in half the butter. Season with salt and pepper. Add bay leaves and wine; cover and cook until the juices are clear when chicken is pierced with a fork. Remove chicken and keep warm. Cook spinach in the butter-wine mixture remaining in pan.

In another pan, melt the rest of the butter and whisk in the flour. Add the cream and stir until sauce is thickened. Add 4 slices of the mozzarella, salt and pepper to taste, and nutmeg. Cook over moderate heat for 3–4 minutes.

Lightly butter four individual casseroles or one large casserole. Place spinach in first, then chicken, then ham (2 slices each for the individual dishes), and the remaining mozzarella (1 slice for each individual dish). Pour on the sauce, sprinkle with the Parmesan, and place under the broiler until hot and bubbly.

YIELD: 4 SERVINGS

Bicentennial Cookbook
THE JUNIOR LEAGUE OF PHILADELPHIA, PENNSYLVANIA

Diana's Company Chicken

5 tablespoons butter
½ pound fresh mushrooms, sliced
2 large onions, thinly sliced
1-1½ pounds boneless chicken, cut into 2 x 2-inch pieces
Flour
⅛ teaspoon thyme
1 teaspoon salt
½ teaspoon curry powder
¼ teaspoon pepper
½ cup chicken broth
½ cup dry white wine
1 cup heavy cream

In electric frying pan or large skillet, melt 3 tablespoons butter. Add mushrooms and onions and sauté until golden and tender. Remove from pan and set aside. Add the 2 remaining tablespoons butter.

Coat chicken lightly with flour. Add to pan and sauté until brown. Add thyme, salt, curry, and pepper, then the broth, wine, mushrooms, and onions. Cover and cook for 20 minutes.

Just before serving, add cream and heat through. Serve with rice or on toast triangles.

YIELD: **4** SERVINGS

THE JUNIOR LEAGUE OF ORANGE COUNTY, NEW YORK

Hot Chinese Chicken Salad

2 whole chicken breasts, skinned and boned
¼ cup cornstarch
¼ cup oil
3-4 cloves garlic, peeled
¼ pound mushrooms, sliced
1 4-ounce can water chestnuts, drained and sliced
1 bunch small green onions including tops, cut into pieces
1 cup diagonally sliced celery
¼ cup soy sauce
2 cups shredded lettuce
1 6-ounce jar pimento, slivered

Cut chicken into thin strips, roll in cornstarch and set aside.

Heat oil in large, deep skillet; add garlic and cook and stir until brown. Discard garlic. Add chicken to garlic oil and stir until lightly browned. Add mushrooms, water chestnuts, green onions, celery, and soy sauce. Cook and stir until heated through. Add lettuce and pimentos. Toss lightly.

Serve at once with rice.

YIELD: 4-6 SERVINGS

Something Special
THE JUNIOR LEAGUE OF YORK, PENNSYLVANIA

Oven-Baked Chicken Delaware Valley

8-10 chicken pieces (breasts and thighs)
Salt and pepper
2-3 tablespoons paprika
1 medium onion, finely chopped
¼ clove garlic, minced
2 stalks celery, finely chopped
Chopped parsley, marjoram, sage,
thyme, basil, rosemary, oregano
¼ cup red wine vinegar
¼ cup water
2/3 cup Burgundy
1 cup dry white wine

Season chicken with salt, pepper, and paprika. Sprinkle onion, garlic, celery, and herbs on both sides of chicken in a 9 x 13-inch pan. Add vinegar, water, and wines. *Cover* and bake at 325° for approximately 1½–2 hours, or until chicken is brown and tender. Add additional liquid if necessary.

YIELD: 5–6 SERVINGS

The Melting Pot
THE JUNIOR LEAGUE OF THE CENTRAL DELAWARE VALLEY, NEW JERSEY

Caribbean Chicken

4 pounds chicken pieces, breasts and thighs
2 cups boiling water
1 tablespoon chili powder
2 teaspoons salt
1/4 teaspoon pepper
1/4 teaspoon cinnamon
1/4 cup minced or chopped onion
1/4 cup butter
1/4 cup cooking oil
2 20-ounce cans pineapple chunks
1 cup seedless green grapes
2 bananas, peeled and sliced lengthwise
1 large avocado, peeled and sliced
1/4 cup cold water
2 tablespoons cornstarch

Wash chicken pieces and put in a Dutch oven or large pot. Add boiling water, chili powder, salt, pepper, cinnamon, and onion. Cover tightly and simmer until chicken is nearly tender, about 30 minutes. Drain chicken pieces and dry well on paper toweling. Strain stock and set aside.

In large heavy skillet, heat butter and oil. Add chicken pieces and brown well on all sides, transfer to a large shallow baking dish as they brown. (Have dish large enough to hold chicken in a single layer.)

Heat oven to 375°.

Drain pineapple chunks, reserving juice. Combine pineapple juice and enough chicken stock to make 4 cups liquid. (Add water if necessary.) Pour over chicken pieces. Sprinkle pineapple chunks over all. Bake for 30 minutes, basting chicken often with pan juices.

Lift chicken out onto a hot platter. Spoon pineapple chunks over chicken and spinkle with grapes. Garnish edge of platter with bananas and avocado.

Combine water and cornstarch. Gradually stir into liquid in baking

Recipe continues . . .

pan and cook, stirring constantly, until sauce is thickened and clear. Serve with the chicken and fruit.

YIELD: 8 SERVINGS

THE JUNIOR LEAGUE OF MONTREAL, QUEBEC

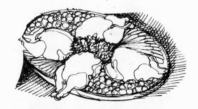

Baked Chicken in Savory Sauce

3 pounds chicken pieces
¼ cup flour
½ teaspoon salt
Dash pepper
¼ teaspoon paprika
½ teaspoon curry powder
¼ cup butter or margarine
Thick tomato slices
½ pound mushrooms, sliced
½ cup thinly sliced onion
1 10¾-ounce can cream of chicken soup
¼ cup white wine or milk

Shake chicken in a bag with flour, salt, paprika, and curry powder.

Melt butter in shallow 2-quart casserole. Place chicken skin side down in the casserole and bake at 400° for 30 minutes. Turn pieces over and top with tomato slices, mushrooms, and onion. Cover with soup mixed with milk or wine. Return to oven for about 20 minutes.

YIELD: 8 SERVINGS

THE JUNIOR LEAGUE OF ELMIRA, NEW YORK

Parmesan Chicken Wings

4 pounds chicken wings
1 cup grated Parmesan cheese
2 tablespoons parsley flakes
1 tablespoon oregano
2 teaspoons paprika
1 teaspoon salt
½ teaspoon pepper

Split chicken wings into three sections at joints. Put remaining ingredients into a large plastic or paper bag. Put chicken wings in bag and shake to coat the wings with the cheese and spice mixture.

Arrange wings in a single layer on greased cookie sheet or in large shallow pan. Bake for 1 hour at 350°.

YIELD: 20–25 SERVINGS

THE JUNIOR LEAGUE OF ALBANY, NEW YORK

Chicken Supreme

1 8-10-ounce package long-grain and wild rice
1 medium onion, chopped
2 tablespoons butter
4 cups diced cooked chicken
1 11¾-ounce can cream of celery soup
1 4-ounce jar diced pimentos
1 15-ounce can French-style green beans, drained
1 cup mayonnaise
1 4-ounce can water chestnuts, thinly sliced

Cook rice according to directions on package. Sauté onion in butter until transparent.

Recipe continues . . .

Combine all ingredients in buttered casserole. Bake at 300°— covered for ½ hour, uncovered for ½ hour.

YIELD: 10 SERVINGS

THE JUNIOR LEAGUE OF TROY, NEW YORK

·   ·   ·   ·   ·   ·   ·   ·   ·   ·   ·   ·   ·   ·   ·   ·

Ducks in Cointreau Sauce

4 ready-to-cook ducks
Garnishes: 16 sauteed, fluted mushroom caps and
six sliced oranges, skin on, fried in butter and sugar

Preheat oven to 350°.

Using poultry shears or kitchen scissors, cut ducks into quarters; remove backbones. Place quarters on a rack, skin side up, in a shallow roasting pan. Roast for 2 hours, or until skin is crisp. Do not baste. Serve with Cointreau sauce and garnish with mushroom caps and orange slices.

Prepare sauce.

YIELD: 8 SERVINGS

COINTREAU SAUCE:
6 tablespoons butter
Thin orange rind of 3 oranges, cut in julienne strips
(use a vegetable peeler)
1½ cups sliced mushrooms (about 18)
3 small cloves garlic, minced
3 tablespoons potato starch or cornstarch
¾ cup dry sherry
¾ cup brandy
1½ cups Cointreau
1½ cups orange juice
3 tablespoons currant jelly
3 tablespoons chopped truffles (optional)
Salt and pepper

Melt butter; sauté orange rind, mushroom slices, and garlic for about 5 minutes. Remove from heat; blend in starch, sherry, brandy, Cointreau, orange juice, currant jelly, and truffles. Return to heat and bring to a boil, stirring, until thick. Season to taste with salt and pepper.

Entirely Entertaining
THE JUNIOR LEAGUE OF MONTCLAIR-NEWARK, NEW JERSEY

Duckling and Wild Rice à l'Orange en Casserole

DUCKS AND STOCK:
2 5-6-pound ducks
Salt
1 onion stuck with 4 cloves
1 teaspoon peppercorns
1 bay leaf
3 sprigs parsley
2 sprigs fresh thyme or ¼ teaspoon dried
2 stalks celery with leaves

Prick ducks all over with the tines of a fork. Remove innards and liver and reserve. Put ducks in a large pot and add cold water to cover. Add salt to taste, the onion with cloves, peppercorns, bay leaf, parsley, thyme, and celery. Bring to a boil and simmer, uncovered, for about 1 hour and 15 minutes, or until the ducks are tender.

Remove ducks from stock and set aside until cool enough to handle. Remove skin and fat and discard. Remove meat from bones and set aside. Return scraps and carcass to stock pot and continue to simmer until it is reduced by half. When the stock is reduced, add the innards and simmer for 10 minutes, or until tender, then add the liver and simmer for 5 minutes more. Strain the stock through a piece of damp cheesecloth or flannel. Pour strained stock into refrigerator containers, cool, then refrigerate overnight. Skim off the fat before using stock.

Recipe continues . . .

SAUCE À L'ORANGE:
3 tablespoons butter
3 tablespoons flour
1 cup reserved duck stock
½ cup currant jelly
½ cup dry white wine
1 clove garlic, minced
1/3 cup orange liqueur (Curaçao, Triple Sec, or Grand Marnier)
Zest of 1 orange, slivered, blanched, and drained
Juice of 1 orange
Salt and freshly ground pepper

Melt butter over low heat. Stir in flour to make a roux and cook gently for 2 minutes. Add the duck stock gradually, stirring constantly, until sauce has thickened. Add currant jelly and stir until melted. Blend in white wine, garlic, liqueur, orange zest, and orange juice. Stir and simmer together for a few minutes. Season with salt and pepper to taste.

WILD RICE:
1 cup wild rice
4 cups reserved duck stock
(if not enough is left, add chicken broth)
2 tablespoons butter
½ cup chopped almonds
Salt and freshly ground pepper

To wash rice, put it in a pan of warm water, stir thoroughly, and drain. Repeat this step twice, then rinse thoroughly in a strainer with cold running water. Return rice to pan; cover with warm water. Bring to a boil and boil for 5 minutes. Drain.

Add stock to the rice. Bring to a boil, cover, and simmer for about 45 minutes, or until grain has opened but the rice is still a bit chewy. Drain. Add butter, almonds, and salt and pepper to taste.

FINAL PREPARATION:
Butter
Salt and freshly ground pepper
Duck or chicken stock or fresh orange juice, if necessary

Preheat oven to 350°.

Butter a shallow, heavy, ovenproof 3-quart casserole. Spread half the rice in the bottom, arrange half the duck meat over the rice, and pour half the sauce over it. Make sure all layers are well salted and peppered. Add the remaining rice, then the duck, and pour the remaining sauce over all. Cover and bake in a 350° oven for ½ hour, or until heated through. If the casserole seems to be drying out, add more hot stock or orange juice.

NOTE: This rather elaborate recipe must be started at least a day in advance, but it can be started as much as five days in advance if the cooked duck is frozen, then defrosted, before the final preparation. It can be doubled and makes a nice main course for a holiday buffet.

YIELD: **6** SERVINGS

New York Entertains
THE JUNIOR LEAGUE OF THE CITY OF NEW YORK, NEW YORK

. . . .

Game Hens with Burgundy

1 teaspoon salt
¼ teaspoon ground cloves
¼ teaspoon nutmeg
¼ teaspoon rosemary
¼ teaspoon thyme
6 Cornish game hens
6 slices bacon, halved
½ cup boiling water
½ teaspoon chicken broth
2 tablespoons chopped onion
½ cup parsley
1½ cups Burgundy wine
3-4 cups cooked rice or rice pilaf
1/3 cup currant jelly
Parsley and orange slices for garnish

Recipe continues . . .

Preheat oven to 350°.

Combine first five ingredients and rub over hens, inside and out. Place hens in shallow roasting pan, breast side up, on rack. Arrange bacon crisscrossed over hens. Mix water, broth, onion, parsley, and wine and pour over hens. Roast uncovered for 1 hour. Increase temperature to 400° and roast for 15 more minutes.

Remove birds to heated platter. Remove bacon and crumble into cooked rice.

Strain juices into saucepan and add currant jelly. Heat and stir constantly until jelly is melted. Spoon sauce over hens and surround with rice. Garnish with fresh parsley and orange sections.

YIELD: 6 SERVINGS

THE JUNIOR LEAGUE OF KINGSTON, NEW YORK

Roast Pheasant Josephine

4 pheasants, cleaned and trussed
8 slices bacon
1½ sticks butter, melted
Watercress

SAUCE:

1 cup Madeira wine
2 10-ounce cans beef gravy
6 tablespoons cognac

Heat oven to 425⁰.

Cover pheasant breasts with bacon, arrange in open roasting pan, and roast for 45 minutes to 1 hour. Baste every 15 minutes with melted butter.

When pheasants are done, discard bacon. Cut birds in half with poultry shears, removing backbones. Cut off breasts, place on a platter, and keep warm.

To prepare sauce, mix together and heat sauce ingredients in a flameproof casserole. Spoon half the sauce over pheasant breasts, garnish with watercress, and serve.

Place the legs and second joints in remaining sauce, along with juice from roasting pan. Bring to a boil. Serve as second helpings.

YIELD: **4** SERVINGS

Entirely Entertaining
THE JUNIOR LEAGUE OF MONTCLAIR-NEWARK, NEW JERSEY

Roast Wild Goose

1 5-6-pound ready-to-cook wild goose
1 apple, diced
1 large onion, chopped
1 stalk celery, chopped
1 tablespoon sage
1 tablespoon marjoram
4 slices bacon
1 cup dry sherry
1½ tablespoons flour
3 tablespoons grated orange rind

Heat oven to 450°.

Put apple, onion, and celery in cavity of goose and put goose on rack in roasting pan. Sprinkle goose with sage and marjoram and cover breast with bacon slices. Brown in the preheated oven for 20 minutes. Pour sherry over goose, reduce heat to 250°, and put lid on roaster. Bake for 4½ hours for well-done goose, basting every 30–40 minutes.

Recipe continues . . .

Remove goose to platter. Pour excess fat from pan and make gravy by mixing flour, orange peel, and ¾ cup water. Add to pan juices and simmer and stir for 5 minutes.

YIELD: 5–6 SERVINGS

THE JUNIOR LEAGUE OF THE LEHIGH VALLEY, PENNSYLVANIA

Fish and Seafood

Inlet Bluefish

1 bluefish, about 2 pounds
½ cup butter (1 stick)
4 tablespoons lemon juice
½ teaspoon onion juice
1 teaspoon steak sauce
¼ teaspoon salt
⅛ teaspoon pepper

Split fish and remove backbone. Place skin side down, spread open, in a buttered or foil-lined pan.

Melt the butter and add the lemon juice, onion juice, steak sauce, salt, and pepper.

Bake at 400° for ½ hour, basting occasionally with the butter sauce.

YIELD: 2 SERVINGS

THE JUNIOR LEAGUE OF THE NORTH SHORE, LONG ISLAND, NEW YORK

Baked Stuffed Red Snapper

STUFFING:

1 medium onion, minced
1 shallot, chopped
1 tablespoon chopped celery
1 tablespoon chopped green pepper
1 clove garlic, minced
2 tablespoons bacon fat
¾ cup shrimp
¾ cup crabmeat
1 teaspoon salt
½ teaspoon pepper
1 tablespoon chopped parsley
1 egg
¾ cup bread crumbs
¼ teaspoon cayenne
Dash Tabasco

Sauté vegetables in bacon fat until soft and transparent. Add shrimp and crabmeat; cook until tender. Combine mixture with remaining ingredients. Set aside.

SAUCE:
¼ cup butter
¼ cup olive oil
½ cup flour
1½ tablespoons tomato paste
3 small onions, sliced
¾ cup sliced green onion tops
1 tablespoon minced garlic
3 tablespoons minced parsley
½ cup chopped green pepper
1 1-pound can peeled whole tomatoes, drained and chopped
2 bay leaves
¾ teaspoon thyme

Recipe continues . . .

1 teaspoon basil
3 tablespoons lemon juice
2 tablespoons salt
2 whole dried red peppers
¾ teaspoon freshly ground black pepper
2 tablespoons Worcestershire sauce
Dash Tabasco
1 cup water

Preheat oven to 375°.

In a heavy pan, melt butter over low heat; add olive oil. Gradually add the flour and cook over low heat, stirring constantly, until mixture is light brown. Stir in tomato paste. Add onions, garlic, parsley, and green pepper; continue cooking over low heat until onion is transparent. Remove pan from heat and stir in remaining ingredients.

Pour contents into baking dish about 3 inches deep and long enough to hold the snapper comfortably.

1 3½-4-pound whole red snapper, split and cleaned,
head and tail left on, eyes removed
10 slices fresh lemon (⅛ inch thick)
2 slices olive

Place generous amount of stuffing in pocket of fish. Sew opening closed with cotton twine. Place fish in the baking dish. It will be practically immersed in the sauce. Arrange lemon slices on top.

Bake fish 45–60 minutes. (If sauce appears too thick, add a few tablespoons of water.) When fish flakes easily with a fork, it is cooked.

Remove from oven and place olive slices for eyes. Remove twine, slice fish crosswise and serve with tomato sauce and stuffing.

YIELD: **4** SERVINGS

THE JUNIOR LEAGUE OF THE NORTH SHORE, LONG ISLAND, NEW YORK

Great Lakes Salmon with Crabmeat Stuffing

Coho salmon fishing is a big sport in the Erie area. The catch is excellent baked or broiled.

> *1 8–10-pound fresh salmon, cleaned*
> *½ cup celery*
> *½ cup chopped onion*
> *¼ cup butter*
> *1 teaspoon salt*
> *½ teaspoon sage*
> *½ teaspoon pepper*
> *1 7½-ounce can crabmeat*
> *2 cups bread cubes*
> *Vegetable oil*

Rinse salmon with water and pat dry. Sprinkle with salt and set aside.

Sauté celery and onion in butter until tender. Add salt, sage, pepper, and crabmeat. Toss this mixture with bread cubes. Fill salmon with stuffing; fasten with skewers or tie with string. Coat outside of fish with oil.

To bake, place salmon in a shallow pan and bake at 350° for 60–90

Recipe continues . . .

minutes, or until fish flakes easily with a fork. Baste with drippings twice during baking.

To grill, wrap oiled fish in a double layer of foil and grill over medium-high heat for 1 hour, turning once.

YIELD: 10 SERVINGS

THE JUNIOR LEAGUE OF ERIE, PENNSYLVANIA

. . . .

Halibut Royale

3 tablespoons lemon juice
1 teaspoon salt
½ teaspoon paprika
6 6-ounce halibut or swordfish steaks
½ cup chopped onion
2 tablespoons butter
6 slices green pepper

In shallow 13 x 9-inch baking dish, combine lemon juice, salt, and paprika. Add fish and marinate 1 hour, turning steaks after 30 minutes.

Cook chopped onion in the butter until tender but not brown. Place steaks in prepared baking dish. Top with pepper rings and sprinkle with cooked onion. Bake at 350° for 15 minutes or until fish flakes easily with a fork.

YIELD: 6 SERVINGS

THE JUNIOR LEAGUE OF KINGSTON, NEW YORK

. . . .

Salmon with Cucumber Sauce

A tradition in New England on the Fourth of July.

1½ *teaspoons salt*
2 *tablespoons lemon juice*
6 *salmon steaks*
1 *cucumber*
½ *cup sour cream*
¼ *cup mayonnaise*
1 *tablespoon minced parsley*
1 *tablespoon grated onion*
2 *teaspoons vinegar*
Salt and pepper to taste
Shredded lettuce
Lemon wedges for garnish

Boil 1 quart water with the 1½ teaspoons salt and the lemon juice in a large skillet. Add 3 salmon steaks and simmer 10 minutes. Remove them and repeat with remaining steaks. Chill.

To make sauce: shred enough cucumber to make 1 cup (do not drain); add remaining ingredients and blend well. Chill.

Arrange salmon on shredded lettuce just before serving. Serve with cucumber sauce and garnish with lemon wedges.

YIELD: **6** SERVINGS

Presenting Boston . . . A Cookbook
THE JUNIOR LEAGUE OF BOSTON, MASSACHUSETTS

Swordfish Steaks Chablis

4 swordfish steaks (2 inches thick)
2 cups Chablis
¼ pound butter
Salt and freshly ground pepper to taste
¼–½ cup bread crumbs
2 lemons, cut into wedges, for garnish

Place swordfish steaks in glass dish just large enough to accommodate them without crowding. Add wine, and let fish marinate for 1 hour, turning once.

Remove steaks from dish and place on broiler pan, reserving marinade. Dot fish with 4 tablespoons butter, season, and broil for 10 minutes, basting once with marinade. Turn the fish, dot with remaining butter and sprinkle with bread crumbs. Broil until brown and fish flakes easily, basting several times with the wine. Remove to a serving platter and garnish with lemon wedges.

YIELD: **4** SERVINGS

Presenting Boston . . . A Cookbook
THE JUNIOR LEAGUE OF BOSTON, MASSACHUSETTS

. . . .

Flounder with Almond Sauce

2 pounds flounder filets
¼ cup melted butter
¼ cup lemon juice
Salt and pepper to taste
2 teaspoons paprika
½ cup slivered almonds

Place filets in well-oiled baking pan. Combine butter, lemon juice, salt and pepper, and paprika; pour over filets. Sprinkle with almonds and bake at 350° for 20–25 minutes. Put under broiler for 2–3 minutes.

YIELD: **6** SERVINGS

THE JUNIOR LEAGUE OF ELMIRA, NEW YORK

Rolled Flounder with Shrimp

4 tablespoons butter
1 clove garlic, minced
1 onion, finely chopped
½ green pepper, finely chopped
8 small shrimp, finely chopped
¼ cup bread crumbs
1 tablespoon parsley
1 tablespoon chives
⅛ teaspoon pepper
¼ teaspoon salt
4 flounder filets

Melt 2 tablespoons butter in a large skillet. Add garlic and onion. Brown lightly. Add green pepper, shrimp, bread crumbs, and seasonings. Remove from stove. Spread 2 tablespoons of the mixture on each filet; roll, and secure with wooden picks.

Melt remaining 2 tablespoons butter in small baking dish in 350° oven. Roll filets in butter and place seam side down close together in dish. Bake at 350° for 25 minutes. Serve with Parmesan Sauce.

Recipe continues . . .

PARMESAN SAUCE:
2 tablespoons butter
2 tablespoons flour
1¼ cups milk
½ cup grated Parmesan cheese
¼ teaspoon salt
⅛ teaspoon pepper

Melt butter in saucepan. Stir in flour and cook 2 minutes. Stir in milk and cook, stirring until thickened. Stir in cheese and seasonings.

YIELD: **4** SERVINGS

THE JUNIOR LEAGUE OF ORANGE COUNTY, NEW YORK

. . . .

Stuffed Flounder

¼ cup chopped onion
¼ cup butter
1 3-ounce can chopped mushrooms, drained (liquid reserved)
1 7½-ounce can crabmeat, drained and flaked
½ cup coarse saltine cracker crumbs
2 tablespoons chopped parsley
1 teaspoon salt
Dash pepper
2 pounds flounder filets
3 tablespoons butter
3 tablespoons flour
Milk
1/3 cup dry white wine
4 ounces Swiss cheese, shredded
½ teaspoon paprika

In skillet, cook onion in the ¼ cup butter until tender. Stir drained mushrooms into skillet with the flaked crabmeat, cracker crumbs, parsley, ½ teaspoon salt, and pepper. Spread mixture over flounder filets. Roll filets and place seam side down in 12 x 10 x 2-inch baking dish.

In saucepan, melt the 3 tablespoons butter; blend in flour and remaining salt. Add enough milk to the reserved mushroom liquid to make 1½ cups; add with white wine to saucepan. Cook and stir until mixture thickens and bubbles. Pour over filets.

Bake in 400° oven for 25 minutes. Sprinkle with cheese and paprika. Return to oven and bake 10 minutes longer, or until fish flakes easily with a fork.

YIELD: 8 SERVINGS

THE JUNIOR LEAGUE OF WILLIAMSPORT, PENNSYLVANIA

Baked Lemon-Stuffed Sole

1/3 cup butter
1/3 cup chopped celery
2 tablespoons onion
1¼ cups herb seasoned stuffing mix
1 tablespoon chopped parsley
1 tablespoon lemon juice
1 teaspoon grated lemon peel
¼ teaspoon salt
¼ teaspoon pepper
4 sole or flounder filets (about 1½ pounds)
½ teaspoon dill
1/3 cup melted butter

Melt 1/3 cup butter. Add celery and onion and sauté until onion is transparent. Stir in stuffing mix, parsley, lemon juice and peel, salt, and pepper. Set aside.

Grease casserole. Place 2 filets on bottom. Top each with about ½

Recipe continues . . .

cup stuffing mixture. Place 2 remaining filets on top. Bake in center of 350° oven for 20–30 minutes.

Mix dill and melted butter. Dribble over fish.

YIELD: 4 SERVINGS

THE JUNIOR LEAGUE OF FALL RIVER, MASSACHUSETTS

·   ·   ·   ·   ·   ·   ·   ·   ·   ·   ·   ·   ·   ·   ·   ·   ·

Filetti Pesce di Sogliola Pesto
(Filet of Sole with Pesto)

3 tablespoons butter
3 ripe tomatoes
Salt and pepper to taste
3 sole filets
3 tablespoons Pesto Sauce
3 sprigs Italian parsley,
chopped, for garnish

Butter an 8 x 8-inch casserole with 1 tablespoon of the butter. Peel, slice, and seed tomatoes. Line bottom of the casserole with two-thirds of the tomato slices. Season with salt and pepper. Place filets on top of the tomatoes. Spread 1 tablespoon Pesto Sauce evenly over each filet and then fold in half. Cover with remaining tomato slices, season with additional salt and pepper, and dot with remaining 2 tablespoons butter.

Bake in a 325° oven for 20–25 minutes, or until fish flakes. Glaze under broiler for about 5 minutes, or until bubbly. Garnish with parsley.

YIELD: 3 SERVINGS

PESTO SAUCE:
(FRESH BASIL SAUCE)

This sauce is almost an Italian staple—used with spaghetti, gnocci, fettuccine, fish, in cold or hot soups. It will keep in freezer for many months.

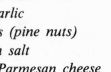

2 cups minced fresh basil leaves
3 cloves garlic
½ cup pignoli nuts (pine nuts)
½ teaspoon salt
½ cup freshly grated Parmesan cheese
½ cup olive oil

In a blender or food processor, blend basil leaves, garlic, and pine nuts until well mixed. Add salt and cheese. Very slowly add olive oil and blend until mixture becomes a fine paste.

YIELD: 1 CUP

From Our House
THE JUNIOR LEAGUE OF HARTFORD, CONNECTICUT

. . . .

Sole Marguery

6 medium mushrooms
6 sole or flounder filets
6 large shrimp
3 tablespoons butter
1 cup water
1 cup white wine
1 tablespoon lemon juice
½ teaspoon salt
3 whole peppercorns
1 slice onion
1 bay leaf
1 tablespoon flour
Dash paprika
1 egg yolk, slightly beaten
¼ cup heavy cream

Recipe continues . . .

Wipe mushrooms and filets with a damp cloth; remove mushroom stems. Peel and clean shrimp.

Melt 1 tablespoon butter in 10-inch skillet over low heat. Fold filets in half and lay in skillet. Add mushrooms, shrimp, water, wine, lemon juice, salt, peppercorns, onion, and bay leaf. Cover and bring to a boil; reduce heat and simmer gently for 8 minutes. Carefully lift out filets, drain well, and arrange in shallow baking dish. Top each filet with 1 shrimp and 1 mushroom.

Boil fish liquid vigorously for 10–12 minutes, or until reduced by half (should be a little more than 1 cup.)

Melt 2 remaining tablespoons butter in small saucepan; add flour and paprika and cook over low heat until bubbly. Strain the fish stock and gradually stir it into the butter-flour mixture. Stir constantly until boiling. Reduce heat and add a small amount to the egg yolk; mix well and pour back into sauce. Add heavy cream and cook 2 minutes longer, stirring constantly.

Pour sauce over filets. Place under broiler about 5 inches below heating unit and broil until lightly browned, about 3 minutes.

YIELD: 6 SERVINGS

THE JUNIOR LEAGUE OF MORRISTOWN, NEW JERSEY

Sole and Scallop Casserole

6 lemon sole filets
Milk
Flour
¼ pound + 2 tablespoons butter
1 medium onion, finely chopped
½ pound mushrooms, finely chopped
½ cup finely chopped parsley
1 clove garlic
Salt and pepper to taste
½ pound small bay scallops (or large
scallops cut into small pieces)
¾ cup shredded Swiss cheese
1 cup light cream

Dip filets in milk, then in flour. Brown in ¼ pound of heated butter for about 2 minutes on each side. Place filets in shallow buttered baking dish.

In separate frying pan, sauté onion in remaining 2 tablespoons butter until clear; add mushrooms, parsley, garlic, salt, and pepper. Cook over high heat for 5 minutes, stirring frequently. Reduce heat and simmer 10 more minutes. Discard garlic. During last 2 minutes of cooking time add scallops. Spoon over sole in baking dish.

Combine cheese and cream in saucepan. Heat, stirring, until cheese is melted and pour over fish. Bake in a preheated 350° oven for 20 minutes, or until golden on top.

YIELD: 6 SERVINGS

THE JUNIOR LEAGUE OF STAMFORD-NORWALK, CONNECTICUT

Baked Filets of Sole

This dish can be prepared in the morning, stored in the refrigerator, and baked at the last minute.

1 tablespoon soft butter
1 teaspoon flour
¼ pound mushrooms, finely chopped
2 shallots, finely chopped
1 teaspoon minced chives
1 tablespoon minced parsley
Fine dry bread crumbs
8 sole or flounder filets
Shredded Swiss cheese
½ cup white wine
½ cup chicken stock
Butter

Butter a shallow baking dish with the soft butter blended with the flour. Mix together the mushrooms, shallots, chives, and parsley. Spread half of this mixture in the baking dish, sprinkle lightly with bread crumbs, and arrange the filets on top. Cover the fish with the rest of the chopped vegetables, sprinkle lightly again with bread crumbs and a little Swiss cheese, and dot with butter. Add white wine and chicken stock and bake in a moderate 350° oven for 20–25 minutes.

YIELD: **4** SERVINGS

THE JUNIOR LEAGUE OF SUMMIT, NEW JERSEY

Fish Wenham

2 10-ounce packages frozen chopped spinach
1/4 cup chopped onion
2 pounds sole filets
4 tablespoons melted butter
1/4 lemon
2 tablespoons sesame seeds
Salt and pepper to taste
1 cup sour cream

Cook spinach according to package directions, drain, and spread in bottom of oblong baking dish. Sprinkle chopped onion over spinach.

Dip fish filets in melted butter and place on bed of spinach. Sprinkle with lemon juice, sesame seeds, and salt and pepper. Spread sour cream over the top. Cover and bake at 350° for 30–45 minutes.

YIELD: 4–6 SERVINGS

THE JUNIOR LEAGUE OF ALBANY, NEW YORK

. . . .

Crabmeat Crepes with Curry Sauce

1/4 cup butter
3 tablespoons oil
1 clove garlic, minced
1 medium onion, finely chopped
1/2 large green pepper, finely chopped
1/2 cup finely diced ham
1 teaspoon salt
1 teaspoon finely chopped orange zest*
1 1/2 pounds crabmeat
1/3 cup cognac
6 luncheon crepes

*Zest is the peel with "white" removed

Recipe continues . . .

CURRY SAUCE:
6 tablespoons butter
5 tablespoons flour
3 teaspoons curry powder
1 teaspoon freshly grated ginger root
1 cup fish or chicken stock
1 cup scalded cream
Chutney and chopped toasted almonds

In a heavy pan, heat the ¼ cup butter and 3 tablespoons oil. Add garlic, onion and pepper, and stew until onion and garlic are translucent and pepper is crisply tender. Add minced ham, salt, orange zest, and crabmeat; cook until heated through. Toss and flame with cognac. Fill 6 luncheon crepes, roll, and arrange on flat baking dish.

To make sauce, melt butter in saucepan over low heat; stir in flour, curry powder, and ginger and cook for a few minutes. Stir in stock and stir constantly until sauce is thickened. Add cream. Blend well and simmer for a few minutes. Correct seasonings.

Spoon the sauce over the crepes and heat in a 375° oven for 10 minutes. Serve with chutney and chopped toasted almonds.

YIELD: 6 SERVINGS

Cooks Book
THE JUNIOR LEAGUE OF GREATER NEW HAVEN, CONNECTICUT

Crab Supreme

½ pound fresh or frozen crabmeat
¼ large green pepper, chopped
⅛ cup sliced pimento
½ tablespoon lemon juice
½ teaspoon Worcestershire sauce
¼ cup mayonnaise
2 drops Tabasco
¼ teaspoon dry mustard
⅛ teaspoon salt
⅛ teaspoon pepper
2 tablespoons bread crumbs
1 tablespoon melted butter

Preheat oven to 375°. Pick over and separate crab into shreds. Combine crab with all ingredients except bread crumbs and butter. Divide mixture into four baking shells or casserole. Top with mixture of bread crumbs and butter. Bake for 15 minutes. Serve bubbling hot.

YIELD: **4** SERVINGS

THE JUNIOR LEAGUE OF ORANGE COUNTY, NEW YORK

Deviled Crab

3 tablespoons butter
1/3 cup flour
2 cups milk
1 cup soft bread crumbs (tear soft
bread apart as you would for stuffing)
3 hard-boiled eggs, chopped
1 pound crabmeat
½ teaspoon salt
⅛ teaspoon pepper
8 ceramic or real scallop shells

Melt butter in a saucepan. Add flour and stir to form a roux. Cook over low heat 2 minutes, stirring. Slowly add the milk and stir until sauce is thickened. Add bread crumbs, eggs, crab, salt, and pepper and mix lightly. Spoon into scallop shells. Bake at 375° for 30 minutes.

YIELD: 8 SMALL LUNCHEON SERVINGS

THE JUNIOR LEAGUE OF WILLIAMSPORT, PENNSYLVANIA

. . . .

Crabmeat Chantilly

4 tablespoons sliced green onion
4 tablespoons vegetable oil
2 tablespoons flour
1 teaspoon salt
2 dashes cayenne
2 cups half and half
½ cup sweet mayonnaise
1 pound lump crabmeat
2 10-ounce packages frozen asparagus spears, cooked,
drained, and cut into bite-size pieces
2 tablespoons grated Parmesan cheese

Cook onion in oil until tender but not brown. Stir in flour, salt, and cayenne. Add half and half and cook, stirring constantly, until thickened. Remove from heat. Stir in salad dressing. Fold in crabmeat.

Arrange asparagus in heatproof platter or shallow baking dish. Spoon crab mixture over asparagus and sprinkle with cheese. *Broil* about 4 inches from heat for 3–5 minutes, or until lightly browned and hot.

YIELD: **6** SERVINGS

THE JUNIOR LEAGUE OF WILMINGTON, DELAWARE

Imperial Crab

1 pound lump crabmeat
½ teaspoon salt
⅛ teaspoon pepper
Dash cayenne
1 tablespoon capers
½ cup mayonnaise
½ cup bread crumbs
Dash paprika
2 tablespoons melted butter

Carefully mix the crab, seasonings, capers, and mayonnaise. Heap into greased crab shells or casserole dish. Sprinkle with bread crumbs and paprika. Drizzle melted butter over top. Bake for 25 minutes in a 350° oven.

YIELD: **4** SERVINGS

THE JUNIOR LEAGUE OF MORRISTOWN, NEW JERSEY

Crab Royale

6 tablespoons butter
2 tablespoons minced shallots
6 tablespoons flour
2¼ cups light cream
1½ teaspoons salt
Dash cayenne
2 teaspoons Dijon mustard
2 egg yolks
¼ cup sherry
2 pounds crabmeat
½ cup buttered bread crumbs

Melt butter over low heat; sauté shallots in it briefly, add flour gradually, and blend. Add cream, ½ cup at a time, stirring vigorously with a whisk. Increase heat slightly and stir constantly until mixture thickens. Reduce heat and add seasonings. Stir to blend and simmer for 15 minutes.

Add some of warm sauce to egg yolks. Carefully add yolks to sauce, whisking to blend. Remove from heat and stir in sherry; gently fold in crabmeat. Pour into large greased au gratin dish, top with buttered crumbs, and bake at 375° for 25–30 minutes.

YIELD: 12 SERVINGS

THE JUNIOR LEAGUE OF WILMINGTON, DELAWARE

Stuffed Lobster Tails Supreme

8 frozen lobster tails, defrosted
5 tablespoons butter or margarine
4 tablespoons flour
1 teaspoon salt
1 teaspoon paprika
Cayenne to taste
2 cups light cream
2 tablespoons lemon juice
1/4 cup cracker crumbs
1/4 cup grated Parmesan cheese

Cook lobster tails in boiling salted water until pink and tender or as package directs. Drain. With scissors, cut meat away from the shells and dice. Rinse the shells and set aside.

Sauté the lobster meat in 4 tablespoons butter in large frying pan for 2–3 minutes. Remove the lobster from the pan. Blend in the flour, salt, paprika, and cayenne and cook for 1–2 minutes.

In a separate pan, heat the cream and then add to the flour mixture, stirring constantly, until mixture thickens and boils 1 minute. Stir in the lemon juice. Add lobster.

Spoon filling into the lobster shells. Mix together the cracker crumbs, cheese, and remaining tablespoon butter and sprinkle this mixture over the lobster. Bake at 450° for 10 minutes, or until top is golden.

YIELD: 4 SERVINGS

Simply Superb
THE JUNIOR LEAGUE OF ELIZABETH-PLAINFIELD, NEW JERSEY

Moules à la Marinière

6 dozen mussels
6 shallots, finely chopped
3 tablespoons butter
1 bay leaf
3 sprigs parsley
1 cup white wine or 2/3 cup white vermouth
½ cup heavy cream
Chopped parsley

Scrub and wash mussels thoroughly, discarding those that do not close when cleaning. Discard the beards.

In a large kettle, sauté shallots in butter for about 2 minutes; add bay leaf and parsley sprigs. Place mussels on top and pour wine over them. Cover kettle tightly and cook until all mussels are open, shaking the pan occasionally. It will take about 7 minutes.

Transfer mussels to a soup tureen, removing the empty shells or just the upper half of each shell if you like. Add cream to sauce in kettle and heat; check seasonings. Pour liquid over mussels and sprinkle with chopped parsley.

YIELD: 4 MAIN COURSE SERVINGS, 6 APPETIZERS

THE JUNIOR LEAGUE OF THE NORTH SHORE, LONG ISLAND, NEW YORK

Oysters Casino

24 oysters on half shell
½ pound butter
1 clove·garlic, minced
1 tablespoon Worcestershire sauce
Freshly ground black pepper
Juice of 1 lemon
1 tablespoon dry mustard
¼ cup parsley
1/3 cup finely minced green onion
½ pound bacon, finely chopped
and partially fried
1 cup dry white wine
2 heads lettuce, finely shredded
Lemon slices, parsley sprigs, and
paprika for garnish

In broiler pan, place oysters in half shell. Mash and mix butter with the garlic and drop a dollop on each oyster. Sprinkle with Worcestershire sauce, pepper, lemon juice, mustard, parsley, green onion, bacon, and wine. Bake at 450° for 5–8 minutes, or until bacon is browned.

Arrange oysters on a platter on a bed of finely shredded lettuce. Pour juices from pan over oysters, letting it spill onto the lettuce when necessary. Garnish with lemon slices, parsley, and paprika.

YIELD: 6 SERVINGS

THE JUNIOR LEAGUE OF STAMFORD-NORWALK, CONNECTICUT

Oyster Pie

1 pint shucked oysters with juice
½ cup chopped green pepper
½ cup chopped celery
4 tablespoons butter
5 tablespoons flour
2 cups hot milk
1 teaspoon salt
Freshly ground pepper
2 tablespoons chopped pimento
Pastry for 1-crust pie

Simmer oysters in their own liquid about 5 minutes, or until edges begin to curl. Sauté peppers and celery in butter until tender. Blend in flour, add milk, and cook, stirring, until sauce thickens. Add oysters, seasonings, and pimento and stir together gently.

Pour into buttered casserole. Top with standard pie pastry. Bake in 425° oven 15–20 minutes, or until crust is brown.

YIELD: 4 SERVINGS

THE JUNIOR LEAGUE OF POUGHKEEPSIE, NEW YORK

· · · · · · · · · · · · · · · · · · ·

Oyster Fritters

30 stewing oysters
2 eggs
¼ teaspoon salt
¼ teaspoon pepper
¼ cup plus 1 tablespoon flour
1 teaspoon baking powder
¼ cup canned evaporated milk
Oil

Clean the oysters. Drain in a strainer. Beat eggs; add salt and pepper, flour, baking powder, and milk. Beat with egg beater. Blend the oysters into this mixture.

Pour 1 inch of oil into large skillet and heat to 365°. Drop the mixture by tablespoonfuls into the hot shortening and fry until brown, turning once, about 6 minutes in all. Drain on paper toweling.

YIELD: 2–3 SERVINGS

Bicentennial Cookbook
THE JUNIOR LEAGUE OF PHILADELPHIA, PENNSYLVANIA

. . . .

Scalloped Oysters

1 pint oysters
2 cups medium–coarse oyster cracker crumbs
½ cup melted butter
Pepper
¾ cup light cream
¼ teaspoon Worcestershire sauce
½ teaspoon salt

Drain oysters, reserving ¼ cup liquid. Combine cracker crumbs and melted butter. Spread one-third of the crumbs in greased 8 x 1¼-inch round or square pan. Cover with half the oysters; sprinkle with pepper. Using another third of the crumbs, spread a second layer and cover with remaining oysters. Sprinkle with pepper.

Combine cream, reserved oyster liquid, Worcestershire sauce, and salt. Pour over oysters. Top with remaining crumbs. Bake uncovered at 350° for 40 minutes.

YIELD: 4–6 SERVINGS

THE JUNIOR LEAGUE OF ELMIRA, NEW YORK

. . . .

Downeast Scallops

1 pound medium-size fresh scallops
2 cups flour, seasoned with
garlic salt and pepper to taste
Italian-flavored bread crumbs
Sweet butter
2 cups light cream

Wash scallops in cold water, drain, and towel-dry.

Roll scallops in flour mixture until each is thoroughly coated. Butter a 9-inch round ovenproof dish generously. Individually place scallops into dish. Sprinkle heavily with bread crumbs and dot small pats of butter on each scallop. Pour all cream over scallops. Bake for 35 minutes at 350°.

YIELD: **4** SERVINGS

THE JUNIOR LEAGUE OF BANGOR, MAINE

. . . .

Scallops in Wine

2 pounds scallops
8 tablespoons butter
3 ounces dry white wine
½ pound fresh mushrooms, sliced
½ cup chopped onion
3 tablespoons flour
3 ounces dry sherry
¾ cup milk
¾ cup heavy cream
Salt
Cayenne
1 egg yolk, beaten
Buttered bread crumbs

Sauté scallops in 3 tablespoons butter until golden, no more than 5 minutes. Add the white wine and transfer mixture to a buttered casserole.

Sauté mushrooms and onion in 2 tablespoons butter until onion is transparent and sprinkle over scallops.

Melt remaining 3 tablespoons butter in another saucepan; add the flour, blending and stirring well. Add the sherry and cook gently for a few minutes. Slowly add the milk and cream, stirring constantly. Season with salt and cayenne. When sauce is thickened, remove from heat and stir in beaten egg yolk. Pour sauce over scallops and top with bread crumbs. Bake at 350° for about 10 minutes, or until top is browned.

YIELD: 4–5 SERVINGS

THE JUNIOR LEAGUE OF GREATER BRIDGEPORT, CONNECTICUT

Greenwich Coquilles Saint Jacques

½ pint scallops
½ cup dry white wine
½ teaspoon mixed dried herbs
½ teaspoon salt
2 teaspoons grated onion
¼ pound mushrooms
6 tablespoons butter
¼ lemon
½ cup light cream
3 tablespoons flour
Salt and pepper to taste
Lemon juice
Fine bread crumbs
1/3 cup shredded Gruyère cheese

Recipe continues . . .

Put the scallops in a saucepan with the wine, herbs, salt, onion, and just enough water to cover. Bring to a boil. Cover and simmer 5 minutes. Set aside.

Wipe and trim mushrooms. Put mushrooms in a small saucepan with 1 tablespoon butter, the juice of ¼ lemon, and enough water to come halfway up the mushrooms. Bring to a boil. Cover and cook gently for 10 minutes.

Strain both scallop and mushroom broth into a 2-cup measure. There should be about 1½ cups liquid. Fill to the 2-cup line with light cream.

Melt 3 tablespoons of the butter. Blend in flour, add half the liquid, and stir until smooth. Coarsely chop the scallops and mushrooms and add to the sauce. Season with salt, pepper, and lemon juice.

Fill scallop shells or ramekins with the mixture. When cool, cover with fine bread crumbs tossed with 2 tablespoons melted butter and the cheese. Bake at 350° for 15 minutes, browning under the broiler for the last few minutes.

YIELD: 6 SERVINGS

Greenwich Recommends
THE JUNIOR LEAGUE OF GREENWICH, CONNECTICUT

.   .   .   .

Scallops in Cream Sauce

½ cup white wine
½ teaspoon lemon juice
1 pound scallops
1 tablespoon butter
2 tablespoons flour
5 ounces light cream
¼ teaspoon salt
¼ teaspoon black pepper
⅛ teaspoon cayenne
¼ cup shredded Gruyère cheese

Heat wine and lemon juice over moderate heat. When it boils, reduce heat and add scallops. Simmer gently 6–8 minutes, or until scallops are firm. Remove from heat and set aside to cool. Strain liquid into a bowl and set aside.

Melt butter in pan over low heat and stir in flour. Gradually add liquid, stirring constantly. Cook sauce 3–4 minutes. Stir in cream, salt, pepper, and cayenne. Cook for 2 minutes more, then fold in scallops. Spoon into scallop shells and sprinkle with cheese. Brown under broiler 4–5 minutes.

YIELD: 4 SERVINGS MAIN COURSE, 6 APPETIZERS

THE JUNIOR LEAGUE OF MONTREAL, QUEBEC

Drunken Scallops

1½–2 pounds sea scallops
1 cup flour
Olive oil
Butter
½ cup chopped fresh parsley
4 slices cooked bacon, crumbled
3 shallots, diced
1 large clove garlic, minced
1 teaspoon dried oregano
1 cup dry white wine

Wash and thoroughly dry scallops, then roll in flour to coat. Heat small, equal amounts of oil and butter in skillet. Cook all ingredients except wine for 4–5 minutes, stirring to prevent sticking. Add more oil or butter if needed. Remove scallops to serving dish and keep warm.

Add wine to the skillet, stirring to loosen all scallop bits, and boil

Recipe continues . . .

until liquid is reduced to half the volume. Pour over scallops. Season with salt and pepper and serve.

YIELD: **4** SERVINGS

Bicentennial Cookbook
THE JUNIOR LEAGUE OF PHILADELPHIA, PENNSYLVANIA

· · · · · · · · · · · · · · · ·

Shrimp and Scallops for Linguine

½ pound shrimp
½ pound sea scallops
1 medium onion, minced
1 clove garlic, minced
2 tablespoons butter
3 large tomatoes, chopped
1 tablespoon tomato paste
1 tablespoon chopped fresh parsley
½ teaspoon oregano
1 small bay leaf
Salt and freshly ground pepper
¼–½ cup dry white wine (or half
dry vermouth, half water)
½ pound linguine cooked according
to package directions
Grated Parmesan cheese

Shell and devein shrimp. Wash scallops.

Sauté the onion and garlic in butter until the onion is tender. Add the chopped tomatoes, tomato paste, parsley, oregano, bay leaf, salt and pepper, and ¼ cup wine (add remaining ¼ cup wine if the sauce thickens while simmering). Simmer about 30 minutes. Check seasonings.

Add the scallops and simmer 5 minutes. Add the shrimp and continue to simmer another 5 minutes, or until the scallops and shrimp are cooked. Serve over linguine and top with Parmesan cheese.

YIELD: 3–4 SERVINGS

THE JUNIOR LEAGUE OF POUGHKEEPSIE, NEW YORK

Deep Fried Scallops

1 pound scallops
2 tablespoons oil
2 tablespoons vinegar
½ teaspoon salt
Flour seasoned with salt and pepper
1 egg
1 tablespoon milk
Fine dry bread crumbs for dredging
Fat for deep frying

Wash scallops; dry on clean towel. (Large scallops should be cut in half.)
   Combine the oil, vinegar, and salt and marinate the scallops for 1 hour. Drain; dredge scallops in the flour mixture. Lightly beat the egg with the milk. Dip the scallops into the egg mixture, then roll in the bread crumbs. Fry for 2 minutes, or until golden brown, in deep fat at 375°. Drain on unglazed paper and serve hot.

YIELD: 4 SERVINGS

THE JUNIOR LEAGUE OF STAMFORD-NORWALK, CONNECTICUT

Scallops in Casserole

1 pound scallops
8 tablespoons butter
3 ounces dry white wine
½ pound fresh mushrooms, sliced
½ cup chopped onion
3 tablespoons flour
3 ounces dry sherry
½ cup milk
1 cup heavy cream
Salt
Dash pepper
1 egg yolk, beaten
Buttered bread crumbs

Sauté scallops in 3 tablespoons butter until golden brown. Add white wine, stirring well. Transfer scallop mixture to a buttered casserole.

Sauté mushrooms and onion in 2 tablespoons butter until soft, not browned. Add to casserole with the scallops.

Melt remaining 3 tablespoons butter in separate pan. Add flour, blending well. Add sherry and cook gently for a few minutes. Slowly add milk and cream, stirring constantly, until well blended. Season to taste with salt and pepper.

When the sauce has thickened, remove from heat and stir in beaten egg yolk. Pour sauce over the scallops, mushrooms, and onion in casserole and top with buttered bread crumbs. Bake in 350° preheated oven for 10 minutes, or until top browns. If the casserole has been made in advance and the ingredients have cooled, bake for 20–25 minutes.

YIELD: **4** SERVINGS

THE JUNIOR LEAGUE OF SPRINGFIELD, MASSACHUSETTS

Coquilles Saint Jacques

¼ cup melted butter
¼ cup flour
1 teaspoon dry mustard
1 teaspoon salt
Dash cayenne
2 cups milk
1 teaspoon Worcestershire sauce
½ cup grated Parmesan cheese
1 teaspoon minced shallot or onion
2 tablespoons butter
2 cups cooked scallops (1 pound)
1 cup cooked small shrimp (½ pound)
1 tablespoon parsley
Additional grated Parmesan cheese

Melt ¼ cup butter; stir in flour, mustard, salt, cayenne, then milk. Cook until thick, stirring constantly. Remove from heat; fold in Worcestershire sauce and ½ cup grated cheese.

In another pan, sauté shallot in 2 tablespoons butter; add scallops, shrimp, parsley, and sauce.

Spoon portions of mixture into shells or individual baking dishes. Sprinkle with more Parmesan cheese and brown under broiler 2–3 minutes, or until bubbling.

Doubles easily. Make ahead or freeze.

YIELD: 6 LUNCH SERVINGS, 4 GENEROUS MAIN COURSE SERVINGS,
8 APPETIZERS

Something Special
THE JUNIOR LEAGUE OF YORK, PENNSYLVANIA

Shrimp India

2 medium onions, finely chopped
½ green pepper, finely chopped
2 cloves garlic, minced
¼ cup butter
2 cups sour cream
2 teaspoons lemon juice
½ teaspoon grated lemon rind
1–2 teaspoons curry powder
¼ teaspoon chili powder
½ teaspoon salt
½ teaspoon freshly ground black pepper
1½ pounds cooked shrimp

Sauté the onions, pepper, and garlic in the butter until the onions are transparent. Stir in the sour cream, lemon juice, lemon rind, curry powder, chili powder, salt, and pepper. When thoroughly blended, add shrimp. Heat through but do not let boil.

Serve immediately with rice and condiments (chutney, coconut, chopped peanuts, crumbled bacon, etc.).

YIELD: 6 SERVINGS

Presenting Boston . . . A Cookbook
THE JUNIOR LEAGUE OF BOSTON, MASSACHUSETTS

.   .   .   .

Melinda's Shrimp de Jonghe

1 cup butter
2 cloves garlic, minced
½ cup chopped fresh parsley
½ teaspoon paprika
Dash cayenne
¼ cup dry sherry
2 cups soft bread crumbs
5–6 cups cleaned shrimp

Melt butter in a medium-size saucepan. Add garlic, parsley, paprika, cayenne, and sherry. Mix and add bread crumbs. Toss.

Place shrimp in an 11 x 7 x 1½-inch greased casserole. Spoon butter-crumb mixture over top. Bake at 325° for 25 minutes, or until crumbs are browned.

YIELD: 6–8 SERVINGS

THE JUNIOR LEAGUE OF ERIE, PENNSYLVANIA

Shrimp Florentine

1 10-ounce package frozen spinach
2 tablespoons chopped onion
3 tablespoons butter
½ teaspoon salt
Pinch mace
Freshly ground black pepper
2 tablespoons flour
¾ cup chicken broth
Dash Worcestershire sauce
⅛ teaspoon dried basil
1 egg yolk
1 teaspoon lemon juice
½ pound shrimp, cooked, peeled, and deveined

Barely cook spinach; drain well. Sauté onion until soft in 1 tablespoon butter. Add to spinach with salt, a pinch mace, and plenty of pepper. Spoon into buttered 1-quart baking dish.

In small pan, melt remaining butter; stir in flour. Stir in chicken broth, Worcestershire sauce, and basil. Cook, stirring, until sauce boils and thickens.

Mix egg yolk with lemon juice and a little of the sauce. Return to

Recipe continues . . .

pan. Stir over low heat for about 1 minute, being careful not to let sauce boil. Add shrimp and pour over spinach. Bake 15–20 minutes at 350°.

YIELD: 2–3 SERVINGS

THE JUNIOR LEAGUE OF ELMIRA, NEW YORK

. . . .

Puffed Butterfly Shrimp

1 teaspoon grated fresh ginger root
½ teaspoon salt
1 teaspoon sherry
1 pound shrimp, shelled, deveined,
and butterflied
1 cup unsifted flour
1 tablespoon baking powder
5 tablespoons oil
2/3 cup cold water
4 teaspoons sesame seeds
3 tablespoons minced green onion
4 cups oil for deep frying

Combine ginger root, ½ teaspoon salt, and the sherry. Brush mixture on split side of shrimp.

Mix flour, baking powder, and remaining salt in bowl. Add oil gradually while stirring. Mix well. Gradually add water to make a thick batter. Add sesame seeds and green onion; mix well. To test consistency of batter, hold shrimp by the tail, dip into batter, then hold over bowl. The batter should drip down slowly from the shrimp.

Heat oil to 365°. Dip shrimp into batter and put into oil. The shrimp will puff up and rise to the surface immediately. Deep fry several shrimp at a time. Turn when batter is set and fry until golden brown. Drain on paper toweling.

Serve hot or warm. You can keep shrimp in warm oven for a ½ hour or more.

YIELD: 8 SERVINGS

Simply Superb
THE JUNIOR LEAGUE OF ELIZABETH-PLAINFIELD, NEW JERSEY

. . . .

Chinese Fried Shrimp and Mushrooms

2 pounds extra large shrimp,
cooked, shelled, and cleaned
4 tablespoons melted butter
2 pounds mushrooms, thickly sliced
1 6-ounce can Chinese bamboo shoots, drained
1 6-ounce can water chestnuts,
drained and sliced
4 teaspoons powdered ginger or
1 tablespoon grated fresh ginger root
2 tablespoons flour
1 cup chicken stock
Salt and pepper to taste
2 tablespoons soy sauce

Sauté shrimp in hot butter until shrimp are heated through. Add sliced mushrooms and continue to sauté until mushrooms are tender. Stir in bamboo shoots and water chestnuts and cook for 2 minutes. Add ginger and cook until shoots and water chestnuts are hot. Push mixture to one side of pan.

Mix flour and chicken stock, salt, and pepper and pour into pan. Simmer for 3–4 minutes or until thickened, stirring often. Then mix in shrimp and vegetables. Add soy sauce and heat thoroughly. Serve over cooked rice.

YIELD: 8 SERVINGS

THE JUNIOR LEAGUE OF HARRISBURG, PENNSYLVANIA

. . . .

Baked Stuffed Shrimp

24 raw jumbo shrimp, shelled
and deveined
2 tablespoons butter
1 small onion, minced
1/4 cup minced celery
1/2 minced green pepper
1 tablespoon chopped parsley
1 pound backfin crabmeat
1 teaspoon salt
1 teaspoon Worcestershire sauce
1/4 teaspoon thyme
Dash tabasco
1/2 cup seasoned bread crumbs
1 egg, beaten
1 cup light cream
1 stick butter
2 cloves garlic, minced
Paprika

Split shrimp lengthwise so they can be opened flat but do not cut all the way through. Spread flat in buttered shallow baking dish and set aside.

In the 2 tablespoons butter, sauté onion, celery, and green pepper until onion is just transparent. Remove from heat; add parsley. Toss vegetable mixture with crabmeat. Add seasonings, bread crumbs, egg, and cream. Toss gently but thoroughly. Mound crab mixture on shrimp.

Melt the stick of butter with garlic. Pour over shrimp. Sprinkle with paprika and bake at 400° for 15 minutes.

This can be prepared early in the day. If so, pour garlic butter over shrimp before baking.

YIELD: 6 SERVINGS

THE JUNIOR LEAGUE OF LANCASTER, PENNSYLVANIA

Scampi in Vermouth

2 pounds shrimp, shelled and deveined
1/3 cup olive oil
2 cloves garlic, minced
¾ teaspoon salt
½ teaspoon freshly ground pepper
½ cup dry vermouth
2 tablespoons chopped parsley
3 tablespoons freshly squeezed lemon juice

Sauté shrimp in olive oil until they begin to color pink. Add garlic, salt, pepper, and vermouth. Cook on high heat so the vermouth reduces to half. This must be done quickly so shrimp do not dry out—total cooking time should not exceed 4 minutes.

Sprinkle with parsley and lemon juice and serve.

YIELD: 6 SERVINGS

THE JUNIOR LEAGUE OF THE NORTH SHORE, LONG ISLAND, NEW YORK

.   .   .   .

Dad's Shrimp Scampi

1 pound large shrimp (about 16–21)
1 teaspoon salt
2 tablespoons vinegar
¾ stick butter (6 tablespoons)
3 cloves garlic, minced
1/3 cup fresh parsley

Clean and devein shrimp. Slice shrimp halfway through from head portion to tail. (When cooked, shrimp will fan open.)

Put shrimp in 3–4 quarts boiling water with the salt and vinegar.

Recipe continues . . .

Bring to boil again and boil 1-1½ minutes. Remove from heat immediately. Drain and place in cold water.

In a heavy frying pan, melt butter with the garlic. Heat shrimp through again in butter and garlic (approximately 3-5 minutes) over low heat. Just before serving, sprinkle with parsley.

Serve with long-grain and wild rice.

YIELD: 4 SERVINGS

THE JUNIOR LEAGUE OF ORANGE COUNTY, NEW YORK

Herbed Shrimp Scampi

1 pound large raw shrimp
¼ pound butter
¼ cup olive oil
1 tablespoon chopped parsley
¾ teaspoon basil
½ teaspoon oregano
½ teaspoon minced garlic
¾ teaspoon salt
½-1 lemon

Peel, devein, and butterfly shrimp, leaving tails attached. Place in a baking dish.

Melt butter and combine with oil, herbs, spices, and juice of lemon. (Can be made ahead to this point.) Broil shrimp for 5 minutes at 450°. Serve with crunchy Italian bread.

YIELD: 2-3 SERVINGS

THE JUNIOR LEAGUE OF THE ORANGES AND SHORT HILLS, NEW JERSEY

Shrimp Rockefeller

2 pounds medium shrimp, shelled
or unshelled
2 10-ounce packages frozen
chopped spinach
4 tablespoons butter
4 tablespoons flour
2 cups warmed milk or light cream
¾ teaspoon salt
White pepper to taste
2 tablespoons sherry
¼ cup Parmesan cheese
Additional Parmesan cheese
Paprika

Preheat oven to 350° ½ hour before serving time.

Bring shrimp to full boil in salted water. Rinse under cold water immediately. Shell, if necessary, devein, and set aside.

Cook spinach according to directions. Drain well and set aside.

Melt butter and add flour, stirring with whisk, for 1 minute. Add warmed milk or cream and cook, stirring, until sauce is thickened. Add salt and pepper, sherry, and Parmesan cheese and stir several minutes until sauce is bubbling and smooth.

Spread spinach in bottom of copper dish or ovenproof shallow casserole. Arrange shrimp on top. Cover with sauce. Sprinkle with a little additional Parmesan cheese and paprika.

Cover with foil and heat in oven until hot, about 20 minutes. Remove foil and place under broiler until brown and bubbling.

Can be prepared ahead of time by layering the spinach and shrimp and covering with foil. Then add hot sauce and proceed as above.

YIELD: 6 SERVINGS

THE JUNIOR LEAGUE OF SPRINGFIELD, MASSACHUSETTS

Shrimp Tempura Okugawa

1 pound jumbo shrimp
2 teaspoons sugar
½ teaspoon baking powder
1 teaspoon salt
2 eggs
½ cup flour (for even crisper batter
use cornstarch)
¾ cup water or beer
Ice cubes
Vegetable oil
Flour for coating

Shell shrimp, leaving tails, and devein. Cut gashes in undersides at ½-inch intervals, then cut lengthwise almost through to back. Fan out into a "butterfly" shape. Rinse under cold water and pat dry with paper toweling.

Combine sugar, baking powder, salt, eggs, flour, and water or beer; mix lightly with chopsticks or fork. Batter should be lumpy. Add a few ice cubes.

Heat a couple of inches of oil in an electric skillet or wok until oil temperature reaches about 365°. (If a drop of batter sinks, then quickly rises to the surface and spins around, the temperature is right.)

Coat shrimp with flour; then dip them, one at a time, into the batter. Fry a few shrimp at a time until golden. Drain on paper toweling. Remove bits of batter from oil with a skimmer.

Serve shrimp with hot rice and soy sauce. Various horseradish or ginger-flavored sauces are also nice.

Do not double recipe.

YIELD: **4** SERVINGS

Hudson River Hospitality
THE JUNIOR LEAGUE OF WESTCHESTER ON HUDSON, NEW YORK

Party Shrimp Creole

1½-2 pounds fresh or frozen raw shrimp
9 tablespoons butter
6 large mushrooms, finely sliced
3 tablespoons sherry
6 tablespoons minced green pepper
½ 6-ounce can tomato paste
½ teaspoon salt
Dash chili powder
Dash cayenne
1 cup light cream
½ cup sour cream
3 onions, thinly sliced

Shell shrimp and remove vein or defrost frozen shrimp. Cook in 4 tablespoons of melted butter for 2 minutes. Remove shrimp, add 2 tablespoons butter, and briskly sauté mushrooms. Add sherry and green pepper and cook until liquid is evaporated. Add 1 tablespoon butter, tomato paste, salt, chili powder, and cayenne. Gradually stir in cream and sour cream. Sauté onion in remaining butter in separate pan and add to sauce, along with the shrimp. Transfer to casserole and bake at 350° for 30 minutes. Serve over rice.

Sauce may be made in advance and frozen. Add shrimp to sauce just before baking.

YIELD: 6 SERVINGS

THE JUNIOR LEAGUE OF WILMINGTON, DELAWARE

Seafood Party Buffet Dish

1 quart mayonnaise
1½ tablespoons Worcestershire sauce
1/3 cup mustard
¾ cup sherry
Dash cayenne or Tabasco
Salt and pepper to taste
1¼ teaspoons curry powder
1/3 cup chopped parsley
1½ cups chopped onion
1½ cups chopped celery
1½ cups coarse fresh bread crumbs
2½ cups water
2 pounds crabmeat, finely picked over
2½ pounds cooked shrimp
Buttered bread crumbs for topping (optional)

Combine all ingredients except topping and place in greased 4-quart casserole or divide into two smaller casseroles. Buttered crumbs on top are optional. Bake at 350° for about 30 minutes.

YIELD: 18 SERVINGS

THE JUNIOR LEAGUE OF BRONXVILLE, NEW YORK

Seafood Casserole

1 pound scallops
1 cup dry white wine
2 teaspoons lemon juice
1 tablespoon chopped parsley
6 tablespoons butter
1/3 cup flour
2-2½ cups cream
¼ cup cognac
1 tablespoon Worcestershire sauce
1/3 cup Parmesan cheese
Salt and pepper to taste
2 egg yolks, beaten
1 pound cooked sliced mushrooms
1 pound cooked lobster or crabmeat
1 pound cooked shrimp
1 cup soft bread crumbs tossed with melted butter
Additional cheese and paprika for topping (optional)

Cook scallops in 1 cup dry white wine with lemon juice and parsley for 3–5 minutes. Do not overcook. Drain scallops and reserve ¾ cup cooking liquid.

Melt the butter and add flour. Gradually stir in reserved scallop liquid, cream, cognac, and Worcestershire sauce. Cook until thickened. Add cheese and stir until melted. Add salt and pepper to taste. Drizzle a small amount of sauce into beaten egg yolks. Slowly combine egg yolk mixture with remaining sauce. Add mushrooms and seafood.

Pour into individual casseroles or one large dish. Cover with bread crumbs and sprinkle with more cheese and paprika, if desired. Bake at 350° for 25–30 minutes, or until heated through and crumbs are brown.

May be made early in the day and refrigerated. Bring casserole to room temperature and bake as directed.

YIELD: 10–12 SERVINGS

THE JUNIOR LEAGUE OF FALL RIVER, MASSACHUSETTS

. . . .

Seafood Curry

¼ cup butter
¼ cup chopped onion
¼ cup chopped celery
½ cup chopped tart apple
1 clove garlic, chopped
1 bay leaf
5 tablespoons + 1 teaspoon flour
½ teaspoon dry mustard
2 teaspoons curry powder, or to taste
½ teaspoon salt
3 cups chicken stock
½ cup light cream
1¼-1½ pounds seafood, preferably a
combination of lobster and shrimp

Melt butter. Add onion, celery, apple, garlic, and bay leaf. Cook until onion is translucent. Sprinkle with flour, mustard, curry powder, and salt. Gradually stir in stock and cook, stirring constantly, until sauce is thickened. Add cream and simmer 10 minutes. Add seafood and cook another 10 minutes.

Serve over rice or in pastry shells with desired condiments.

YIELD: 6 SERVINGS

THE JUNIOR LEAGUE OF SPRINGFIELD, MASSACHUSETTS

Egg and Cheese Dishes

COVE HOLLOW FARM

REGISTERED HOLSTEINS

Egg over the Falls

2 slices white bread
2 tablespoons soft margarine
2 eggs

With a small juice glass, cut a round circle out of the center of each slice of bread. Spread one side of bread with margarine. Place bread butter side up in a buttered frying pan and break an egg in each hole. When egg is set, turn egg and bread over and brown other side.

YIELD: 1 SERVING

THE JUNIOR LEAGUE OF BUFFALO, NEW YORK

Savory Eggs

2 cups shredded American cheese
¼ cup butter
1 cup light cream
½ teaspoon salt
¼ teaspoon pepper
2 teaspoons mustard
12 eggs, lightly beaten

Sprinkle cheese on bottom of a 13 x 9-inch glass baking dish. Dot with butter. Combine cream, salt, pepper, and mustard. Pour half this mixture over the cheese. Pour the eggs over the cream mixture and then pour in the remaining cream mixture.

Bake in a 325° oven for about 40 minutes, or until set.

YIELD: 6–8 SERVINGS

THE JUNIOR LEAGUE OF BUFFALO, NEW YORK

Oeufs à la Fermière (Farmer's Eggs)

9 eggs
3 tablespoons heavy cream
1 8-ounce package cream cheese, softened
3 tablespoons chopped chives
2 tablespoons chopped fresh parsley
½ teaspoon salt
¼ teaspoon white pepper
Dash nutmeg

SAUCE:
¼ cup butter
¼ cup flour
1½ cups hot milk
½ teaspoon salt
¼ teaspoon white pepper
2 tablespoons heavy cream

Put eggs in cold water, bring to a boil, and simmer for 10 minutes. Plunge into cold water and cool. Peel eggs, slice lengthwise, and remove yolks. Arrange whites in a buttered bake-and-serve dish.

Mash yolks with cream, cheese, herbs, and spices. Mix thoroughly and stuff eggs. Any extra filling may be mixed into the sauce.

For sauce: Melt butter, stir in flour, and cook for 3–4 minutes, being careful not to brown the flour. Add milk all at once, stirring constantly. Cook 3 minutes to thoroughly cook flour. Add salt and pepper, then stir in the heavy cream.

Pour sauce over eggs and bake at 375° for 10 minutes.

YIELD: 6 SERVINGS

THE JUNIOR LEAGUE OF GREATER UTICA, NEW YORK

Brunch Egg Casserole

2 cups plain croutons
4 ounces shredded natural cheddar
cheese (1 cup)
4 eggs, lightly beaten
2 cups milk
½ teaspoon salt
½ teaspoon mustard
⅛ teaspoon onion powder
Dash pepper
4 slices bacon, cooked, drained, and crumbled
Parsley and bacon curl for garnish

Grease 10 x 6 x 1¾-inch baking dish.

Combine croutons and cheese and put in bottom of pan. Combine eggs, milk, salt, mustard, onion powder, and pepper; mix until blended. Pour over crouton mixture in casserole. Sprinkle crumbled bacon on top.

Bake at 325° for 50–60 minutes. Garnish with bacon and parsley.

YIELD: 6 SERVINGS

THE JUNIOR LEAGUE OF WORCESTER, MASSACHUSETTS

. . . .

Maple Omelet

3 eggs, separated
3 tablespoons maple syrup
½ teaspoon vanilla
Few grains salt
2-3 teaspoons butter
½ cup finely sliced almonds

Preheat oven to 350°.

Beat egg yolks until thick and lemon-colored. Beat in maple syrup, vanilla, and salt. Beat egg whites until stiff but not dry. Fold into the yolk mixture.

Melt butter in a hot, heavy 8- or 9-inch skillet; cover the bottom with sliced almonds. Add the egg mixture. Turn the heat to low and cook slowly to a light brown color underneath, about 8 minutes. Transfer to oven for 8–10 minutes. Crease and fold onto a hot platter and serve at once with warm maple syrup.

YIELD: 2 SERVINGS

THE JUNIOR LEAGUE OF HAMILTON-BURLINGTON, ONTARIO

.   .   .   .

Father Samanski's Cheese Bread

1 stick margarine
2 tablespoons mustard
2 tablespoons poppy seeds
1 large loaf Italian bread
10–12 slices mozzarella cheese
(about ¼ inch thick)
4 slices bacon

Combine margarine, mustard, and poppy seeds. Slice bread and spread all sides with the margarine mixture.

Cut a piece of aluminum foil large enough to wrap bread and place around bread, leaving the top open. Keeping loaf intact, place 1 slice cheese between each slice bread. Arrange bacon strips on top of loaf and bake at 350° for 30 minutes, or until bacon is crisp.

Serve with a salad for luncheon or Sunday night supper.

YIELD: 4–6 SERVINGS

THE JUNIOR LEAGUE OF MORRISTOWN, NEW JERSEY

.   .   .   .

Cheese Strata

8 slices bread, trimmed and cut
into cubes
1 cup shredded cheddar cheese
1 cup shredded Swiss cheese
3 eggs
1½ cups milk
½ cup sour cream
¼ teaspoon nutmeg
¾ teaspoon salt
⅛ teaspoon pepper
1 teaspoon mustard

Line an 8 x 8-inch greased baking dish or medium casserole with half the bread cubes. Top with half the cheese. Add remaining bread cubes and sprinkle remaining cheese on top.

Beat the eggs lightly and add milk, sour cream, and seasonings. Beat again. Pour this mixture over the bread and cheese and let stand at least 30 minutes. Bake at 325° for 45 minutes. (If refrigerated ahead, bake 50–55 minutes.)

YIELD: 6 SERVINGS

THE JUNIOR LEAGUE OF TROY, NEW YORK

.　.　.　.　.　.　.　.　.　.　.　.　.　.　.　.　.

Cheese Berege

8 ounces Swiss cheese
8 ounces Muenster or Monterey Jack cheese
1 cup minced fresh parsley
1 egg, beaten
2 packages frozen patty shells
Flour
Butter

Dice cheeses. Add parsley and egg and mix well. (This can be done a day ahead and refrigerated.)

Thaw patty shells and let sit at room temperature for a while. Flour board and rolling pin. Roll each shell out into a rectangle and cut lengthwise into two strips. Put some of cheese mixture at one end of each strip and roll up as you would a package, sealing edges so cheese will not run out during the baking.

Arrange in baking pan with edges touching. Dot with lots of butter. Bake at 350° for 45 minutes, or until lightly browned.

Great for breakfast, brunch, or hors d'oeuvres. Can be made ahead and frozen.

YIELD: 22–24 PIECES

THE JUNIOR LEAGUE OF SYRACUSE, NEW YORK

Featherweight Cottage Cheese Pancakes

Butter
3 eggs, separated
1/4 teaspoon salt
1/4 cup flour
3/4 cup large curd cottage cheese

Heat griddle slowly and butter it lightly.

Beat egg whites until stiff but not dry. Beat yolks with same beater until light and lemon-colored. Stir in salt, flour, and cheese. Fold in egg whites.

Drop by small spoonfuls on griddle. Turn once when brown on one side and brown the other. Serve immediately with butter and syrup.

YIELD: 2–3 SERVINGS

Cooks Book
THE JUNIOR LEAGUE OF GREATER NEW HAVEN, CONNECTICUT

Laurana's Cottage Cheese Roast

Your guests will guess you are serving veal or beef.

2 cups creamed cottage cheese
3 eggs, beaten
¼ cup milk
½ cup chopped onion
2 bouillon cubes, shaved, or equivalent amount powdered
¼ cup cooking oil
½ cup finely chopped pecans
4½ cups cereal flakes
¼ cup shredded sharp cheddar cheese
2 tablespoons sour cream
Sage to taste

Beat together the cottage cheese, eggs, and milk. Add remaining ingredients; mix very well. Place in an oiled 9 x 5 x 3-inch loaf pan. Bake at 375° for 45 minutes.

Serve hot or cold.

YIELD: 12 SERVINGS

THE JUNIOR LEAGUE OF ERIE, PENNSYLVANIA

Finnish Pancake

1 cup milk
2/3 cup flour
2 tablespoons sugar
½ teaspoon salt
2 eggs
½ teaspoon grated fresh lemon peel
½ teaspoon ground cardamom
¼ cup butter

Place all ingredients except butter in blender. Blend, and scrape sides. Meanwhile, place butter in 9-inch pie plate and melt in a 400° preheated oven. Remove pie plate from oven and pour batter into plate.

Bake for 30 minutes, or until pancake puffs and turns golden brown. Cut into quarters. Serve hot with syrup and/or fruit.

Great for brunch because it bakes while you set the table and make the coffee.

YIELD: **4** SERVINGS

THE JUNIOR LEAGUE OF SCHENECTADY, NEW YORK

. . . .

Little Pancakes Filled with Cheese

THE CREPES:
½ cup flour
Pinch salt
1 large egg
1 cup milk
Butter

Sift flour and salt into bowl. Combine egg and milk. Add to flour and mix until smooth.

Cook the crepes by heating a small frying pan from 5 to 6 inches in diameter until very hot. Put a little butter in pan and swirl pan to coat bottom and sides. As soon as butter begins to brown, pour in about 2 tablespoons of the batter and swirl pan in a circular motion to spread batter evenly and thinly to the edge. Cook about 1 minute, or until set and brown on underside. Turn and cook for 20 seconds more. Turn out on towel to cool. Repeat, making 12 crepes.

Recipe continues . . .

CHEESE FILLING:

½ cup dry white wine
8 ounces shredded Emmenthal Swiss cheese
2 teaspoons cornstarch
1 tablespoon kirsch
Black pepper

In saucepan, heat white wine, but do not boil. Stir in cheese and cook, stirring, until cheese is smooth and creamy. Stir in cornstarch dissolved in kirsch and continue to stir until the cheese bubbles. Sprinkle with pepper. Keep warm over hot water.

SAUCE:

Make your favorite hollandaise sauce. Measure ¾ cup and fold in ¼ cup whipped cream.

Preheat oven to 450°.

To assemble, spread each crepe with about 1½ tablespoons of the cheese filling; roll up and arrange in a buttered dish.

Bake for 4–5 minutes. Remove from oven. Spoon sauce over the crepes and run under broiler for 30–60 seconds, or until sauce is lightly browned.

YIELD: 12 CREPES (5–6 INCHES IN DIAMETER), 4 LUNCHEON SERVINGS, OR 10 APPETIZERS

Show House Recipes
THE JUNIOR LEAGUE OF BINGHAMTON, NEW YORK

Zucchini Puff

*3 large or 6 small yellow squash
or zucchini
2 tablespoons melted butter
1 teaspoon salt
½ teaspoon pepper
4 eggs, well beaten
1½ cups milk
1 tablespoon flour
2/3 cup shredded Gruyère cheese*

Peel and dice squash; put in a saucepan with the butter, salt, and pepper. Cover and cook over low heat until the squash is soft.

Beat together eggs, milk, and flour. Add squash to egg mixture. Blend well and pour into a buttered 2-quart casserole. Sprinkle with cheese and bake at 400° for 20 minutes.

YIELD: **4–6** SERVINGS

Presenting Boston . . . A Cookbook
THE JUNIOR LEAGUE OF BOSTON, MASSACHUSETTS

Vegetable-Cheese Casserole

This is a nutritious main or side dish, and it can be varied with the addition of other vegetables.

1 medium onion, chopped
1 clove garlic, minced
2 tablespoons butter or oil
2 carrots, diagonally sliced
⅛ inch thick
2 medium potatoes (sweet or
white), peeled and cubed
1 cup chopped green vegetable(s):
peas, snap beans, broccoli
(Optional) ½ cup chopped mushroom,
½ cup chopped celery,
1 teaspoon wheat germ,
2 tablespoons sunflower seeds,
2 tablespoons sesame seeds
1–2 tablespoons soy sauce
2 cups shredded sharp cheddar cheese

Sauté onion and garlic in butter. As these cook, add sliced carrots, potatoes, the green vegetable(s), and any other vegetable desired. Sauté until just crunchy. For added nutrition, add wheat germ and/or sunflower or sesame seeds. Sprinkle with soy sauce.

In a casserole, alternate layers of the vegetable mixture with layers of cheese. Bake at 350° until bubbly, approximately 20–25 minutes.

YIELD: 6–8 SERVINGS

THE JUNIOR LEAGUE OF NEW BRITAIN, CONNECTICUT

·   ·   ·   ·   ·   ·   ·   ·   ·   ·   ·   ·   ·   ·   ·   ·   ·

Rarebit à la Italienne

3-4 medium onions, chopped
¼ cup butter
2 tablespoons flour
1 14½-ounce can stewed tomatoes
2-3 teaspoons Worcestershire sauce
¾ pound fresh mushrooms, sliced
10 ounces extra sharp cheddar cheese, shredded

Sauté onions in butter until onions are transparent. Stir in flour and tomatoes and simmer for 20 minutes. Add Worcestershire sauce and mushrooms. Slowly add cheese, stirring constantly over low heat. When cheese is melted, pour into chafing dish and keep warm.

Serve over rice or toast.

YIELD: 2 SERVINGS

THE JUNIOR LEAGUE OF TROY, NEW YORK

. . . .

Frozen Cheese Soufflé with Broccoli Sauce

6 tablespoons butter or margarine
1/3 cup all-purpose flour
2 cups milk
12 ounces sharp American cheese,
shredded (3 cups)
6 egg yolks
6 egg whites
½ teaspoon cream of tartar

In medium saucepan, melt the butter. Blend in the flour. Add the milk all at once and cook and stir until thickened and bubbly. Add cheese and stir until melted. Remove from heat.

Recipe continues . . .

Beat egg yolks until thick and lemon-colored. Slowly add cheese mixture to yolks, stirring constantly; cool slightly. Beat egg whites and cream of tartar to stiff peaks. Gradually pour yolk mixture over whites and fold together well. Pour into 8 ungreased individual (1-cup) soufflé dishes. Cover tightly with freezer wrap or foil and freeze until needed.

To serve, set dishes in shallow pan filled with hot water to depth of ½ inch. Bake in 300° oven for 1¼ hours, or until knife inserted comes out clean.

Serve with Broccoli Sauce.

YIELD: 6 SERVINGS

BROCCOLI SAUCE:

½ *cup chopped onion*
2 tablespoons butter
2 tablespoons flour
1 chicken bouillon cube
½ *cup boiling water*
1 cup milk
1 10-ounce package frozen chopped broccoli,
cooked and drained

In saucepan, cook onion in butter until tender. Blend in flour. Dissolve bouillon cube in boiling water and add to saucepan with the milk. Cook and stir until sauce is thickened and bubbly. Stir in barely cooked broccoli. Cook until heated through.

Cooks Book
THE JUNIOR LEAGUE OF GREATER NEW HAVEN, CONNECTICUT

Skyscraper Cheese Soufflé with Crabmeat Sauce

¼ pound butter
½ cup instant flour
1 teaspoon salt
¼ teaspoon pepper
2 cups milk
2 cups shredded cheddar cheese
8 eggs, separated

Butter a 2½-quart soufflé dish; butter or oil a 6-inch band of aluminum foil and tie it around the soufflé dish, buttered side in, to form a collar.

Melt ¼ pound butter in a heavy saucepan. Stir in flour, salt, and pepper. Add milk and cook over low heat, stirring constantly, until sauce is thickened and completely smooth. Add cheese and stir until it melts. Beat egg yolks; stir into cheese sauce and cook, stirring constantly, for 2–3 minutes, or until hot. Do not let it boil. Remove from heat.

Beat the egg whites until stiff but not dry. Carefully fold sauce into beaten egg whites. Pour into prepared soufflé dish. For an attractive "top hat," run the tip of a knife around the soufflé dish 1 inch in from the edge.

Preheat oven to 475° and bake soufflé for 10 minutes; lower heat to 400° and continue baking for 45 minutes, or until nicely browned.

Remove foil collar and serve at once with Crabmeat Sauce.

YIELD: 6 SERVINGS

CRABMEAT SAUCE:
¼ cup butter
2 tablespoons instant flour
Salt and pepper to taste
1 cup light cream
½ cup chopped crabmeat
2 tablespoons dry sherry

Recipe continues . . .

Melt butter in pan over moderate heat. Stir in flour, salt, and pepper and cook until mixture becomes frothy. Add the cream and continue stirring until sauce is thickened and smooth. Carefully stir in the crabmeat. Remove from heat and stir in the sherry.

THE JUNIOR LEAGUE OF THE CITY OF NEW YORK, NEW YORK

Pasta, Grains, and Beans

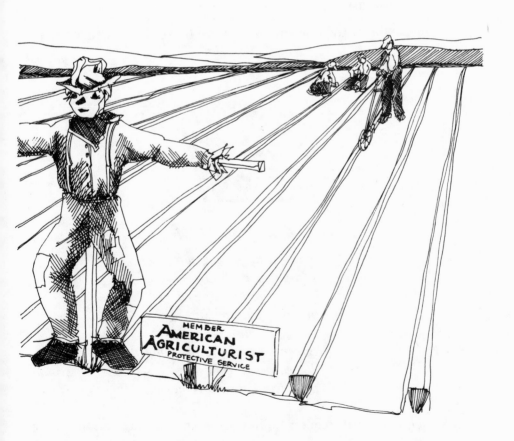

MEMBER
AMERICAN
AGRICULTURIST
PROTECTIVE SERVICE

Homemade Noodles

3 cups sifted unbleached flour
3 large eggs
Pinch salt
2 tablespoons vegetable oil
5 tablespoons milk

Mix the above ingredients until you have the consistency of dough. Knead about 2 minutes and roll out on a floured surface about ⅛ inch thick. Cut the dough the width of desired noodles. Let the noodles dry for at least 24 hours. Either freeze noodles or bag in airtight bags.

To cook, put in boiling salt water for 3 minutes. Drain and serve with your favorite sauce.

YIELD: APPROXIMATELY 1 POUND NOODLES

THE JUNIOR LEAGUE OF THE ORANGES AND SHORT HILLS, NEW JERSEY

· · · · · · · · · · · · · · · · · ·

Noodles Romanoff

2 8-ounce packages egg noodles
3 cups large curd cottage cheese
2 cloves garlic, minced
2 teaspoons Worcestershire sauce
2 cups sour cream
1 bunch green onions, finely chopped
½ teaspoon Tabasco
1 cup grated Parmesan cheese

Cook noodles until tender; drain. Combine all ingredients except

Parmesean cheese and turn into a greased 1¾–2-quart casserole. Sprinkle with cheese. Bake at 350° for 25 minutes.

YIELD: 8 SERVINGS

THE JUNIOR LEAGUE OF WILLIAMSPORT, PENNSYLVANIA

. . . .

Noodle Bake

1 pound chopped chuck
3 tablespoons cooking oil
1 teaspoon salt
1 teaspoon pepper
16 ounces tomato sauce
1 teaspoon sugar
1 8-ounce package noodles
6–8 green onions, chopped
5 ounces softened cream cheese
1½ cups sour cream
1 cup shredded cheddar cheese

In a frying pan, sauté the meat in oil. Add salt and pepper, tomato sauce, and sugar. Simmer, covered, for 20 minutes.

In a large pot, bring 3 quarts salted water to a boil and cook the noodles as directed on package. Drain, rinse under cold water, and drain again.

Mix chopped onions and cream cheese. In a 3-quart casserole, layer the noodles, half the onion-cream cheese mixture, all the meat mixture, the remaining onion-cream cheese mixture, and top with shredded cheese.

Bake at 350° for 45 minutes.

YIELD: 6 SERVINGS

THE JUNIOR LEAGUE OF GREATER BRIDGEPORT, CONNECTICUT

. . . .

Noodles and Spinach Casserole

1 8-ounce package medium noodles
1 large onion, chopped
½ pound mushrooms, sliced
2 tablespoons vegetable oil
1 10-ounce package frozen creamed
spinach, thawed

Cook noodles according to instructions on package. Sauté onion and mushrooms in vegetable oil. Drain and empty noodles into a casserole. Stir in mushroom mixture. Spread thawed spinach on top of noodles, cover, and bake at 350° for 1 hour.

YIELD: 4–6 SERVINGS

THE JUNIOR LEAGUE OF BUFFALO, NEW YORK

. . . .

Fettucine Alfredo

¼ pound butter
¼ cup heavy cream
½ cup freshly grated Parmesan cheese
1 pound fettucine
6–8 quarts water
1 tablespoon salt
Freshly ground pepper

Cream butter until light and fluffy; beat in the cream a bit at a time and the grated cheese until all is used. This may be made ahead and set aside in a covered bowl, but be sure to bring to room temperature before using.

Boil the fettucine in salted water until tender; do not overcook. Drain and transfer to a hot serving dish or chafing dish. Add the butter and cheese mixture and toss until every strand is well coated. Dust with pepper.

YIELD: 4 SERVINGS

The Melting Pot
THE JUNIOR LEAGUE OF THE CENTRAL DELAWARE VALLEY, NEW JERSEY

Baked Noodles à la Bronxville

1 pound fine noodles
1 pound mozzarella cheese, shredded
1 stick butter, melted
Salt and pepper to taste
1 pint heavy cream
1½ pounds Parmesan cheese, grated
2 tablespoons soft butter

Cook noodles according to directions; drain and empty into a large mixing bowl. Add mozzarella, the melted butter, salt and pepper, ¾ cup of the cream, and three-quarters of the Parmesan cheese. Mix well. Butter sides and bottom of an ovenproof baking dish. Empty mixture into dish and add rest of cream with remaining Parmesan on top. Dot top with soft butter. Bake in a 350° oven for 40 minutes.

Can be made the day before.

YIELD: 12 SERVINGS

THE JUNIOR LEAGUE OF BRONXVILLE, NEW YORK

Jayhawk Noodles

4 tablespoons butter
2 tablespoons Worcestershire sauce
8 medium green onions, finely chopped
1 clove garlic, minced
8 ounces sour cream
1 8-ounce package egg noodles
1 tablespoon salt
½ teaspoon pepper
Grated Parmesan cheese

Melt butter in skillet. Add Worcestershire sauce, green onions, and garlic. Cook mixture slowly over low heat. Add sour cream, stirring constantly.

Cook noodles according to directions on package in boiling water with the salt. Drain noodles and add pepper.

Add noodles to sour cream mixture. Sprinkle with Parmesan cheese.

YIELD: 6 SERVINGS

THE JUNIOR LEAGUE OF SYRACUSE, NEW YORK

.   .   .   .

Sou-Berag

1 8-ounce package medium noodles
1 pound Monterey Jack or Muenster
cheese, chopped
2 eggs, beaten
½ teaspoon salt
½ cup minced fresh parsley
½ pint cottage cheese
Butter

Boil noodles in salted water until tender. Drain and rinse with cold water.

Mix cheese with beaten egg and salt. Divide into equal portions. Mix chopped parsley with one portion of cheese.

Put half the noodles in buttered square or rectangular casserole, then add cheese with parsley. Add remaining noodles and sprinkle remaining cheese over top. Dot well with butter.

Bake at 350° until cheese melts and browns on top. Cut into squares.

YIELD: **4–8** SERVINGS

THE JUNIOR LEAGUE OF SYRACUSE, NEW YORK

Carbonara

*½ pound thickly sliced bacon,
cut into 2-inch pieces
4 cloves garlic, thinly sliced
2 tablespoons olive oil
1 tablespoon margarine or butter
¼ cup dry white wine
5 tablespoons grated Romano cheese
¾ cup grated Parmesan cheese
8 twists pepper
2 tablespoons Italian parsley
3 eggs, beaten
1 pound linguine*

Fry bacon and reserve ¼ of the drippings. Saute garlic in olive oil and butter, then add the bacon and drippings. Add wine and cook over medium heat until wine boils away. Set aside.

In a large bowl, combine cheeses, pepper, parsley, and the beaten eggs; mix. Cook the linguine and drain it, then put in bowl with egg

Recipe continues . . .

mixture. While linguine is draining, reheat the bacon mixture. When hot, pour over top of linguini and serve.

YIELD: 4–6 SERVINGS

THE JUNIOR LEAGUE OF WILKES-BARRE, PENNSYLVANIA

Fettucine with Bacon

12 ounces noodles
4 ounces butter
1 cup ricotta cheese, at room temperature
¼ teaspoon salt
⅛ teaspoon black pepper
3 tablespoons freshly chopped parsley
¼ cup hot water
½ pound cooked bacon, cut in small pieces,
or ½ pound cooked ham, cubed
¾–1 cup grated Parmesan cheese

Cook noodles al dente. While noodles are cooking, melt butter and set aside.

Combine ricotta, salt, pepper, parsley, and hot water in bowl and mix thoroughly. Set mixing bowl over a pan of hot water (not boiling) and stir frequently.

Drain noodles in colander and transfer to serving platter. Quickly pour melted butter over noodles, add the bacon or ham, and toss lightly. Add ricotta mixture and half the grated cheese. Continue to toss lightly. Add remaining Parmesan, toss, and serve.

YIELD: 6–8 SIDE DISH SERVINGS OR 4 MAIN COURSES

THE JUNIOR LEAGUE OF KINGSTON, NEW YORK

Clam Sauce for Pasta

¼ pound butter
2 cloves garlic, split
1 7-ounce can minced clams
1 teaspoon oregano, or to taste
Salt and pepper to taste
½ cup dry white wine

Melt butter in saucepan with garlic over low heat. Drain clams, reserving liquid. Turn off heat under butter and let sit for 10 minutes. Remove garlic. Add minced clams and spices and cook for 5 minutes over low heat. Add clam liquid and wine and heat just to boiling. Serve over hot linguini or spaghetti.

May be doubled.

YIELD: 2 SERVINGS

THE JUNIOR LEAGUE OF NEW BRITAIN, CONNECTICUT

. . . .

Lemon-Clam Linguini

2 6½-ounce cans minced clams
1 small onion, chopped
3 cloves garlic, minced
2 tablespoons oil
2 tablespoons butter
1 teaspoon oregano
½ teaspoon salt
⅛ teaspoon pepper
2 tablespoons chopped fresh parsley
1-2 tablespoons lemon juice
1 teaspoon grated lemon rind
1 8-ounce package linguini,
cooked according to package directions
Grated Parmesan cheese

Recipe continues . . .

Drain off clam juice and reserve. Sauté onion and garlic in oil and butter in saucepan until tender, but do not brown. Add reserved clam juice, oregano, salt, and pepper. Bring to a boil over high heat; cook until reduced to 1 cup. Lower heat and add clams, parsley, lemon juice, and lemon rind. Heat thoroughly. Toss with linguini. Serve with Parmesan cheese.

YIELD: 4 SERVINGS

THE JUNIOR LEAGUE OF LANCASTER, PENNSYLVANIA

Linguini with Herbed Clam Sauce

2 cloves garlic, minced
¼ cup olive oil
4 tablespoons butter
1 8-ounce can minced clams with broth
½ cup dry white wine
¼ cup finely chopped flat Italian parsley
¼ teaspoon partially crumbled rosemary
¼ teaspoon oregano
Salt
Freshly ground black pepper
1 pound linguini or spaghetti

Lightly brown the garlic in the oil and butter. Add the clam broth, white wine, parsley, rosemary, oregano, salt, and pepper. Bring to a boil, then simmer for 10 minutes. Add the clams and cook 5 minutes.

Cook the linguini in rapidly boiling water until al dente, 6–8 minutes.

Add the clam sauce to the linguini and serve.

YIELD: 8 APPETIZERS OR 4 MAIN COURSE SERVINGS

The Melting Pot
THE JUNIOR LEAGUE OF THE CENTRAL DELAWARE VALLEY, NEW JERSEY

Pasta Spring Medley

1 cup sliced zucchini
1½ cups broccoli flowerets
1½ cups snow peas
1 cup peas
6 stalks asparagus, sliced in
1-inch pieces
1 pound spaghetti
12 cherry tomatoes
10 large mushrooms, sliced
3 tablespoons olive oil
2 teaspoons minced garlic
Salt and fresh black pepper to taste
¼ cup chopped Italian parsley
1/3 cup pine nuts
1/3 cup butter
1 cup heavy cream
½ cup grated Parmesan cheese
1/3 cup chopped fresh basil or
1 teaspoon dried

Blanch first five vegetables separately in boiling salted water for 1–2 minutes until just crisply tender. Drain and run under cold water. Set aside. This can be done in advance.

Cook pasta until al dente and drain. While pasta is cooking, sauté tomatoes and mushrooms in 1 tablespoon oil with 1 teaspoon garlic, salt, pepper, and parsley for 1–2 minutes. Set aside.

In large pan with 2 tablespoons oil, sauté pine nuts until brown. Add remaining 1 teaspoon garlic and all vegetables and heat thoroughly.

In pan large enough to hold pasta and vegetables, melt butter and add cream, cheese, and basil. Stir until cheese melts. Add pasta and toss

Recipe continues . . .

to coat with sauce. Add vegetables and toss again. Top with cherry tomatoes and mushrooms and serve with Parmesan cheese.

YIELD: **6** SERVINGS

Simply Superb
THE JUNIOR LEAGUE OF ELIZABETH-PLAINFIELD, NEW JERSEY

Midsummer Spaghetti with Uncooked Tomato Sauce

8 tablespoons olive oil
1½ pounds ripe tomatoes, skinned,
seeded, and chopped
2 cloves garlic, chopped
3 leaves fresh basil, chopped
Salt and pepper to taste
1 pound spaghetti or vermicelli

Put olive oil in a deep serving dish with the chopped tomatoes, garlic, and basil and marinate for 4 hours at room temperature. Then season to taste with salt and pepper and stir gently.

Cook the pasta in a large amount of rapidly boiling, well-salted water until tender. Drain well. Add sauce and stir gently. Serve immediately.

YIELD: **3–4** SERVINGS

The Everyday Gourmet
THE JUNIOR LEAGUE OF NORTHERN WESTCHESTER, BEDFORD HILLS, NEW YORK

Canadian Baked Beans (Fèves au Lard)

Although Boston is famous for its baked beans, every self-respecting village in Quebec boasts of its Fèves au Lard (Beans with Pork Fat) or Fèves au Canard (Beans with Duck).

1 pound navy beans
1 quart water
1 bay leaf
2 sprigs celery leaves
¼ teaspoon thyme
1 small onion stuck with 6 cloves
2 cloves garlic
1 medium onion, sliced
1 tablespoon salt
2 teaspoons vinegar
1½ teaspoons dry mustard
3 tablespoons brown sugar
2 tablespoons Worcestershire sauce
¼ cup molasses
¼ cup maple syrup
½ cup catsup
Dash black pepper
¼ pound salt pork or bacon or
½ duck, boned and diced

Soak beans overnight in a quart of cold water. Rinse.

Boil the beans in the 1 quart of water with the next five ingredients for 30 minutes. Drain, strain, and reserve the liquid.

Put the sliced onion in the bottom of the bean pot or a casserole. Mix the rest of the ingredients (except the beans and the pork, bacon, or duck) and add to the pot. Add the beans and the reserved liquid to cover. Arrange the pork, bacon, or duck on top. Cover and bake at 300° for 7 hours. At the end of the first 4 hours, remove 1 cup of the beans, mash,

Recipe continues . . .

and stir back into the pot. Keep beans covered with bean liquid during the cooking.

One hour before serving, remove cover to let the beans brown.

YIELD: 10 SERVINGS AS A SIDE DISH

THE JUNIOR LEAGUE OF HAMILTON-BURLINGTON, ONTARIO

Connecticut Baked Beans

4 cups navy, kidney,
pea, soldier, or yellow beans (2 pounds)
1–2 pounds salt pork, diced
1 teaspoon salt
¾ cup maple syrup or
½ cup brown sugar
½ teaspoon ginger
½ teaspoon cinnamon
¼ teaspoon nutmeg
¼ teaspoon mace
1 tablespoon dry mustard
2 medium onions, chopped
1 cup molasses
1 clove garlic, chopped
1 20-ounce can tomato juice or
1 29-ounce can tomatoes

Soak beans overnight; keep water level above beans. Next day, simmer beans for 2–3 hours until tender. Drain and reserve liquid.

Add and mix in other ingredients with beans; add enough bean liquid to cover. Cover and bake slowly for 6–8 hours at 250°. Add boiling water as needed to cover beans while baking. Uncover during last ½ hour of baking to brown top.

YIELD: 10–12 LARGE SERVINGS

THE JUNIOR LEAGUE OF NEW BRITAIN, CONNECTICUT

Lentil Cassoulet

1 cup lentils
3 cups water
1 small piece salt pork
1 teaspoon salt
2 medium onions, chopped
2 teaspoons olive oil
2 tablespoons olive oil
½ pound mushrooms, sliced
1 teaspoon curry powder, or to taste
Dash ground pepper
1 tablespoon parsley
1 cup sour cream or plain yogurt
1 cup chopped green onion for garnish

Wash lentils. Combine lentils, water, and salt pork in 1½-quart saucepan. Bring to a boil, then turn down to simmer; cover and cook 40 minutes. Add salt and set aside.

Preheat oven to 350°.

In skillet, sauté onions in olive oil and add mushrooms, curry powder, pepper, and parsley. Check curry at this point for taste.

Combine lentils and mixture from skillet. Put in 2-quart baking dish. Bake, covered, for 30 minutes. Remove and serve with yogurt or sour cream and chopped green onion as garnish.

Recipe continues . . .

VARIATION:

Add 4 pork sausage links, chopped and sautéed or 4 Italian sausages, removed from casings and sautéed or any German sausage. All sausages should be cooked before adding to the recipe.

YIELD: 4–6 SERVINGS

Hudson River Hospitality
THE JUNIOR LEAGUE OF WESTCHESTER-ON-HUDSON, NEW YORK

. . . .

Purée of Lentils

½ pound lentils, yellow split
peas, or green split peas
2 onions
2 cloves
3 carrots
2 leeks, white part only
1 stalk celery
3 sprigs parsley
1 cup water
Dash thyme
1 bay leaf
Salt and pepper to taste
5–6 tablespoons butter

Soak the lentils for about 3 hours in cold water. Drain lentils well.

Peel the onions and stick 1 clove in each. Peel carrots and slice thinly. Wash leeks thoroughly and chop. Scrape celery and chop.

In a heavy pot, put lentils, onions with cloves, carrots, leeks, celery, and parsley. Add water, thyme, bay leaf, salt, and pepper. Bring to a boil and cook at a gentle simmer for about 1 hour. Discard cloves and bay leaf.

If still liquid, drain. Pass lentils through a vegetable mill or purée in blender or food processor. Reheat the purée and slowly whisk in butter. Correct seasoning and serve with a roast.

YIELD: **4** SERVINGS

THE JUNIOR LEAGUE OF THE CITY OF NEW YORK, NEW YORK

. . . .

Barley Casserole

¹/₂ cup pine nuts
¹/₂ cup butter
1 cup finely chopped onion
1 cup pearled barley (not instant)
¹/₂ cup finely chopped parsley
¹/₂ cup finely chopped chives
6 cups beef broth (4 cans beef
broth + 1 can water is ok)

Sauté the nuts in the butter for 5 minutes, or until golden brown. Remove the nuts and sauté the onion for 5 minutes. Add the pearled barley and brown, stirring constantly. Add the parsley, chives, and half the nuts. Mix. Add the broth and pour into a casserole. Bake 1½ hours at 350°. Stir once after 30 minutes. Sprinkle with remaining nuts and bake 20 more minutes.

YIELD: **4–6** SERVINGS

THE JUNIOR LEAGUE OF TROY, NEW YORK

. . . .

Quick "Lasagna" Casserole

1 pound lean ground beef
10 green onions, chopped
2 8-ounce cans tomato sauce
2 tablespoons grated Parmesan or
Romano cheese, or to taste
1½ teaspoons salt
¼ teaspoon basil
1 clove garlic, minced
¼ teaspoon oregano
⅛ teaspoon pepper
1 8-ounce package wide noodles,
cooked and drained
1 cup cottage cheese
1 cup sour cream

Brown beef in skillet. Drain off fat. Add onions and cook for a few minutes. Add tomato sauce, grated cheese, salt, and other seasonings. Simmer 10 minutes.

Combine noodles, cottage cheese, and sour cream.

In a 2-quart baking dish, alternate layers of noodle mixture and meat sauce, starting with noodles and ending with meat sauce. Bake at 350° for 25–30 minutes.

YIELD: 6 SERVINGS

THE JUNIOR LEAGUE OF BROOKLYN, NEW YORK

Cavatelli with Broccoli

1 pound cavatelli (small stuffed
macaroni shapes)
½ cup olive oil
2 tablespoons butter
1–2 cloves garlic
Salt and pepper to taste
1 10-ounce package frozen chopped broccoli,
cooked until barely tender
Grated Parmesan cheese

Cook cavatelli in 6 quarts rapidly boiling salted water. Meanwhile, heat olive oil and butter in saucepan and in it sauté garlic just until brown. Discard garlic.

When cavatelli is done, drain; empty into a large bowl and toss with the olive oil, broccoli, and salt and pepper to taste. Serve topped with grated Parmesan.

YIELD: 4–6 SERVINGS

THE JUNIOR LEAGUE OF BERGEN COUNTY, NEW JERSEY

Maracelli à la Happy

2 pounds ground beef
¼ pound hot Italian sausage,
removed from skin
1 medium onion, chopped
½ green pepper, chopped
32 ounces marinara sauce
6 ounces canned sliced mushrooms
2 ounces dry red wine
1 teaspoon oregano
1 tablespoon grated Parmesan cheese
½ pound size 22 macaroni shells
Garlic salt
1 tablespoon butter
½ pound Port Salut cheese,
thinly sliced

Sauté ground beef, sausage, onion, and green pepper, breaking meat into small pieces. Add marinara sauce, mushrooms, red wine, oregano, and Parmesan cheese. Simmer for 1 hour.

Cook macaroni shells 12–15 minutes. Drain and add garlic salt and butter. Combine shells and sauce. Spoon into shallow casserole. Place thin slices of Port Salut cheese on top. Bake at 325° for 30 minutes.

This dish freezes well.

YIELD: 8–10 SERVINGS

THE JUNIOR LEAGUE OF MONMOUTH COUNTY, NEW JERSEY

Rice Pilaf

2 cups rice
1 large onion, chopped
1 cup sliced mushrooms
2 teaspoons oregano
½ pound margarine (2 sticks)
3 cans consommé
2 cans water

Simmer rice, onion, mushrooms, and oregano in melted margarine for 20 minutes, stirring occasionally. Empty mixture into large ovenproof casserole; add consommé and water. Cook, covered at 400° for 1–1½ hours.

YIELD: 8–12 SERVINGS

THE JUNIOR LEAGUE OF THE ORANGES AND SHORT HILLS, NEW JERSEY

Rice Savoy

1 small onion, finely chopped
1 garlic clove, minced
2 tablespoons butter
2 tablespoons vegetable oil
1 cup long-grain rice
2 cans beef consommé
1 teaspoon paprika
1 teaspoon soy sauce
1 teaspoon chopped parsley

Recipe continues . . .

Brown onion and garlic in butter and oil. Add remaining ingredients and mix all together. Bake in covered dish at 350° for 1 hour.

YIELD: 4 SERVINGS

THE JUNIOR LEAGUE OF LANCASTER, PENNSYLVANIA

Mushroom Almond Rice

1 cup chopped onion
4 tablespoons butter
1½ cups converted rice
2 10¾-ounce cans beef bouillon
¼ teaspoon pepper
½ cup slivered almonds
1 cup sliced mushrooms

In a heavy saucepan, cook onion in 2 tablespoons of the butter until tender. Add rice and stir until rice is golden. Add bouillon and pepper; stir well. Heat to boiling. Cover pan, reduce heat, and cook for 15–20 minutes, or until liquid is absorbed.

Sauté almonds and mushrooms in remaining 2 tablespoons butter. When rice is tender add almonds and mushrooms and toss lightly.

YIELD: 6 SERVINGS

THE JUNIOR LEAGUE OF BUFFALO, NEW YORK

Vegetables

Pennsylvania Fresh Corn Fritters

2 eggs, separated
2 cups fresh corn kernels
2 tablespoons sugar
½ teaspoon salt
1 slice bread, crumbled

Mix together egg yolks, corn, sugar, salt, and bread crumbs. Beat egg whites until stiff. Fold corn mixture into egg whites. Fry, one side at a time, until golden brown, on a buttered hot griddle or skillet. Serve immediately.

YIELD: **4–6** SERVINGS

THE JUNIOR LEAGUE OF HARRISBURG, PENNSYLVANIA

Long Island Summer Corn

2 cups fresh corn kernels
(about 5 ears)
½ cup melted butter (1 stick)
2 eggs
1 cup sour cream
1 cup diced Monterey Jack cheese
½ cup corn meal
1 4-ounce can diced green chilies
1½ teaspoon salt

Preheat oven to 350°. Generously butter a 2-quart casserole.

Purée 1 cup corn with butter and eggs in blender or food processor. Mix remaining ingredients. Add puréed mixture and blend well. Pour into prepared pan and bake uncovered for 50–60 minutes.

This can be made ahead of time and reheated before serving. It also freezes beautifully—defrost before reheating.

YIELD: 6 SERVINGS

THE JUNIOR LEAGUE OF THE NORTH SHORE, LONG ISLAND, NEW YORK

Corn Pudding

12 ears fresh corn, scraped
Pinch salt
Pinch pepper
2 eggs
2 tablespoons sugar (for
fully ripe corn)
1 cup light cream
2 tablespoons butter

Mix scraped corn with salt, pepper, eggs, sugar, and cream in buttered casserole dish. Dot with butter. Bake, uncovered, at 350° for 1 hour.

YIELD: 6 SERVINGS

THE JUNIOR LEAGUE OF ELMIRA, NEW YORK

Teller Corn Pudding

2 eggs
2 cups fresh corn kernels (5 ears)
1 tablespoon cornstarch
1 cup milk
1/3 cup sugar
1 tablespoon butter
1/3 teaspoon salt
1/8 teaspoon pepper

Beat eggs; add to corn. Mix cornstarch in milk. Combine all. Pour into greased casserole. Bake at 325° for about 1 hour, or until firm.

YIELD: 4 SERVINGS

THE JUNIOR LEAGUE OF POUGHKEEPSIE, NEW YORK

. . . .

Our Favorite Eggplant

1 medium onion, chopped
4-6 slices bacon, cooked
(reserve drippings)
1 pound eggplant, ~~unpeeled~~ and peel
cut into 1-inch cubes
1 16-ounce can crushed tomatoes
1 teaspoon sugar
½ teaspoon salt
¼ teaspoon pepper
2 tablespoons finely chopped parsley
1 teaspoon crushed dried basil
1 cup shredded cheddar cheese

Sauté onion in bacon drippings until tender. Add eggplant, tomatoes, sugar, salt, and pepper. Cover and simmer 10 minutes.

Combine parsley and basil with crumbled bacon and add to eggplant mixture. Spoon into 1-quart casserole. Sprinkle with cheese. Bake at 350° for 20 minutes, or until cheese is thoroughly melted.

YIELD: 4–6 SERVINGS

THE JUNIOR LEAGUE OF GREATER BRIDGEPORT, CONNECTICUT

Haricots Verts

1 pound fresh string beans,
trimmed but left whole
¼ pound fresh mushrooms, finely
chopped lengthwise
4 tablespoons butter
3 large cloves garlic, minced
3 tablespoons chopped fresh parsley
Salt and freshly ground pepper to taste

Steam beans and mushrooms over medium heat until tender but not too soft, 15–20 minutes.

In large frying pan, melt butter until hot and add cooked beans and mushrooms, then garlic. Fry at high heat for several minutes uncovered, stirring often. Reduce heat, add parsley, and continue frying until well blended and moisture is gone. Sprinkle with salt and pepper to taste.

YIELD: 6 SERVINGS

Hudson River Hospality
THE JUNIOR LEAGUE OF WESTCHESTER-ON-HUDSON, NEW YORK

Hodge Podge

6 onions
6 carrots
8 potatoes
Salt and pepper to taste
½ cup hot rich milk
1½ teaspoons butter

Dice and boil onions and carrots. Drain. Boil potatoes. Drain thoroughly. Add onions and carrots to potatoes and mash. Beat in salt, pepper, and hot milk.

Good served with pot roast.

YIELD: 6 SERVINGS

THE JUNIOR LEAGUE OF POUGHKEEPSIE, NEW YORK

. . . .

Purée of Frozen Lima Beans

3 10-ounce packages frozen lima beans
3 tablespoons butter
5 tablespoons heavy cream
Salt and pepper

Cook lima beans as directed on package. Drain and purée in blender or food processor. Over low heat or boiling water, melt butter. Add lima bean purée. Stir in heavy cream and season with salt and pepper.

If a thinner purée is preferred, add more butter and/or heavy cream. Serve with any roast.

YIELD: 6 SERVINGS

THE JUNIOR LEAGUE OF THE CITY OF NEW YORK, NEW YORK

. . . .

Mushrooms au Gratin

1 pound fresh mushrooms
2 teaspoons butter
1/3 cup sour cream
¼ teaspoon salt
Dash ground black pepper
1 tablespoon flour;
¼ cup chopped parsley
½ cup shredded Swiss cheese

Slice mushrooms ¼ inch thick. Sauté in butter until lightly browned. Cover pan and cook for 2 minutes at medium-low heat.

In a small bowl, blend sour cream, salt, pepper, and flour until smooth. Stir mixture into mushrooms and bring to a simmer. Remove from heat and pour into a shallow dish. Sprinkle with parsley and cheese. Heat uncovered at 425° for 10–15 minutes.

YIELD: **4** SERVINGS

Simply Superb
THE JUNIOR LEAGUE OF ELIZABETH-PLAINFIELD, NEW JERSEY

. . . .

Mushroom Casserole

1 pound fresh mushrooms
1/3 cup butter
1 tablespoon snipped parsley
1 tablespoon grated onion
1 tablespoon mustard
⅛ teaspoon cayenne
⅛ teaspoon nutmeg
1½ tablespoons flour
1 cup heavy cream

Recipe continues . . .

Wash and slice mushrooms. Mash the butter with parsley, onion, spices, and flour.

In 1½-quart greased casserole, layer the mushrooms and dot with the butter mixture. Pour cream over all and bake, uncovered, at 375° for 55 minutes.

Excellent with steak and can be prepared early in the day.

YIELD: 6–8 SERVINGS

Greenwich Recommends
THE JUNIOR LEAGUE OF GREENWICH, CONNECTICUT

Escalloped Mushrooms

1 pound fresh mushrooms, sliced
2 tablespoons butter
3 tablespoons flour
½ teaspoon parsley
1 cup + 2 tablespoons light cream
Juice of ½ lemon
Dash paprika
½ teaspoon salt
1 egg yolk, beaten
2 tablespoons cream
1 cup cracker crumbs
½ cup melted butter

Sauté mushrooms in the 2 tablespoons butter. Sprinkle flour over mushrooms; add parsley. Stir and cook until flour is absorbed. Add 1 cup cream, bring to a boil and simmer for 10 minutes. Add lemon juice, paprika, and salt.

Beat egg yolk with the 2 tablespoons cream. Stir into mushroom mixture. Pour into 8 x 8-inch baking dish. Cover with cracker crumbs and pour melted butter over top. Bake for 1 hour at 350°.

YIELD: **4** SERVINGS

THE JUNIOR LEAGUE OF LANCASTER, PENNSYLVANIA

Rose D's "Mushroom Monterey"

1 pound mushrooms, sliced
2 tablespoons butter or margarine
2 tablespoons flour
1 cup sour cream
¼ teaspoon salt, or to taste
Freshly ground pepper
¾ cup freshly grated Parmesan cheese
¼ cup chopped parsley

Sauté mushrooms in butter about 2 minutes. Add flour to sour cream; add cream mixture to mushrooms and heat just until it begins to boil. Turn into a greased shallow baking dish. Sprinkle with salt, pepper, Parmesan cheese, and parsley. Bake in preheated 425° oven 10 minutes, or until bubbly.

YIELD: **6** SERVINGS

THE JUNIOR LEAGUE OF WILKES-BARRE, PENNSYLVANIA

Stuffed Mushrooms

1 pound mushrooms
3 teaspoons butter
¼ cup finely chopped green pepper
¼ cup finely chopped onion
1½ cups soft bread crumbs
½ teaspoon salt
¼ teaspoon turmeric
¼ teaspoon pepper
1 tablespoon butter

Preheat oven to 350°.

Wash mushrooms. Trim and dry thoroughly. Remove and finely chop stems.

Melt the 3 teaspoons butter in skillet. Cook and stir chopped mushroom stems, green pepper, and onion in butter until tender, about 5 minutes. Remove from heat. Stir in bread crumbs and seasonings.

Melt the 1 tablespoon butter in shallow baking dish. Fill mushroom caps with stuffing mixture. Place mushrooms filled side up in baking dish. Bake at 350° for 15 minutes. Then broil about 2 minutes 3–4 inches from heat. Serve hot as a vegetable or appetizer.

YIELD: 6 SERVINGS

THE JUNIOR LEAGUE OF ORANGE COUNTY, NEW YORK

Mushrooms and Wine en Casserole

1 tablespoon ground marjoram
1 tablespoon chives
1 pound mushrooms, trimmed and cleaned
½ cup melted butter
½ cup chicken broth
¼ cup dry white wine
1 tablespoon salt
Freshly ground pepper to taste

Put raw mushrooms in ungreased casserole. Combine all other ingredients and pour over mushrooms. Cook uncovered at 350° for 30 minutes.

YIELD: 6 SERVINGS

THE JUNIOR LEAGUE OF SYRACUSE, NEW YORK

•   •   •   •   •   •   •   •   •   •   •   •   •   •   •   •   •   •

Onion Shortcake

1 large Spanish onion
¼ cup butter
1½ cups corn muffin mix
1 egg, beaten
1/3 cup milk
1 cup cream-style corn
1 cup sour cream
¼ teaspoon salt
1 cup shredded sharp cheddar cheese

Recipe continues . . .

Slice onion into rings and cook slowly in butter until transparent.

Combine mix, egg, milk, and corn. Pour into buttered 8-inch square pan.

Add sour cream, salt, and half the cheese to onion. Mix well and spread evenly over corn batter. Sprinkle with remaining cheese. Bake at 425° for 30 minutes. Serve hot.

YIELD: 9 SERVINGS

THE JUNIOR LEAGUE OF BANGOR, MAINE

Peas and Cucumber

2 10-ounce packages frozen peas
Salt
1 tablespoon sugar
1 cucumber, peeled, seeded, and diced
½–¾ cup sour cream

Cook peas in salted water with sugar until barely tender. Add diced cucumber and cook 1 minute to heat. Drain. Stir in sour cream and serve hot.

YIELD: 8 SERVINGS

THE JUNIOR LEAGUE OF WORCESTER, MASSACHUSETTS

Mashed Potato Casserole

5 pounds potatoes, peeled (9 large)
6 ounces cream cheese
1 cup sour cream
2 teaspoons onion salt
1 teaspoon garlic salt
1 teaspoon salt
Pinch white pepper
2 tablespoons butter

Cook potatoes in salted water until tender. Drain, then mash until smooth. Add remaining ingredients and beat until light and fluffy. Cool slightly and spoon into a large greased casserole. Dot with a little more butter. Bake in 350° oven for 30–45 minutes.

This can be prepared and refrigerated 1–2 days in advance. Remove from refrigerator about 1 hour before serving and bake.

YIELD: 10 SERVINGS

THE JUNIOR LEAGUE OF MONTREAL, QUEBEC

Artichokes au Gratin

1½–2 tablespoons flour
2 tablespoons butter
2 10-ounce packages frozen artichokes,
cooked and drained (reserve liquid)
¼ cup milk
½ pint heavy cream
White pepper
½ cup finely shredded Gruyère cheese
Paprika

Recipe continues . . .

Make a cheese sauce: Stir flour and butter vigorously with a whisk over low heat. Slowly add 1/3 cup artichoke cooking broth, milk, and heavy cream, stirring vigorously. Season with white pepper. Add all but 1 tablespoon cheese to sauce. Stir briskly until cheese is melted and sauce is smooth.

Arrange artichokes in buttered baking or au gratin dish. Pour sauce over artichokes; sprinkle with remaining cheese and paprika. Bake at 350° for 35–40 minutes.

YIELD: 4–6 SERVINGS

THE JUNIOR LEAGUE OF THE ORANGES AND SHORT HILLS, NEW JERSEY

Asparagus Chinese-Style

2 pounds fresh asparagus
½ cup finely chopped onion
2 tablespoons oil
1 tablespoon cornstarch
¾ cup chicken broth
1 tablespoon soy sauce
⅛ teaspoon pepper
1/3 cup thinly sliced water chestnuts
2 tablespoons slivered toasted almonds

Remove ends and scales of asparagus stalks, wash thoroughly, and cut in thin diagonal slices. Cook asparagus and onion in hot oil over medium heat until tender-crisp, stirring constantly, about 2 minutes.

Combine cornstarch, chicken broth, soy sauce, and pepper. Add to asparagus and bring to a boil; simmer 2 minutes. Stir in water chestnuts and almonds. Serve immediately.

YIELD: 6 SERVINGS

The Everyday Gourmet
THE JUNIOR LEAGUE OF NORTHERN WESTCHESTER, BEDFORD HILLS, NEW YORK

Broccoli Pie

4 ounces cream cheese, softened
1 cup heavy cream
½ cup soft bread crumbs
¼ cup grated Parmesan cheese
2 eggs, lightly beaten
1 cup chopped cooked broccoli
1 large onion, chopped
½ pound mushrooms, chopped
4 tablespoons butter
½ teaspoon oregano
¾ teaspoon salt
⅛ teaspoon pepper
1 uncooked 10- or 11-inch pastry shell

Preheat oven to 425°.

Blend cream cheese and cream together. Add the bread crumbs, Parmesan cheese, and eggs. Stir in broccoli.

Sauté the onion and mushrooms in butter until tender. Stir in the seasonings. Beat this mixture into the cheese mixture. Let cool. Fill the pie shell and bake in the preheated oven for 25 minutes.

The filling may be prepared a day in advance and kept in the refrigerator until ready to use.

YIELD: 6 SERVINGS

THE JUNIOR LEAGUE OF HAMILTON-BURLINGTON, ONTARIO

Skillet Cabbage

4 cups shredded cabbage
1 green pepper, chopped
2 cups chopped celery
2 large onions, chopped
2 large tomatoes, chopped
1 tablespoon bacon drippings
2 teaspoons sugar
Salt and pepper to taste

Combine all ingredients in a large skillet and cook over medium heat for 5 minutes, stirring frequently.

YIELD: 4–6 SERVINGS

THE JUNIOR LEAGUE OF ELMIRA, NEW YORK

Fluffy Potato Casserole

2 cups hot or cold mashed potatoes
1 8-ounce package cream cheese
1 small onion, finely chopped
2 eggs
2 tablespoons flour
Salt and pepper to taste
1 3½-ounce can French fried onions

Put potatoes into the large bowl of an electric mixer. Add cream cheese, chopped onion, eggs, and flour. Beat at medium speed until ingredients are blended, then beat at high speed until light and fluffy. Taste and season if needed.

Spoon into a greased 9-inch square baking dish. Bake uncovered at

300–325° for about 35 minutes. During the last 10 minutes, spread onions over top of the casserole.

YIELD: 4–6 SERVINGS

THE JUNIOR LEAGUE OF SCRANTON, PENNSYLVANIA

Pommes de Terre à la Dauphinoise

2½ cups heavy cream
1 tablespoon butter
2 cloves garlic, minced
2½ pounds red potatoes
1/3 cup freshly grated Parmesan cheese
Salt and pepper

Simmer cream, butter, and garlic in saucepan until the mixture is half its original quantity.

Slice the potatoes very thinly and dry roughly. Butter a small, deep 2-quart casserole and layer the potatoes, sprinkling each layer with a little Parmesan, salt, and pepper. Cover the potatoes with the reduced cream, pouring it through a strainer. If necessary, add additional cream to cover potatoes.

Cover casserole and bake in a 350° oven for about 1 hour.

YIELD: 6 SERVINGS

The Melting Pot

THE JUNIOR LEAGUE OF THE CENTRAL DELAWARE VALLEY, NEW JERSEY

Gourmet Potatoes

6 medium potatoes
2 cups shredded cheddar cheese
¼ cup butter
1½ cups sour cream
1/3 cup finely chopped onion
¼ teaspoon pepper
1 teaspoon salt
2 tablespoons butter
Paprika

Cook potatoes in skins; cool, peel, and shred or mash coarsely.

Over low heat, combine cheese and the ¼ cup butter, stirring until the ingredients are almost melted. Remove from heat and blend in sour cream, onion, and seasonings. Fold in potatoes and put into 2-quart casserole. Dot with butter and sprinkle with paprika. Bake at 350° for 30 minutes.

YIELD: 8 SERVINGS

THE JUNIOR LEAGUE OF WILKES-BARRE, PENNSYLVANIA

. . . .

Potatoes Louise

Idaho baking potatoes, peeled
1 tablespoon melted butter per potato
Grated Parmesan cheese
Salt
Paprika

Fill a shallow casserole with cold water. Slice potatoes ⅛-inch thick, but *do not* cut through completely. Stand potatoes in rows in water. When casserole is full, cover with lid and drain off water.

Pour melted butter over potatoes and sprinkle with cheese to taste.

Add salt and paprika to taste. Bake at 350° for 1–1½ hours, or until crisp on top.

THE JUNIOR LEAGUE OF BRONXVILLE, NEW YORK

* * * * * * * * * * * * * * * * * * *

Potatoes O'Brien

6–8 potatoes (about 1½ pounds)
Salt to taste
3 tablespoons peanut, vegetable,
or corn oil
1/3 cup finely chopped onion
Salt and freshly ground pepper to taste
1 cup cubed green pepper
1 tablespoon butter
1/3 cup cubed pimento (optional)

Peel potatoes and cut into ½-inch cubes. There should be about 3 cups. As they are cubed, drop them into a saucepan of cold water. Add salt, bring to a boil, and simmer for 1–2 minutes. Drain well.

Heat the oil in a skillet and add potatoes. Cook, stirring and shaking the skillet as necessary, until potatoes become golden, about 8–10 minutes. Add the onion, salt, and pepper and cook briefly. Add the green pepper and cook, stirring gently as necessary, about 3 minutes. Add the butter and cook about 2 minutes. Add the pimento and stir gently. Cook until heated through.

YIELD: 4 SERVINGS

The Everyday Gourmet
THE JUNIOR LEAGUE OF NORTHERN WESTCHESTER, BEDFORD HILLS, NEW YORK

* * * * * * * * * * * * * * * * * *

Potato Pancakes

2 cups shredded raw potato
2 whole eggs, well beaten
Pinch baking powder
1½ teaspoons salt
1 tablespoon flour
1 onion, grated
Dash pepper

Combine potato and eggs, and mix with the other ingredients. Drop by tablespoonfuls into ¼ inch hot oil and fry until crisp and brown on both sides. Drain on paper toweling. Serve with applesauce.

The fried cakes can be frozen and reheated in a 350° oven.

YIELD: 16 3-INCH PANCAKES

THE JUNIOR LEAGUE OF BUFFALO, NEW YORK

Swiss Scalloped Potatoes

3 pounds potatoes, peeled and thinly sliced
1 medium onion, grated
¾ pound shredded Swiss cheese
3 eggs
2¼ cups milk
2 teaspoons salt
½ teaspoon pepper
½ teaspoon paprika
Dash parsley

Boil potatoes, uncovered, for 5 minutes. Drain. Place alternating layers of potatoes, onion, and cheese in a buttered baking dish. Combine eggs, milk, salt, and pepper in a small bowl and beat well. Pour over potatoes and sprinkle top with paprika. Cover dish with foil and bake at 325° for 1¾ hours.

YIELD: 8–10 SERVINGS

The Melting Pot
THE JUNIOR LEAGUE OF THE CENTRAL DELAWARE VALLEY, NEW JERSEY

Braised Celery

3 bunches celery
3 tablespoons butter
¼ cup minced onion
1 cup beef broth
2 teaspoons Worcestershire sauce
¾ teaspoon salt
⅛ teaspoon pepper

Cut the celery bunches in half lengthwise and discard the leaves. Cut in 1-inch pieces. Melt the butter in a skillet and in it sauté the celery and onion for 10 minutes, shaking the pan frequently. Add all other ingredients, cover, and cook over low heat for 25 minutes, or until celery is tender but firm.

YIELD: 4–6 SERVINGS

Recipes by Request
THE JUNIOR LEAGUE OF GREATER WATERBURY, CONNECTICUT

Herbed Spinach Bake

1 10-ounce package frozen chopped spinach,
cooked and drained
1 cup cooked rice
1 cup shredded cheddar cheese
2 eggs, lightly beaten
½ cup milk
2 tablespoons chopped onion
½ teaspoon Worcestershire sauce
1 teaspoon salt
¼ teaspoon rosemary
2 tablespoons soft butter

Mix all ingredients together. Pour into baking dish. Bake at 350° for 30 minutes.

If using as side dish for large crowd, triple recipe but use only 2 packages spinach.

YIELD: 4–6 SERVINGS

THE JUNIOR LEAGUE OF SUMMIT, NEW JERSEY

•   •   •   •   •   •   •   •   •   •   •   •   •   •   •   •   •   •   •

Spinach Pie

¼ pound mushrooms, sliced
1 medium zucchini, thinly sliced
1 small green pepper, diced
6 tablespoons butter
1 pound ricotta cheese
1 cup shredded mozzarella cheese
3 eggs, lightly beaten
1 10-ounce package frozen chopped spinach,
cooked and squeezed dry
2 tablespoons olive oil
Salt and pepper to taste

Sauté the mushrooms, zucchini, and green pepper in half the butter until soft. Let cool.

Combine ricotta, mozzarella, eggs, spinach, olive oil, salt, and pepper and the cooled vegetable mixture. Turn into 9-inch oiled pie plate. Sprinkle with remaining butter, melted. Bake at 350° for 45 minutes.

Delicious and versatile. Use as main luncheon dish, to accompany dinner as a vegetable, or cut into small pieces for appetizer.

YIELD: 1 9-INCH PIE

THE JUNIOR LEAGUE OF WORCESTER, MASSACHUSETTS

Spinach Roulade with Mushroom Filling

A "roulade" is a flat soufflé baked in a rectangular shape, then rolled with a filling. Serve as a first course, as the main course for a luncheon or supper, or as the vegetable accompaniment to a main course.

> *3 pounds well washed fresh spinach or*
> *3 10-ounce packages frozen spinach,*
> *finely chopped*
> *Salt and pepper*
> *Nutmeg*
> *6 tablespoons butter*
> *4 eggs, separated*
> *Bread crumbs*
> *¼ cup grated Parmesan cheese*

If using fresh spinach, cook it before chopping. Drain the spinach well, place it in a large bowl, and add the seasonings to taste. Beat in the butter and the egg yolks. Beat the egg whites until stiff. Fold the whites into the spinach mixture by hand.

Oil a jelly roll pan and line with wax paper, leaving an inch or so

Recipe continues . . .

hanging over the ends. Oil the wax paper and sprinkle with bread crumbs.

Spread spinach mixture in the pan and sprinkle with Parmesan cheese. Bake in a preheated 350° oven for 15 minutes. Unmold the roulade onto foil or a linen towel. Spread the Mushroom Filling evenly over it and roll lengthwise.

Serve the roulade either at room temperature or warm. May be made ahead and reheated covered with foil in a 180° to 200° oven.

YIELD: 8 SERVINGS

MUSHROOM FILLING:
½ pound mushrooms, finely minced
3 tablespoons finely minced green onion
2 tablespoons butter
1 8-ounce package cream cheese
2–3 tablespoons sour cream
Salt and pepper
1 tablespoon chopped dill

Sauté the mushrooms and onion in the butter. In a bowl, blend together the cream cheese and sour cream. Add the mushrooms and onion and mash well. Add salt and pepper to taste and the dill. If necessary, chill for a few minutes until slightly firm.

THE JUNIOR LEAGUE OF HARTFORD, CONNECTICUT

Spanakopeta

¼ cup butter
3 pounds fresh spinach or 6 10-ounce
packages frozen spinach, slightly thawed
2 bunches green onions, chopped
¼ cup chopped parsley
6 eggs
½ pound feta cheese, drained and crumbled
Salt and pepper to taste
1 pound phyllo pastry, thawed
Melted butter

Melt the ¼ cup butter in large skillet. Add spinach, green onions, and chopped parsley and sauté until vegetables are wilted. Drain well.

In a large mixing bowl, beat eggs. Add cheese and salt and pepper. Add cooled spinach mixture. Taste for seasoning.

Line a 9 x 13-inch baking dish with 4-6 sheets phyllo pastry, brushing each sheet with melted butter as you place it in the pan. Top with one-third of the spinach mixture. Repeat layers of phyllo, butter, and spinach and top with pastry. Trim edges and score top in serving portions. Bake in a preheated 300° oven for 40-50 minutes.

YIELD: 12 SERVINGS

THE JUNIOR LEAGUE OF ERIE, PENNSYLVANIA

Baked Squash

*1 quart Hubbard squash, peeled and
thinly sliced (any other winter squash
may be substituted)
2 teaspoons salt
¼ cup sugar
½ cup heavy cream
1 teaspoon cinnamon*

Butter a casserole and add the squash. Sprinkle with salt and sugar. Pour cream over. Sprinkle with cinnamon and bake, covered, for 50 minutes in 250–300° oven.

YIELD: 6 SERVINGS

THE JUNIOR LEAGUE OF ELMIRA, NEW YORK

. . . .

Tomato Stacks

*3 large ripe tomatoes
Salt
4 ounces aged Swiss cheese, shredded
¼ cup chopped onion
1 10-ounce package frozen chopped
broccoli, cooked and drained*

Cut tomatoes into slices ¾ inch thick. Sprinkle each lightly with salt.

Set aside 2 tablespoons shredded cheese. Combine remaining cheese, "hot" broccoli, and onion.

Place tomato slices on baking sheet. Spoon broccoli mixture onto tomatoes completely covering them. Sprinkle with remaining cheese.

Broil 8 inches from heat for 10–12 minutes, or until cheese bubbles and tomatoes are hot. Do not let cheese burn.

YIELD: 6 SERVINGS

THE JUNIOR LEAGUE OF BERGEN COUNTY, NEW JERSEY

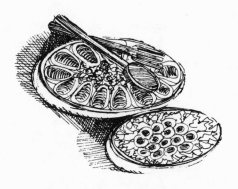

Escalloped Tomatoes

1 medium onion, chopped
Butter
1 22-ounce can stewed tomatoes
1 teaspoon sugar
Salt and pepper to taste
Bread cubes
Oregano (optional)
Shredded cheddar cheese

Sauté onion in butter. Add onion to mixture of tomatoes, sugar, salt, and pepper. Put seasoned tomatoes in shallow greased casserole or pie plate. Cover with bread cubes. Sprinkle with oregano if desired and cover *generously* with cheese. Bake in 400° oven for about 20 minutes.

YIELD: 3–4 SERVINGS

THE JUNIOR LEAGUE OF WORCESTER, MASSACHUSETTS

Tomato-Zucchini Scallop

2 small zucchini, thinly sliced
1 medium onion, thinly sliced
2 medium tomatoes, peeled and sliced
1 cup plain croutons
1 teaspoon salt
6 ounces shredded sharp cheese (1½ cups)

In a greased 1½-quart casserole, layer the zucchini, onion, tomatoes, croutons, salt, and 1 cup of the cheese. Bake, covered, at 350° for 1 hour. Remove cover, sprinkle with remaining cheese, and return to oven until cheese is melted.

YIELD: 6 SERVINGS

THE JUNIOR LEAGUE OF SCHENECTADY, NEW YORK

. . . .

Tourlou Tava

Freshness of ingredients is the key to this Greek ratatouille. It is always tastier when made the day before serving; it can be kept in the refrigerator for up to a week or frozen.

2 pounds fresh string beans
2 large onions, quartered and sliced
¼ cup chopped dill
½ cup olive oil
4 cloves garlic
1 cup chopped parsley
1 pound tomatoes, chopped
Salt and pepper to taste
4-6 medium zucchini, sliced
2 packages frozen okra, thawed

Combine all ingredients except zucchini and okra in a large casserole. Cover and bake at 450° for about 10 minutes, or until liquid starts to simmer. Reduce heat to 350° and bake for 1 hour. Add the zucchini and okra and bake for an additional hour, or until the vegetables are tender.

YIELD: 10–12 SERVINGS

Presenting Boston . . . A Cookbook
THE JUNIOR LEAGUE OF BOSTON, MASSACHUSETTS

• • • • • • • • • • • • • • • •

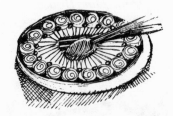

Yugoslavian Vegetable Casserole

1 potato, diced
1 medium zucchini, unpeeled and diced
1 medium eggplant, unpeeled and diced
2 green peppers, diced
2 small carrots, quartered lengthwise
and cut in 1-inch strips
1 Bermuda onion, coarsely chopped
½ cup shelled fresh peas
2 tablespoons chopped parsley
1/3 cup olive oil
1 tablespoon salt
1 teaspoon Tabasco
1 teaspoon freshly ground black pepper
4 large tomatoes, sliced
1/3 cup raw rice
½ cup olive oil
2 tablespoons white wine vinegar
1¾ cups shredded cheddar cheese

Recipe continues . . .

Combine potato, zucchini, eggplant, green peppers, carrots, onion, peas, and parsley with the 1/3 cup olive oil, salt, Tabasco, and pepper. Line an oiled 9 x 11-inch baking dish with half the vegetable mixture. Layer with half the tomato slices and sprinkle with rice. Add remaining vegetables and top with remaining tomato slices.

Mix the ½ cup olive oil with vinegar and pour over casserole. Bake, covered, at 350° for 1¾ hours. Sprinkle with cheese and place under broiler until cheese is melted.

YIELD: 12 SERVINGS

From Our House
THE JUNIOR LEAGUE OF HARTFORD, CONNECTICUT

Zucchini Boats

6 small zucchini
1½ cups peeled, chopped tomato
¾ cups toasted bread cubes
Salt and pepper to taste
Grated Parmesan cheese

Trim and steam zucchini for 7-10 minutes, or until tender. Cut in half and scoop out pulp. Combine tomato, bread cubes, salt, and pepper. Spoon into zucchini shells and sprinkle with cheese. Bake at 400° about 15-20 minutes.

YIELD: 6 SERVINGS

THE JUNIOR LEAGUE OF BERGEN COUNTY, NEW JERSEY

Zucchini with Cherry Tomatoes

1½ pounds small zucchini
3 tablespoons butter
1 teaspoon salt
⅛ teaspoon freshly ground black pepper
1 pint cherry tomatoes, halved
2 teaspoons lemon juice
¼ teaspoon sugar

Wash but don't peel zucchini. Slice ½-inch thick. Place in skillet and add boiling water to cover. Cook, covered, until barely tender. Drain well.

Return zucchini to skillet and add remaining ingredients. Toss gently, cover, and simmer until tomatoes are heated through. Do not overcook.

YIELD: 8 SERVINGS

THE JUNIOR LEAGUE OF ELMIRA, NEW YORK

Zucchini in Cream

6 small zucchini, cut in ½-inch slices
2/3 cup sour cream
1 tablespoon butter
6 tablespoons shredded sharp cheddar cheese
½ teaspoon salt
3 tablespoons bread crumbs
1 teaspoon dill weed, or to taste

Recipe continues . . .

Preheat oven to 375°.

Simmer zucchini for 10 minutes in water to cover; drain and turn into ovenproof casserole.

In small saucepan, combine sour cream, butter, 4 tablespoons of the cheese, and salt. Heat, stirring until blended. Pour over zucchini. Top with bread crumbs, 2 remaining tablespoons cheese, and dill. Bake in preheated oven for 10 minutes, or until crumbs are golden. Let stand 5 minutes, then serve.

YIELD: 4 SERVINGS

THE JUNIOR LEAGUE OF KINGSTON, NEW YORK

. . . .

Zucchini Fritters

1 cup milk
1 cup flour
1 teaspoon baking powder
2 tablespoons shredded cheddar cheese
2 eggs
Pepper and paprika to taste
1 zucchini
Vegetable oil

Mix all ingredients except the zucchini and oil in a bowl. Grate the zucchini into a sieve and let it drain. Add zucchini to the other ingredients and mix. Drop by tablespoonfuls into vegetable oil heated to 365°. Remove when brown and drain on absorbent paper.

YIELD: 15 FRITTERS

THE JUNIOR LEAGUE OF SYRACUSE, NEW YORK

. . . .

Zucchini with Sour Cream and Dill

4–6 large zucchini
1 stick butter
2 tablespoons finely chopped fresh dill
Salt and pepper to taste
8 ounces sour cream

Slice zucchini thinly. Sauté zucchini in butter, sprinkling with dill and salt and pepper to taste. When zucchini is fork-tender, stir in sour cream and heat to serving temperature.

YIELD: 6 SERVINGS

THE JUNIOR LEAGUE OF BROOKLYN, NEW YORK

. . . .

Zesty Zucchini

4 slices American cheese
8 ounces sharp cheese, shredded
¼ cup shredded Swiss cheese
1 large zucchini, unpeeled and sliced
1 large onion, sliced
1 large tomato, peeled and sliced
6 slices bacon, cooked

Grease a 2-quart casserole. Line bottom with American cheese. Alternate layers of zucchini, onion, tomato, and mixture of shredded cheeses, ending with cheeses. Bake at 350° for 1 hour. Fifteen minutes before serving, put bacon slices on top.

YIELD: 4–6 SERVINGS

Bicentennial Cookbook .
THE JUNIOR LEAGUE OF PHILADELPHIA, PENNSYLVANIA

. . . .

Salads

Broccoli and Celery Salad

2 large bunches broccoli
2 cups sliced celery
2 tablespoons minced onion
¼ cup diced pimento
2 teaspoons celery seed
2 tablespoons lemon juice
1 cup mayonnaise
¼ cup sour cream
¼ teaspoon freshly ground pepper

Cut broccoli into 1-inch pieces. Cook in a small amount of boiling salted water about 5 minutes, or until crisp-tender. Drain and cool. Add next five ingredients.

Combine mayonnaise and sour cream and pour over broccoli mixture. Add pepper and toss gently. Refrigerate 4–6 hours or overnight before serving.

YIELD: 6 SERVINGS

THE JUNIOR LEAGUE OF MORRISTOWN, NEW JERSEY

. . . .

Marinated Carrots

5 cups cooked sliced carrots
1 green pepper, seeded and chopped
1 onion, chopped
1 cup sugar
½ cup salad oil
½ cup white vinegar, or to taste
1 teaspoon each salt, pepper, dry
mustard, Worcestershire sauce
1 6-ounce can tomato sauce

Mix ingredients and let stand 12–24 hours.

YIELD: 6 SERVINGS

THE JUNIOR LEAGUE OF SYRACUSE, NEW YORK

French Carrot Salad

1 pound fresh carrots, scraped
1/3 cup chopped fresh parsley
¼ cup finely chopped green onion
½ teaspoon minced garlic
3 tablespoons olive oil
2 tablespons vinegar
1 tablespoon lemon juice
1 tablespoon sugar

Finely shred carrots—the pound will yield about 4–5 cups shredded carrot. Add parsley, onion, and garlic. Add remaining ingredients, toss all, and adjust with additional oil or vinegar according to taste. Let stand 1 hour to blend flavors.

An inexpensive and vitamin-filled salad.

YIELD: 6–8 SERVINGS

THE JUNIOR LEAGUE OF KINGSTON, NEW YORK

Our Favorite Caesar Salad

3 cloves garlic, minced
½ teaspoon dry mustard
½ teaspoon Worcestershire sauce
6 tablespoons grated Parmesan cheese
2 tablespoons wine vinegar
2 tablespoons lemon juice
8 tablespoons olive oil
2 egg yolks
1 large head romaine lettuce, washed,
dried, and torn into large pieces
½ cup croutons (hopefully homemade!)

In a large *wooden* salad bowl, put garlic, mustard, Worcestershire sauce, and 1 tablespoon Parmesan cheese. Mix with a fork. Add vinegar, lemon juice, and olive oil. Mix again with a fork. Add egg yolks and mix well. Let stand ½ hour at room temperature.

At serving time, put romaine on top of dressing, sprinkle with remaining 5 tablespoons Parmesan cheese, add croutons, toss, and enjoy!

YIELD: 4–6 SERVINGS

The Everyday Gourmet
THE JUNIOR LEAGUE OF NORTHERN WESTCHESTER, BEDFORD HILLS, NEW YORK

· · · · · · · · · · · · · · · · · ·

Genesee Country Sauerkraut Salad

1 green pepper, seeded and chopped
1 cup finely chopped celery
1 cup finely chopped onion
1 1-pound can sauerkraut
1 4-ounce jar pimento, drained
½ cup vinegar
1½ cups sugar
1 teaspoon celery seed

Combine pepper, celery, and onion. Drain sauerkraut and rinse lightly. Add sauerkraut, pimento, and celery seed to chopped vegetables. Heat vinegar and sugar until sugar is dissolved. Pour over all ingredients. Refrigerate for at least 24 hours before serving.

YIELD: **4** SERVINGS

THE JUNIOR LEAGUE OF ROCHESTER, NEW YORK

Swedish Chicken Salad

1 3½-pound chicken, poached
1 cup long-grain rice
1 green apple
1 red apple
2 bananas
Lemon juice
½ cup heavy cream
2/3 cup mayonnaise
1 teaspoon curry powder
Salt and pepper

Cut chicken meat into bite-size pieces. Cook rice. Core and thinly slice the apples. Peel and thickly slice the bananas. Sprinkle fruit with lemon juice to keep it from turning brown.

Whip the cream to same consistency as mayonnaise and fold together. Add curry powder. Fold in chicken, apple, banana, and rice. Add more lemon juice and salt and pepper to taste.

Serve cold with tossed green salad and crusty bread.

YIELD: **4** SERVINGS

THE JUNIOR LEAGUE OF BERGEN COUNTY, NEW JERSEY

Fruit and Chicken Salad

3 cups cooked, diced chicken
1 cup diced celery
1 cup mandarin orange sections (seedless
white grapes may be substituted)
1 cup pineapple chunks
2 tablespoons vegetable oil
2 tablespoons orange juice
2 tablespoons vinegar
Mayonnaise

Combine the first four ingredients. Blend the oil, orange juice, vinegar and toss with the chicken mixture. Chill 1 hour. Drain and add enough mayonnaise to moisten the ingredients.

Serve on lettuce leaves.

YIELD: 4–6 SERVINGS

Presenting Boston . . . A Cookbook
THE JUNIOR LEAGUE OF BOSTON, MASSACHUSETTS

Luncheon Salad

This recipe can be easily multiplied to serve a larger group. A 20-pound turkey equals approximately 8 quarts turkey meat.

1 20-ounce can water chestnuts
2 quarts diced, cooked chicken or
turkey breast
2 pounds seedless grapes
2 cups sliced celery
2–3 cups toasted slivered almonds
2 cups mayonnaise
1 cup sour cream
1 teaspoon curry powder
1 tablespoon soy sauce
1–2 tablespoons lemon juice
Boston or Bibb lettuce
1 1-pound 13-ounce can pineapple chunks

Slice or dice the water chestnuts and mix with the turkey meat. Add grapes, celery, and half the toasted almonds.

Mix mayonnaise and sour cream with curry powder, soy sauce, and lemon juice. Combine with turkey mixture, chill for several hours, then spoon into nests of lettuce. Sprinkle with remaining toasted almonds and garnish with pineapple chunks.

YIELD: 12–15 GENEROUS SERVINGS

THE JUNIOR LEAGUE OF BRONXVILLE, NEW YORK

Mushroom Salad

1 head lettuce or any combination
greens, shredded
½ pound mushrooms, sliced

FRENCH DRESSING:
½ cup oil
¼ cup cider vinegar
¼ cup chopped onion
¼ cup minced fresh parsley
1 teaspoon chopped green pepper
1 teaspoon sugar
1 teaspoon salt
1 teaspoon dry mustard
⅛ teaspoon red pepper

Combine dressing ingredients. This may be done ahead. Pour over lettuce and mushrooms at serving time, and toss lightly.

YIELD: **4** SERVINGS

THE JUNIOR LEAGUE OF MORRISTOWN, NEW JERSEY

．　．　．　．　．　．　．　．　．　．　．　．　．　．　．　．　．

Mushroom-Cress Salad

1/3 cup oil
2 tablespoons tarragon or
white wine vinegar
½ teaspoon salt
Freshly ground pepper to taste
4 bunches watercress, washed and trimmed
½ pound mushrooms, thinly sliced

In bowl, mix oil, vinegar, salt, and pepper. Add watercress and mushrooms. Toss lightly before serving.

YIELD: **4** SERVINGS

THE JUNIOR LEAGUE OF BANGOR, MAINE

. . . .

Mushroom-Bacon Salad

1 pound medium-size fresh mushrooms
2/3 cup salad oil or olive oil
3 green onions, including tops,
thinly sliced (about ¼ cup)
4 tablespoons lemon juice
1 teaspoon Worcestershire sauce
½ teaspoon salt
⅛ teaspoon pepper
½ teaspoon dry mustard
12 slices thin bacon
Lettuce

Rinse mushrooms and pat dry. Slice about ⅛ inch thick into a bowl.

In small bowl or jar, combine oil, onions, lemon juice, Worcestershire sauce, salt, pepper, and mustard. Shake or stir until well blended. Pour over mushrooms and mix gently. Cover and refrigerate for at least 4 hours or overnight; uncover and stir several times.

Shortly before serving, cook bacon until crisp; drain.

To serve, spoon mushrooms and onions into lettuce-lined bowl. Top with crumbled bacon. Drizzle with any remaining marinade.

YIELD: **8** SERVINGS

THE JUNIOR LEAGUE OF WILMINGTON, DELAWARE

. . . .

Pea Salad

2 10-ounce packages frozen green peas
1½ large cucumbers, thinly sliced
9 green onions, chopped
3 stalks celery, chopped
¾ cup oil
½ cup wine vinegar
3 tablespoons sugar
3 tablespoons chopped parsley
1½ teaspoons garlic salt
1½ teaspoons salt
¾ teaspoon oregano
½ teaspoon pepper

Put peas in a bowl and cover with boiling water. Drain off boiling water immediately. Add sliced cucumbers, onions, and celery to peas.

In separate bowl, combine remaining ingredients to make dressing. Blend thoroughly. Toss vegetables with dressing.

YIELD: 8 SERVINGS

Hudson River Hospitality
THE JUNIOR LEAGUE OF WESTCHESTER-ON-HUDSON, NEW YORK

. . . .

German Potato Salad

4 potatoes, boiled in skin
2 stalks celery, chopped
1 small onion, chopped

Peel potatoes and slice. Mix with celery and onion.

DRESSING:
3 slices bacon, diced
2 teaspoons flour
1/4 cup vinegar
1/4 cup sugar
1/4 cup cold water
1/8 teaspoon dry mustard
1/4 teaspoon salt
1/8 teaspoon pepper

Fry bacon until crisp. Add to vegetables. Add the remaining ingredients to hot drippings in frying pan and cook until thick. Pour over vegetables. Toss and serve warm.

YIELD: 4 SERVINGS

THE JUNIOR LEAGUE OF LANCASTER, PENNSYLVANIA

. . . .

Tangy Potato Salad

5 cups diced cooked potato
1 cup sliced celery
1/4 cup finely chopped green onion
1/2 cup sliced radish
2 tablespoons chopped parsley
1 cup plain yogurt
1/2 cup mayonnaise
1 teaspoon prepared horseradish
1/2 teaspoon dill weed
1 1/2 teaspoons salt
1/8 teaspoon pepper
Lettuce
Hard-boiled eggs for garnish

Recipe continues . . .

Combine potato, celery, onion, radish, and parsley. Lightly mix together yogurt, mayonnaise, horseradish, dill weed, salt, and pepper. Add to potato mixture and toss lightly. Chill 1 hour.

Serve in lettuce cups garnished with hard-boiled eggs.

YIELD: 6–8 SERVINGS

THE JUNIOR LEAGUE OF MONTREAL, QUEBEC

Garden Rice Salad

1 package long-grain and wild rice mix
¼ cup mayonnaise
½ cup plain yogurt
1 cup sliced celery
1 cup cubed tomato
½ cup diced cucumber
2 tablespoons chopped parsley
⅛ teaspoon pepper
¼ cup chopped dry-roasted peanuts
for garnish

Cook rice as directed on package but omit butter or margarine; cool. Toss lightly with all remaining ingredients except peanuts. Cover and chill. Garnish with peanuts—the crunch adds so much!

YIELD: 4½ CUPS

THE JUNIOR LEAGUE OF ROCHESTER, NEW YORK

Sea Scallops Ceviche Salad

½ pound sea scallops
Juice of 4 limes
4 tablespoons chopped onion
2 tablespoons chopped parsley
4 tablespoons chopped green pepper
6 tablespoons olive oil
Salt and freshly ground pepper to taste

Cut raw scallops into quarters and cover with lime juice. Marinate 1 hour or more in refrigerator, stirring occasionally. Drain; combine other ingredients and add to scallops. Mix well and serve on a bed of shredded romaine lettuce.

YIELD: 4 SERVINGS

Entirely Entertaining
THE JUNIOR LEAGUE OF MONTCLAIR-NEWARK, NEW JERSEY

Shrimp-Cauliflower Salad

1 cup cold cooked rice
1 pound cooked shrimp
¾ teaspoon salt
1 tablespoon lemon juice
1 tablespoon minced green onion
2 tablespoons French dressing
1 tablespoon chopped olive
1 cup diced cauliflower
1/3 cup mayonnaise

Recipe continues . . .

Combine all the above ingredients and enjoy!

YIELD: 6 SERVINGS

THE JUNIOR LEAGUE OF THE ORANGES AND SHORT HILLS, NEW JERSEY

Spinach Salad

1 pound fresh spinach
1 egg
3 tablespoons Parmesan cheese
2 tablespoons Dijon mustard
1 capful Worcestershire sauce
1 teaspoon sugar
Salt and freshly ground pepper
Juice of 1 lemon
1/3 cup salad oil
8 slices crisply cooked bacon, crumbled
2 hard-boiled eggs, coarsely mashed

Wash spinach and break into bite-size pieces. Chill.

Mix next seven ingredients in small bowl. Add oil and mix again.

Before serving, put spinach in large bowl. Add crushed bacon and egg. Pour dressing on and toss until spinach is coated.

YIELD: 4 SERVINGS

THE JUNIOR LEAGUE OF WILKES-BARRE, PENNSYLVANIA

Hot Spinach Salad

1 pound fresh spinach
4 large fresh mushrooms
1 teaspoon sugar
¼ cup vinegar
4–5 slices bacon
4 tablespoons brandy
Salt and pepper

Clean spinach, removing stems, and place leaves in a salad bowl. Slice mushrooms finely and add to spinach. Add sugar and vinegar and toss well. Fry bacon until crisp and crumble. Add brandy to bacon in skillet, flame, and pour over the salad. Season to taste, toss well, and serve.

YIELD: 2–4 SERVINGS

THE JUNIOR LEAGUE OF SCRANTON, PENNSYLVANIA

Cold Steak Salad

2 pounds boneless sirloin,
cut into ½-inch cubes
½ cup butter
¾ pound mushrooms, sliced
1 9-ounce package frozen artichoke
hearts, cooked and cooled
1 cup finely diced celery
1 pint small cherry tomatoes
2 tablespoons chopped chives
2 tablespoons chopped parsley
2 cups Salad Dressing
2 teaspoons Dijon mustard

Recipe continues . . .

In a large skillet over high heat, sauté meat cubes, a few at a time, in the butter until browned on all sides. Drain meat on absorbent paper and put into salad bowl. Quickly sauté mushrooms in butter remaining in skillet and add to bowl with the meat. Add artichoke hearts, celery, tomatoes, chives, and parsley. Mix lightly.

Pour dressing mixed with mustard over salad; toss, cover, and marinate overnight.

YIELD: 6 SERVINGS

SALAD DRESSING:
2¼ cups oil
¾ cup wine vinegar
6 shallots, finely chopped
1/3 cup chopped parsley
1/3 cup chopped fresh dill weed
Salt and freshly ground black pepper
⅛ teaspoon Tabasco

Combine all ingredients in glass jar and shake. Store in refrigerator.

YIELD: ABOUT 3 CUPS

THE JUNIOR LEAGUE OF SUMMIT, NEW JERSEY

.   .   .   .

Layered Salad

1 package lemon-flavored gelatin
2 large bananas, sliced
1 8-ounce can crushed pineapple,
drained (reserve juice)
8 cherries, chopped
2 egg yolks
½ cup sugar
1 tablespoon flour
1-2 tablespoons butter
1 cup heavy cream, whipped

Make gelatin according to package directions and add fruit as it thickens. Pour into 8 x 8-inch pan.

Make dressing by mixing together egg yolks, sugar, flour, butter, and reserved pineapple juice. Cook until thick. Cool. Fold into whipped cream. Spread over the firm gelatin.

YIELD: 6 SERVINGS

Recipes by Request
THE JUNIOR LEAGUE OF GREATER WATERBURY, CONNECTICUT

. . . .

Strawberry Salad

2 packages strawberry-flavored gelatin
1½ cups boiling water
1 12-ounce package frozen strawberries
1 cup crushed pineapple
½ cup pecans
1 cup sour cream

Dissolve gelatin in water. Add strawberries. Chill until slightly congealed. Add pineapple and nuts; mix. Put half the mixture into oiled mold. Chill until firm. When set, mix the other half with sour cream. Gently pour into mold and chill until ready to serve.

YIELD: 6 SERVINGS

THE JUNIOR LEAGUE OF SUMMIT, NEW JERSEY

. . . .

Tabooley

1 cup bulgur (cracked wheat)
2 cups water
1 large bunch mint, chopped
2 large bunches parsley, chopped
3 cucumbers, peeled and chopped
6 medium tomatoes, peeled, seeded, and chopped
4 bunches green onions (including tops)
6 stalks celery, chopped
1 cup oil
1 cup lemon juice
1 teaspoon cumin
Salt to taste

Soak bulgur in water for at least 1 hour. Drain and squeeze out excess moisture. Combine with vegetables, oil, lemon juice, cumin, and salt. Mix thoroughly. Let marinate for 1 hour before serving.

YIELD: 8–10 SERVINGS

Show House Recipes
THE JUNIOR LEAGUE OF BINGHAMTON, NEW YORK

. . . .

Waldorf Cider Salad

½ cup seedless raisins
1 tablespoon unflavored gelatin
2 tablespoons lemon juice
1¾ cup apple cider
Salt to taste
1 large red apple
¾ cup diced celery
Salad greens
Mayonnaise
Sour cream

Cover raisins with water and boil 5 minutes. Drain and cool. Soften gelatin in lemon juice. Heat cider to boiling and dissolve the gelatin in it. Add salt to taste. Cool until slightly thickened but not set.

Core and dice apple. Fold raisins, apple, and celery into gelatin. Spoon into individual molds and chill until firm.

Unmold on crisp salad greens and serve with dressing made by blending equal parts of mayonnaise and sour cream.

YIELD: **6** SERVINGS

THE JUNIOR LEAGUE OF STAMFORD-NORWALK, CONNECTICUT

Salade de Cresson

½ cup olive oil
¼ cup wine vinegar
2 tablespoons heavy cream
½ teaspoon sugar
Salt to taste
Freshly ground pepper
½ pound fresh mushrooms, thinly sliced
1 bunch green onions (white part only),
sliced, or one small onion
2 bunches watercress
2 apples, peeled and diced
Chopped chervil

Recipe continues . . .

Combine the oil, vinegar, cream, sugar, salt, and pepper. Marinate the mushrooms and onion in the mixture for 1 hour.

Just before serving, arrange watercress on each plate. Stir the apple into the dressing. Spoon mixture onto cress. Top with a sprinkling of fresh herbs.

YIELD: **4** SERVINGS

Presenting Boston . . . A Cookbook
THE JUNIOR LEAGUE OF BOSTON, MASSACHUSETTS

·   ·   ·   ·   ·   ·   ·   ·   ·   ·   ·   ·   ·   ·   ·   ·   ·   ·

Wild Rice Salad

2 cups wild rice
1/3 cup olive oil
4 cups hot chicken broth
French dressing (vinaigrette)
2/3 cup thinly sliced water chestnuts
¼ cup sliced green onion
½ teaspoon salt
⅛ teaspoon pepper
¾ pound snow peas
½ pound fresh mushrooms, thinly sliced

Wash and soak wild rice for ½ hour. Drain and pat dry. Heat olive oil for 1 minute; add rice and cook, stirring, for about 5 minutes. Empty into casserole with tight cover along with the chicken broth. Cover and bake for 50–60 minutes in 325° oven. Rice should absorb all liquid, so let it sit on counter until it does so.

While rice is still warm, toss with 1/3 cup French dressing and let cool. Add water chestnuts, green onion, salt, pepper, and ¼ cup more dressing. Chill 1 hour.

Blanch snow peas for 30 seconds. Drain, refresh under cold water, and pat dry. (If fresh snow peas are not available, use frozen, but do not cook.) Cut into 1-inch pieces and toss with 2 tablespoons French dressing. Chill for 30 minutes. Add mushrooms, ¼ cup more dressing, and salt and pepper to taste; toss with rice mixture. Chill.

This may all be done in stages—the rice can be cooked the day before serving the salad.

YIELD: 10 SERVINGS

THE JUNIOR LEAGUE OF MORRISTOWN, NEW JERSEY

Zucchini Tomato Salad

2 large zucchini
2 large tomatoes
1 clove garlic, minced
1-2 teaspoons salt, or to taste
2 tablespoons wine vinegar
1/3 cup olive oil
⅛ teaspoon pepper
¼ teaspoon mixed Italian herbs
(oregano, parsley, etc.)
¼ teaspoon chili powder

Slice zucchini and tomatoes very, *very* thinly!
Mix all ingredients together. Chill thoroughly.

YIELD: 6 SERVINGS

Hudson River Hospitality
THE JUNIOR LEAGUE OF WESTCHESTER-ON-HUDSON, NEW YORK

Sweet and Sour Sauce for Greens

This recipe has passed through central Pennsylvania families for generations. It is especially interesting in the spring with young dandelion greens. If different greens are used, the recipe changes character.

4 slices bacon, cut into 1-inch squares
1/3 chopped onion
½ cup sugar
1/3 cup vinegar
3 quarts greens (spinach, chard,
dandelion), washed and torn loosely
into bite-size pieces
1 hard-boiled egg, grated or chopped

Fry bacon over high heat in saucepan or pot that is large enough to accommodate greens for tossing. Remove bacon bits when crisp. Drain on paper toweling. Add chopped onion to hot bacon drippings and reduce heat to medium. Cook onion 5 minutes, or until soft and golden. Add sugar and vinegar and cook at high heat until sugar is melted. Add greens and toss until wilted.

Remove from heat to serving dish and garnish with bacon and egg. Serve immediately.

YIELD: 4–6 SERVINGS

THE JUNIOR LEAGUE OF HARRISBURG, PENNSYLVANIA

Breads and Coffee Cakes

Steamed Brown Bread

1 cup unbleached flour
1 cup rye flour
1 cup yellow corn meal
1 teaspoon baking soda
½ teaspoon salt
½ cup seedless raisins
2/3 cup chopped walnuts
2 cups buttermilk
¾ cup dark molasses
Butter

Mix together the dry ingredients. Stir in raisins and nutmeats. Blend buttermilk and molasses in mixing bowl. Add dry ingredients and stir until well blended. Pour batter into three greased food cans or molds. Cover with aluminum foil and tie. Place molds on rack in kettle; pour in water to a depth of 1 inch. Cover and simmer over low heat 2½–3 hours. Add more hot water as necessary. Remove bread from cans, brush with a little melted butter, and cool on racks.

YIELD: 3 SMALL LOAVES

THE JUNIOR LEAGUE OF POUGHKEEPSIE, NEW YORK

Dill Bread

1 envelope active dry yeast
¼ cup water
1 cup small curd cottage cheese
2 tablespoons butter
1 tablespoon onion flakes
2 tablespoons sugar
1 teaspoon salt
1 tablespoon dill seed
¼ teaspoon baking soda
1 egg, beaten
2½ cups flour

Soften yeast in water. Put cottage cheese, butter, onion flakes, sugar, salt, dill seed, and baking soda in a medium saucepan and heat until just warm. Add yeast and egg to mixture. Add the flour a little at a time until dough is difficult to stir. Turn dough out on floured board and knead in the rest of the flour until dough is smooth. Put dough in a 2-quart casserole and let rise in warm place until double in bulk, about 2 hours. Bake at 350° for 30–40 minutes.

YIELD: 1 LOAF

THE JUNIOR LEAGUE OF WILKES-BARRE, PENNSYLVANIA

Honey Bread

1¼ cups milk
2 teaspoons salt
4 tablespoons butter
¼ cup light honey
¼ cup sugar
2 envelopes active dry yeast
½ cup lukewarm water (105–110°)
Pinch sugar
1 large egg
5 cups unsifted unbleached flour

Combine milk, salt, butter, honey, and ¼ cup sugar in a large pot and cook over low heat until the butter melts. Remove from heat.

Put yeast in the water with the pinch of sugar. Add the egg, flour, and yeast mixture to the heated milk and mix well.

Knead the dough for 10 minutes. Grease a mixing bowl and put dough in it. Cover with transparent film and place it in the oven with a bowl of hot water beneath. Let the dough rise until double in bulk, approximately 1 hour.

Remove dough from oven and divide in half. Knead each half about 1 minute and put into a greased loaf pan. Place pans in the oven with bowls of hot water beneath until the dough rises to 1 inch above the edge of the pans, approximately 1 hour.

Bake at 350° for 30 minutes or until bread tests done.

YIELD: 2 LOAVES

THE JUNIOR LEAGUE OF THE ORANGES AND SHORT HILLS, NEW JERSEY

Honey Whole Wheat Bread

4 cups scalded milk
¼ pound margarine
½ cup honey
½ cup dark brown sugar
4 teaspoons salt
2 envelopes active dry yeast or
2 cakes compressed yeast
½ cup lukewarm water (about 95°)
About 4 pounds stone ground
whole wheat flour

Combine first five ingredients in large mixing bowl. Mix well and cool to lukewarm. Soften yeast in water. (Adding 1 teaspoon sugar will speed the activation of the yeast.) Stir into the milk mixture. Gradually stir in flour as needed to make a stiff dough. (A wooden spoon is best for this.) Beat well after each addition.

Cover bowl with damp tea towel. Let rise in warm, draft-free place until double in bulk, about 1½ hours. Punch down. Knead dough on board or pastry cloth lightly sprinkled with flour until dough is smooth and elastic. Divide into four parts for small loaves; three parts for large loaves. Shape into loaves and place in greased loaf pans. Let rise until double in bulk, about 1 hour. Bake in 375° oven until done—40–50 minutes if you like it crusty. Remove from pans and cool on wire racks.

This bread is made with natural stone ground whole wheat flour which contains no preservatives, so it should be refrigerated if it is necessary to keep it awhile. It makes good toast, as well as being delicious plain with butter or for sandwiches.

YIELD: 3 LARGE LOAVES OR 4 SMALL LOAVES

Bicentennial Cookbook
THE JUNIOR LEAGUE OF PHILADELPHIA, PENNSYLVANIA

Thrifty Whole Wheat Bread

This recipe uses those leftover cereals that are sitting on your shelves getting stale. Some of the more sugared cereals would not be appropriate for use.

½ cup shortening
3 tablespoons salt
½ cup brown sugar
½ cup dark molasses
½ cup honey
2 cups wheat germ
2 or more cups leftover dry cereal
1½ cups dry milk
3 cups whole wheat flour
2 cups hot water
4 envelopes active dry yeast
3 cups warm water (110–115°)
4-8 cups unbleached white flour as needed

In a very large bowl, combine the first ten ingredients. Mix to melt shortening and blend. Meanwhile soften yeast in warm water.

Combine yeast mixture with flour mixture and beat until smooth. Add as much unbleached white flour as necessary to make a manageable dough. Turn dough out onto floured surface and knead until smooth, about 10 minutes.

Transfer dough to well-greased bowl. Turn dough so all sides are covered with oil. Place in a warm spot to double in bulk. Punch down and allow to rise a second time. Punch dough and shape into loaves. Allow to rise a third time.

Preheat oven to 425°. Bake loaves at that temperature for 10 minutes. Reduce heat to 325° and continue to bake for 40 minutes more, or until loaves sound hollow when tapped on bottom. Turn onto racks to cool.

YIELD: 4 LARGE LOAVES OR 6 SMALL LOAVES

THE JUNIOR LEAGUE OF ERIE, PENNSYLVANIA

Grape-Nut Shredded Wheat Bread

1 cup grape-nuts cereal
2 squares shredded wheat
½ cup molasses
½ cup brown sugar
½ cup shortening
3 teaspoons salt
2 cups boiling water
2 cups scalded milk
1 compressed yeast cake
8 or more cups flour

Combine first six ingredients in large bowl. Pour boiling water over; let stand 10 minutes. Add scalded milk and mix.

When lukewarm, add yeast cake and dissolve. Then add enough flour to form moderately stiff dough. Knead for 10 minutes. Let rise in greased bowl. Divide in three parts and form into loaves. Place in greased pans and allow to rise.

Bake at 350° for 45–50 minutes.

YIELD: 3 LOAVES

THE JUNIOR LEAGUE OF BANGOR, MAINE

Aunt Nana's Banana Bread

½ cup soft butter or margarine
1 teaspoon vanilla
1 cup sugar
2 eggs
4 medium ripe bananas, mashed
1 tablespoon milk
2 cups unsifted all-purpose flour
1 teaspoon baking soda
¼ teaspoon salt

Cream butter, vanilla, and sugar until light and fluffy. Beat in eggs.

Combine bananas and milk. Mix flour, soda, and salt. Blend dry ingredients into creamed mixture alternately with bananas. Turn into greased 9 x 5 x 3-inch loaf pan. Bake at 350° for 1 hour and 10 minutes, or until bread tests done.

YIELD: 1 LOAF

THE JUNIOR LEAGUE OF MONMOUTH COUNTY, NEW JERSEY

.   .   .   .

Cranberry Coffee Cake

¾ cup sugar
¼ cup soft butter
1 egg
½ cup milk
2 cups flour
2 teaspoons baking powder
¼ teaspoon salt
1½ cups cranberries
½ cup chopped walnuts

TOPPING:
2/3 cup brown sugar
1/3 cup flour
1 teaspoon cinnamon
1/3 cup melted butter

Mix together sugar, butter, and egg. Stir in milk. Sift together and add dry ingredients. Blend in cranberries and nuts. Spread batter into floured, well-greased 9 x 9-inch pan.

Mix topping ingredients together into crumbs and sprinkle over batter. Bake at 375° for 30–40 minutes, or until cake tester comes out clean.

YIELD: 8–12 SERVINGS

THE JUNIOR LEAGUE OF GREATER BRIDGEPORT, CONNECTICUT

Old-Fashioned Hot Water Gingerbread

½ cup sugar
½ cup melted butter
1 cup molasses
1 egg
2½ cups sifted flour
1½ teaspoons baking soda
½ teaspoon salt
1 teaspoon ginger
1½ teaspoons cinnamon
½ teaspoon cloves
½ teaspoon nutmeg
1 cup boiling water

Recipe continues . . .

Combine sugar, butter, molasses, and egg and beat well. Sift together dry ingredients and stir into egg mixture. Lastly stir in the hot water.

Bake in two greased and floured loaf pans at 375° for 30–40 minutes, or until cake tester comes out clean.

Serve with a topping of whipped cream if desired.

YIELD: 2 LOAVES

THE JUNIOR LEAGUE OF GREATER BRIDGEPORT, CONNECTICUT

Nutmeg Tea Cake

2 cups light brown sugar
2 cups flour
½ pound butter, softened (2 sticks)
1 egg
1 teaspoon nutmeg
1 cup sour cream
1 teaspoon baking soda
½ cup chopped nuts

Preheat oven to 350°.

With fingers, blend brown sugar, flour, and butter into crumbs. Spread half the crumbs in a greased 9-inch square pan.

Stir egg, nutmeg, and sour cream mixed with the soda into remaining crumbs. Pour batter over crumbs in pan and sprinkle with chopped nuts.

Bake for 35–40 minutes.

YIELD: 9-INCH SQUARE CAKE

THE JUNIOR LEAGUE OF THE ORANGES AND SHORT HILLS, NEW JERSEY

Oatmeal Cake

1½ cups boiling water
1 cup quick oats
½ cup butter
1 cup brown sugar
1 cup granulated sugar
2 eggs
1½ cups sifted flour
1 teaspoon cinnamon
1 teaspoon nutmeg
1 teaspoon baking soda
½ teaspoon salt

Pour water over oats. Set aside.

Cream butter and sugars. Beat in eggs and then add water and oatmeal mixture.

Sift flour and spices together with baking soda and salt. Stir into other mixture. Spoon into greased 13 x 9-inch pan and bake at 350° for 30–35 minutes. Spread topping on cake and broil until bubbly and slightly brown.

TOPPING:

½ cup sugar
¼ cup brown sugar
1 cup coconut
1 cup nuts
6 tablespoons margarine
¼ cup milk
¼ teaspoon vanilla

Heat all ingredients, except vanilla, until bubbly. Remove from heat and stir in vanilla.

YIELD: 1 13 x 9-INCH CAKE

THE JUNIOR LEAGUE OF WILLIAMSPORT, PENNSYLVANIA

Sour Cream Pound Cake

½ pint sour cream
¼ teaspoon baking soda
½ pound butter
3 scant cups sugar
1 teaspoon almond extract
5-6 egg yolks
2½ cups flour
5-6 egg whites

Mix the sour cream and baking soda; let stand while mixing remaining batter.

Cream together the butter and sugar. Add the extract and egg yolks, one at a time, beating well after each addition. Sift flour three times and stir in alternately with the sour cream mixture. Beat the egg whites until stiff and fold in.

Bake in a greased 8-inch tube pan 1½ hours at 325°.

YIELD: 1 8-INCH CAKE

THE JUNIOR LEAGUE OF YORK, PENNSYLVANIA

· · · · · · · · · · · · · · · · ·

Pumpkin Bread

1½ cups sugar
¼ teaspoon baking powder
1 teaspoon baking soda
¾ teaspoon salt
½ teaspoon cloves
½ teaspoon cinnamon
1 2/3 cups flour
½ cup oil
½ cup water
1 cup mashed, cooked pumpkin
2 eggs

Mix all ingredients together and pour into a greased loaf pan. Bake at 350° for 70 minutes, or until the bread tests done.

YIELD: 1 LOAF

THE JUNIOR LEAGUE OF WILLIAMSPORT, PENNSYLVANIA

Grandma's Raisin Bread

1 cup raisins
1 teaspoon baking soda
1 cup boiling water
1½ cups flour
½ cup sugar
½ teaspoon salt
1 egg
1 tablespoon salad oil

In a small bowl, combine raisins and soda. Add water, cover, and set aside until cool.

In a medium-size bowl, stir together flour, sugar, and salt. Mix in raisins with liquid, egg, and salad oil. Stir until mixed.

Turn into a greased and floured 9 x 5-inch loaf pan and bake at 350° for 35–45 minutes.

YIELD: 1 LOAF

THE JUNIOR LEAGUE OF GREATER UTICA, NEW YORK

Rhubarb Bread

¾ cup dark brown sugar
1/3 cup salad oil
1 egg
½ teaspoon baking soda
½ teaspoon salt
1 teaspoon vanilla
½ cup sour milk
1¼ cups flour
1 cup fresh or frozen rhubarb
¼ cup granulated sugar
¾ tablespoon butter

Beat together brown sugar, oil, and egg. Mix soda, salt, vanilla, and sour milk; add to first mixture. Stir in flour and rhubarb.

Pour batter into greased and floured loaf pan. Sprinkle top with mixture of sugar and butter. Bake in 350° oven for 1 hour. Let stand about 10 minutes before removing from pan.

YIELD: 1 LOAF

THE JUNIOR LEAGUE OF BANGOR, MAINE

Sour Cream Coffee Cake

¼ *pound butter or margarine*
1 cup granulated sugar
2 eggs
1½ cups flour
1½ teaspoons baking powder
1 teaspoon vanilla
½ pint sour cream
1 teaspoon baking soda
1 teaspoon cinnamon
½ cup chopped nuts
¼ cup brown sugar

Cream together the butter, granulated sugar, and eggs. Add the flour, baking powder, and vanilla. Beat and mix well. Mix the baking soda with the sour cream and add to flour mixture. In a separate bowl, mix together the cinnamon, chopped nuts, and brown sugar.

Grease an 8-inch tube pan and put in half the cinnamon mixture, then the batter, then the rest of the cinnamon mixture. With a knife, cut through the mixture, turning pan five times. Bake at 350° for 60–65 minutes. Cool in pan for 1 hour.

YIELD: 1 8-INCH CAKE

THE JUNIOR LEAGUE OF YORK, PENNSYLVANIA

Pennsylvania Dutch Spice Cake

2 cups brown sugar
1 cup shortening
2 eggs
1 cup buttermilk
Pinch salt
2 teaspoons cinnamon
1 teaspoon cloves
1 teaspoon allspice
1 teaspoon baking soda
2½ cups flour

Cream brown sugar and shortening. Beat in eggs, one at a time. Stir in buttermilk. Sift dry ingredients and add slowly to buttermilk mixture. Beat thoroughly. Pour into greased loaf pan and bake at 350° for 1 hour.

YIELD: 1 LOAF CAKE

THE JUNIOR LEAGUE OF THE LEHIGH VALLEY, PENNSYLVANIA

Streusel-Filled Coffee Cake

FILLING:

½ cup brown sugar

2 teaspoons flour

2 teaspoons cinnamon

2 teaspoons melted butter

½ cup nuts

CAKE:

1½ cups flour

3 teaspoons baking powder

¼ teaspoon salt

¾ cup sugar

¼ cup shortening

1 egg

1/3 cup milk

1 teaspoon vanilla

To make filling, mix sugar, flour, and cinnamon; blend in butter, then add nuts.

To make batter, sift dry ingredients, cut in shortening; add egg and milk, then vanilla.

Pour half the batter mixture into a buttered 8-inch pan and sprinkle with half the filling. Add remaining batter and filling mixture, either in one or many layers. Bake for 20–30 minutes at 350°.

YIELD: 6–8 SERVINGS

THE JUNIOR LEAGUE OF TROY, NEW YORK

Swedish Coffee Bread

2 cups milk
3 envelopes active dry yeast
1 cup sugar
¼ pound butter or margarine
Grated rind of 1 lemon
1 teaspoon salt
1 teaspoon crushed cardamom seeds
6¼ cups flour
2 eggs, well beaten
1 teaspoon crumbled saffron* (optional)
1 egg white, beaten
½ cup or more finely chopped
blanched slivered almonds
1/3 cup sugar

Warm milk to 110–115° on yeast thermometer. Add yeast with a teaspoon of the sugar. Let stand 5–10 minutes.

Meanwhile, in a large bowl beat butter, lemon rind, remaining sugar, salt, and cardamom until light and fluffy. Add 4 cups flour. Beat very hard. Add eggs, saffron if desired, and yeast mixture. Add remaining flour and turn dough onto a lightly floured surface. Allow to rest 5–10 minutes.

Knead 5–8 minutes. Place dough in a large greased bowl. Cover with wax paper and a clean dishtowel and let stand in a warm place (about 80°) until dough is doubled, about 2 hours.

Punch down with fist; pull edges into center and turn dough over in bowl. Cover and let rise again until nearly double. Punch down again and place on floured surface.

Divide dough into two portions. Shape into loaves. Lightly grease two baking sheets; place loaves onto sheets. Cover with towels and let rise about 45 minutes, or until double in bulk.

---

*Into a small cup, crumble enough saffron to yield 1 teaspoon. Pour about 2 tablespoons hot milk over the saffron. Stir and set aside for 2–3 hours. Strain the saffron from the milk before adding it with the eggs.

Brush loaves with beaten egg white. Sprinkle each loaf with half of the mixture of chopped almonds and 1/3 cup sugar.

Bake at 375° for 15–25 minutes, or until golden. Cool completely on cooling racks.

YIELD: 2 LOAVES

THE JUNIOR LEAGUE OF SYRACUSE, NEW YORK

· · · · · · · · · · · · · · · ·

Swedish Tea Ring

3¼–3½ cups all-purpose flour
1 envelope active dry yeast
1 cup milk
6 tablespoons butter or margarine
1/3 cup granulated sugar
½ teaspoon salt
1 egg
Confectioners' sugar

In large mixer bowl, combine 2 cups of the flour and the yeast. In saucepan, beat together milk, butter, granulated sugar, and salt until just warm (115–120°), stirring constantly, until butter almost melts. Add to dry mixture in mixer bowl. Add egg and beat at low speed of electric mixer for ½ minute, scraping bowl constantly. Beat 3 minutes at high speed.

By hand, stir in enough of the remaining flour to make a soft dough. Knead on lightly floured surface until smooth, about 3–5 minutes, adding a small amount of additional flour if too sticky. Shape into a ball. Place in a greased bowl; turn once to grease surface. Cover and let rise in warm place until doubled, about 1 hour. Punch dough down. Let rest 10 minutes.

Recipe continues . . .

Roll into an 18 x 12-inch rectangle. Spread with filling. Roll lengthwise, jelly-roll style. Pinch to seal edge. Place seam side down and form into a ring. Place on a greased 15-inch round baking tray. Cut with kitchen shears every ½ inch to within ½ inch of bottom. Gently pull slices alternately to the left and to the right.

Let ring rise in a warm place until nearly doubled, about 45 minutes. Bake at 375° for 15–20 minutes. While still hot, sprinkle with confectioners' sugar.

ALMOND FILLING:
2 tablespoons butter
1/3 cup granulated sugar
¼ cup ground almonds
¼ teaspoon almond extract

Cream the butter until light and fluffy, gradually adding the sugar. Stir in the ground almonds and the almond extract.

YIELD: 1 LARGE COFFEE BREAD

THE JUNIOR LEAGUE OF NEW BRITAIN, CONNECTICUT

. . . .

Pennsylvania Dutch Funnel Cake

1 1/3 cups flour
¼ teaspoon salt
½ teaspoon baking soda
¾ teaspoon baking powder
2 tablespoons sugar
1 egg
2/3 cup milk
¼ teaspoon vanilla
Cooking oil
Confectioners' sugar

Sift flour, salt, baking soda, baking powder, and sugar. Beat egg; blend in milk and vanilla. Add to dry mixture and beat until smooth.

In a large frying pan or skillet, preferably iron, pour enough cooking oil to cover the bottom by ½ inch. Heat to just short of smoking, about 365°. Carefully pour batter into a small funnel while holding finger over the bottom of the funnel. Drop the batter through the funnel into the oil by releasing the finger. Move the funnel around to form a circle, star, or zigzag patterns—do not fill the entire bottom of pan. The cake will swell slightly. Cook for 30 seconds, then turn with tongs. Cook 30 seconds more, or until crisp and golden. Drain on absorbent paper. Sprinkle with confectioners' sugar and serve.

YIELD: 4–6 SERVINGS

THE JUNIOR LEAGUE OF HARRISBURG, PENNSYLVANIA

· · · · · · · · · · · · · · · · · · · ·

Sue's Refrigerator Rolls

2 envelopes active dry yeast
2 cups warm water (105–115°)
¼ cup shortening
½ cup sugar
1 egg
2 teaspoons salt
6½–7 cups flour

In a mixing bowl, dissolve yeast in warm water. Add shortening, sugar, egg, and salt. Mix thoroughly, mashing the shortening. Add half the flour. Blend with an electric mixer. Add remaining flour, 1 cup at a time, working it into the dough with hands.

Place dough in greased bowl; turn once to bring greased side of dough to top. Cover loosely with foil or plastic wrap and let rise in

Recipe continues . . .

refrigerator 2 hours or more. Punch dough down at least once during that period.

Two hours before baking, shape into rolls and arrange on oiled baking sheet. Cover; let rise in warm place until double. Bake for 15 minutes at 400°. If browner top is desired, brush tops with melted butter or milk before baking.

This dough recipe keeps in refrigerator about three days.

VARIATION:

Recipe can be used to make hamburger rolls. Roll out dough and cut with "old-fashioned" size glass. Proceed as above.

YIELD: 3 DOZEN ROLLS

THE JUNIOR LEAGUE OF ALBANY, NEW YORK

. . . .

Original Refrigerator Rolls

1 cup milk
1 cup margarine
¼ cup warm water (100°)
1 tablespoon sugar
1 cake or envelope active dry yeast
2 eggs
½ cup sugar
1 teaspoon salt
1 teaspoon baking powder
4½ cups flour
Melted butter

Scald and cool the milk and margarine. In a small bowl, mix the warm water, 1 tablespoon sugar, and yeast.

In a large bowl, beat together eggs, ½ cup sugar, and salt. Add the milk and yeast mixtures to the egg mixture. Mix in baking powder and flour. Cover bowl with damp cloth and refrigerate overnight. Remove from refrigerator 1 hour before rolling.

Divide dough into four balls. Roll each ball into a circle and cut each into twelve (or sixteen) wedge-shaped pieces. Roll each wedge, starting at wide end, to form a crescent. Brush each with melted butter and place on lightly greased cookie sheet. Cover rolls with damp cloth and leave at room temperature at least 4 hours.
Bake at 400° for 8–10 minutes.

YIELD: **48–64** ROLLS

THE JUNIOR LEAGUE OF ROCHESTER, NEW YORK

Frosty Morning Bran Muffins

1 cup whole-bran cereal
1 cup boiling water
1½ cups sugar
½ cup melted shortening
2 eggs, beaten
2 cups buttermilk
2½ cups unsifted flour
2½ teaspoons baking soda
1 teaspoon salt
2 cups bran flake cereal
1 cup raisins

In a small pan, mix cereal and boiling water. Cover and set aside.

In a large mixing bowl, cream sugar and shortening. Beat in eggs, then stir in reserved bran mixture and buttermilk.

Sift together flour, soda, and salt right into mixing bowl. Stir in bran flakes and raisins.

Fill greased muffin tins two-thirds full and bake at 400° for 20 minutes.

Recipe continues . . .

Batter will keep 4 weeks, tightly covered, in the refrigerator.

YIELD: 30 MUFFINS

THE JUNIOR LEAGUE OF GREATER UTICA, NEW YORK

. . . .

Popovers

1 cup milk
1 cup all-purpose flour
Dash salt
2 eggs

Mix all ingredients together by hand. Disregard lumps. (Do not use a mixer or popovers will not rise.) Pour into cold, greased muffin tins, filling each cup half full. Place in a cold oven. Set the oven at 450° and bake for 30 minutes. Serve immediately.

These are great for breakfast, brunch, or with roast beef.

YIELD: 6 SERVINGS

THE JUNIOR LEAGUE OF HAMILTON-BURLINGTON, ONTARIO

. . . .

Squash Muffins

2 cups sifted flour
2 teaspoons baking powder
1/2 teaspoon salt
1/2 cup sugar
1/4 teaspoon cinnamon
1/4 teaspoon allspice
1 egg, beaten
1 cup mashed winter squash
(butternut or acorn)
1 cup milk

Blend dry ingredients in large mixing bowl. Beat egg, add squash and milk, and blend. Add squash mixture to dry ingredients and stir just until ingredients are moistened. Fill greased muffin tins three-quarters full. Bake in 400° oven for 20–25 minutes.

YIELD: 18 MUFFINS

THE JUNIOR LEAGUE OF POUGHKEEPSIE, NEW YORK

Desserts

PICK YOUR OWN

STRAWBERRIES

Apple Country Kuchen

¹/₂ cup margarine
1 cup sugar
2 eggs
2 cups flour
1 teaspoon baking powder
1 teaspoon baking soda
¹/₂ teaspoon salt
1 cup sour cream
1 teaspoon vanilla
2 medium apples, peeled and thinly sliced
1 teaspoon cinnamon
¹/₄ cup sugar

Cream margarine, sugar, and eggs. Mix flour, baking powder, baking soda, and salt. Mix sour cream and vanilla. Combine the three mixtures alternately until smooth.

Pour evenly into two greased 9-inch cake pans. Top batter with sliced apples, cinnamon, and sugar. Bake at 350° for 35–40 minutes.

YIELD: 2 9-INCH CAKES

THE JUNIOR LEAGUE OF GREATER UTICA, NEW YORK

.   .   .   .

Bavarian Apple Torte

¹/₂ cup margarine
1 cup sugar minus 1¹/₂ tablespoons
³/₄ teaspoon vanilla
1 cup flour
1 8-ounce package cream cheese, softened
1 egg
¹/₂ teaspoon cinnamon
4 cups peeled, sliced apple
¹/₄ cup sliced almonds

Cream margarine, 1/3 cup sugar, and ¼ teaspoon vanilla. Blend in flour. Spread dough in bottom of a greased and floured 9-inch spring-form pan and up the sides 1½ inches.

Combine cream cheese with ¼ cup sugar. Add egg and ½ teaspoon vanilla; mix. Pour into pastry.

Combine 1/3 cup sugar, cinnamon, and apple slices. Toss well. Arrange attractively (in circles) over cream cheese mixture and sprinkle with almonds.

Bake at 400° for 30 minutes. (Place sheet of aluminum foil under spring-form pan before baking.)

Let cool before removing sides of pan. Store in refrigerator but set out a few minutes before serving.

YIELD: 10–12 SERVINGS

Show House Recipes
THE JUNIOR LEAGUE OF BINGHAMTON, NEW YORK

Apricot Whip

1 cup cooked dried apricots
½ cup cream
3 egg whites
1 tablespoon apricot brandy

Put 1 cup apricots without juice through a strainer or food mill. Whip separately the cream and the egg whites until stiff. Add the brandy to the apricot pulp, then mix with the whipped cream. Lastly, fold in egg whites, put in glass bowl for serving, and chill for several hours.

YIELD: 4 SERVINGS

Cooks Book
THE JUNIOR LEAGUE OF GREATER NEW HAVEN, CONNECTICUT

Bananas Barbara

4 tablespoons brown sugar
2 tablespoons butter
2 ripe bananas, peeled and sliced lengthwise
1 ounce banana liqueur
2 ounces brandy
4 scoops vanilla ice cream

Melt brown sugar and butter in a skillet. Add bananas and sauté until tender. Pour on liqueur and brandy. Flame. Baste with liquid until flame is out. Serve immediately over ice cream.

YIELD: 4 SERVINGS

THE JUNIOR LEAGUE OF KINGSTON, NEW YORK

. . . .

Berry Baked Alaska Flambé

1 8-9-inch round sponge cake
1 cup fresh or frozen strawberries or
raspberries (if frozen, drain first)
5 egg whites
2/3 cup sugar
1 quart ice cream
½ cup brandy or cognac

Preheat oven to 500°.

Cut a circle in top of cake 1 inch deep and 2 inches smaller in diameter than diameter of cake. Remove circle and use for another purpose. Fill center of cake with berries.

Make meringue: Beat egg whites until soft peaks form. Gradually add sugar and beat until meringue is stiff.

Scoop ice cream on top of berries. Spread meringue over ice cream and down sides of cake, making sure all ice cream and cake are covered with a thick layer. Sprinkle lightly with sugar. Bake in preheated oven about 3 minutes, or until meringue is golden.

To flambe: Heat brandy or cognac in saucepan (do *not* boil). Ignite. When flaming, pour contents of pan on top of browned Alaska, turn out lights, and present immediately.

YIELD: 8 SERVINGS

THE JUNIOR LEAGUE OF MONMOUTH COUNTY, NEW JERSEY

Blueberry Buckle

2 cups sifted flour
2 teaspoons baking powder
½ teaspoon salt
¼ cup margarine
¾ cup sugar
1 teaspoon vanilla
1 large egg
½ cup milk
1 15-ounce can blueberries

TOPPING:
½ cup sugar
1/3 cup flour
½ teaspoon cinnamon
¼ cup soft margarine

Recipe continues . . .

Sift together flour, baking powder, and salt. Cream margarine, sugar, and vanilla. Add egg and beat well. *Stir* in sifted ingredients in three additions alternately with milk. Fold in drained blueberries and turn into greased and floured 8 x 8-inch pan.

Combine topping ingredients until crumbly. Sprinkle on top of batter and bake at 375° for 40 minutes.

YIELD: 10 SERVINGS

THE JUNIOR LEAGUE OF SCHENECTADY, NEW YORK

Iced Blueberries Brûlée

1 quart blueberries or other fruit
1 tablespoon kirsch
3 tablespoons brandy
1 pint heavy cream, whipped
1 cup brown sugar

Cover bottom of a 3-quart soufflé dish with berries. Add kirsch and brandy to cover. Spread whipped cream evenly over coated berries. Sprinkle with brown sugar.

When just ready to serve, place under broiler to carmelize the sugar. Don't let sugar burn.

YIELD: 8 SERVINGS

Greenwich Recommends
THE JUNIOR LEAGUE OF GREENWICH, CONNECTICUT

Carrot Pudding

1 cup sifted flour
½ teaspoon baking soda
1 teaspoon baking powder
½ teaspoon salt
½ cup shortening
½ cup brown sugar
2 cups grated raw carrot
2 eggs, unbeaten
¼ cup orange juice
Rind of ½ orange, grated

Sift flour, baking soda, baking powder, and salt together. Cream together shortening and brown sugar. Mix together the carrot, eggs, orange juice, and orange rind. Combine the carrot mixture with the sugar and shortening; mix well. Gradually add the dry ingredients to this mixture; blend well.

Pour into a greased casserole. Bake at 350° for 45 minutes.

YIELD: 6–8 SERVINGS

THE JUNIOR LEAGUE OF WILLIAMSPORT, PENNSYLVANIA

· · · · · · · · · · · · · · · · · · ·

Cheese Romanoff

¼ pound sweet butter, softened
¾ cup sugar
1 pound pot cheese
1¼ cups sour cream
2 teaspoons vanilla
Fresh strawberries

Recipe continues . . .

Beat butter and sugar together. Add the cheese, beating with an electric mixer at medium speed. Add sour cream and vanilla and continue beating until smooth.

Spoon mixture on round dish to form a mound and refrigerate at least 4 hours. Garnish with strawberries. Serve very cold with Rasberry Sauce.

RASPBERRY SAUCE:
1 10-ounce package frozen raspberries
½ cup sugar
2 tablespoons lemon juice

Cook all ingredients in a small saucepan over a low heat for 30 minutes. Strain and refrigerate.

YIELD: 6 SERVINGS

THE JUNIOR LEAGUE OF THE LEHIGH VALLEY, PENNSYLVANIA

.   .   .   .

Cherries Jubilee

¾ cup currant jelly
2 cups pitted Bing cherries
½ cup brandy
1½ quarts vanilla ice cream

In an electric skillet, melt jelly over low heat. Add fruit. Pour brandy into center of fruit; heat by stirring. Light carefully with match. Spoon over ice cream.

YIELD: 6 SERVINGS

Recipes by Request
THE JUNIOR LEAGUE OF GREATER WATERBURY, CONNECTICUT

.   .   .   .

Chocolate Bread Pudding

2 cups bread crumbs
2 cups scalded milk
2/3 cup sugar
2 ounces unsweetened chocolate, melted
1 teaspoon vanilla
½ cup chopped walnuts (optional)
Whipped cream (optional)

Soak the bread crumbs in the scalded milk; add the sugar, chocolate, vanilla, and nuts. Mix well and bake in a buttered 1-quart baking dish at 350° for 1 hour, or until set.

Serve hot with whipped cream if desired.

YIELD: 6 SERVINGS

THE JUNIOR LEAGUE OF STAMFORD-NORWALK, CONNECTICUT

Frozen Chocolate Mousse

1 package ladyfingers
18 ounces semisweet chocolate pieces
3 tablespoons instant coffee
½ cup boiling water
6 egg yolks
½ cup sugar
1 teaspoon vanilla
6 egg whites
1½ cups heavy cream

Recipe continues . . .

Split ladyfingers and line the sides of an oiled 9-inch spring-form pan, with rounded sides of ladyfingers against the pan.

Melt chocolate in double boiler over hot water, stirring occasionally. Dissolve instant coffee in the ½ cup boiling water. Set chocolate and coffee aside to cool.

Beat egg yolks in small bowl of electric mixer at high speed until foamy. Gradually beat in sugar until mixture is thick. Reduce speed to low and beat in vanilla, coffee, and melted chocolate.

Beat egg whites in large bowl until stiff and glossy peaks form. Whip 1½ cups heavy cream in another bowl.

Stir about 1 cup of beaten egg whites into the chocolate mixture to lighten it. Then fold the chocolate mixture into the remaining egg whites. Fold in the whipped cream. Spoon and pour into lined spring-form pan.

Cover with foil and a freezer bag and freeze until firm. (It can be stored in the freezer as long as a month.)

Run a knife gently around the sides before removing the ring. Let the mousse sit in the refrigerator 2–3 hours before serving. To serve, remove sides of pan and place dessert on a large serving plate.

YIELD: 12–16 SERVINGS

THE JUNIOR LEAGUE OF MONMOUTH COUNTY, NEW JERSEY

· · · · · · · · · · · · · · · · · · · ·

Patsy's Chocolate Rum Cream

1 cup sugar
¼ cup strong coffee
½ cup water
6 egg yolks
6 ounces semisweet chocolate, melted
3 tablespoons dark rum
2½ cups heavy cream
Confectioners' sugar

Make syrup of sugar, coffee, and water. Cool. Beat egg yolks in double boiler and slowly beat in syrup. Cook over hot water until creamy, stirring constantly. Remove from heat and add chocolate and rum. Whip the cream and fold in 2 cups. Pour into mold and chill several hours. To serve, unmold, sprinkle with confectioners' sugar, and pass the remaining ½ cup whipped cream.

YIELD: 6 SERVINGS

Recipes by Request
THE JUNIOR LEAGUE OF GREATER WATERBURY, CONNECTICUT

.   .   .   .

Coffee Parfait

¾ *cup sugar*
1/3 cup water
4 egg yolks
Dash salt
2 cups heavy cream
2 tablespoons instant coffee
2 teaspoons vanilla
1 1-ounce square bitter chocolate, shaved or grated*

Cook sugar and water in a saucepan until syrup spins a thread or it reaches 230° on a candy thermometer.

Meanwhile, beat egg yolks and salt thoroughly. Beat hot syrup into egg yolks in a thin gradual stream and continue beating until cool.

Beat heavy cream with coffee and vanilla until cream holds definite peaks. Fold in cooled yolk mixture along with three-quarters of the chocolate. Reserve remaining chocolate for garnish.

Spoon into ramekins and freeze until firm. Remove from freezer and put in refrigerator about 1 hour before serving.

*Put the squares of bitter chocolate in the freezer for several hours; it is then easy to shave with a heavy knife.

Recipe continues . . .

YIELD: 12 SERVINGS

The Everyday Gourmet
THE JUNIOR LEAGUE OF NORTHERN WESTCHESTER, BEDFORD HILLS, NEW YORK

• • • • • • • • • • • • • • • • •

Frozen Grand Marnier Mousse

2 egg whites
Pinch salt
6 tablespoons sugar
1 cup heavy cream
¼ cup Grand Marnier

BERRY SAUCE:
1 10-ounce package frozen strawberries or raspberries
Grand Marnier to taste

Beat egg whites with salt to a soft peak, then gradually beat in ¼ cup sugar until meringue is stiff and shiny. Whip cream until stiff, then beat in remaining sugar. Gently stir in Grand Marnier. Fold in egg whites.

Turn into 1-quart mold or soufflé dish. Freeze until firm.

Defrost fruit just enough to drain excess juices. Purée in blender until smooth. Put through sieve to remove seeds. Add Grand Marnier (or any favorite liqueur) to taste. Spoon over frozen mousse before serving.

YIELD: 6–8 SERVINGS

Show House Recipes
THE JUNIOR LEAGUE OF BINGHAMTON, NEW YORK

• • • • • • • • • • • • • • • • •

Easy Indian Pudding

2 tablespoons butter
4 tablespoons corn meal
1 teaspoon cinnamon
Dash each nutmeg and salt
½ cup molasses
¼ cup honey or sugar
1 quart milk
½ cup raisins

Grease 1½-quart baking dish with butter.

Mix dry ingredients with molasses and honey. Scald milk to 170°. Add milk to dry ingredients and blend. Add raisins.

Pour into prepared dish and bake at 300–350° for 2–4 hours. Test as for custard. The longer the cooking, the better the flavor.

Serve cool or cold with heavy whipped cream or ice cream.

YIELD: 6–8 SERVINGS

THE JUNIOR LEAGUE OF BANGOR, MAINE

Everett's Lemon Bread Pudding

10 slices bread, trimmed
1 quart milk
6 egg yolks
2 cups sugar
4 tablespoons grated lemon rind
½ cup lemon juice
½ teaspoon vanilla

Recipe continues . . .

MERINGUE:

6 egg whites
½ cup sugar
½ teaspoon vanilla

Soak bread in milk, then crumble with fingers. Beat yolks with sugar and grated lemon rind. Add lemon juice slowly, then vanilla. Blend well. Combine this mixture with bread mixture. Turn into greased casserole and place in pan of hot water. Cook at 350° for 1 hour, or until knife inserted in center comes out clean. Cool.

May be prepared 3–4 hours ahead before serving.

Whip egg whites until stiff with sugar and vanilla. Top pudding with meringue and brown briefly under broiler.

YIELD: 8–10 SERVINGS

THE JUNIOR LEAGUE OF SUMMIT, NEW JERSEY

.   .   .   .

Fresh Lemon Charlotte Russe

1 tablespoon unflavored gelatin
½ cup fresh lemon juice
4 eggs, separated
1½ cups sugar
Pinch salt
3 tablespoons butter
1½ teaspoons grated lemon peel
1 teaspoon vanilla
2 packages ladyfingers
2 cups heavy cream
Fresh strawberries for garnish

Soften gelatin in lemon juice. Beat egg yolks with 1 cup sugar until thick. Add salt. Turn into the top of a double boiler. Cook over hot, but not boiling water, stirring until thick, about 5–10 minutes. Add the butter while stirring. Once thickened, add lemon peel and vanilla. Set aside to cool.

Line bottom and sides of 9-inch spring-form pan with ladyfingers.

Beat 1 cup of the heavy cream until stiff. Beat egg whites until stiff. In a large bowl, fold cream and egg whites into cooled lemon mixture. Pour into prepared spring-form pan and chill overnight.

Before serving, remove side of pan and place russe on crystal plate or silver tray. Garnish with remaining cup of cream, whipped, using a pastry bag, and fresh strawberries.

YIELD: 6 SERVINGS

THE JUNIOR LEAGUE OF BRONXVILLE, NEW YORK

. . . .

Pennsylvania Dutch Lemon Cups

1 cup granulated sugar
4 tablespoons flour
⅛ teaspoon salt
5 tablespoons lemon juice
Grated rind of 1 lemon
3 egg yolks, well beaten
1½ cups milk
2 tablespoons melted butter
3 egg whites, stiffly beaten

Combine sugar, flour, and salt; add lemon juice and rind. Add egg yolks, milk, and butter. Mix well. Fold in egg whites. Pour into greased custard cups. Set cups in a pan of warm water that comes halfway up sides of cups. Bake at 325° for 45 minutes.

When ready to serve, turn out of cups so custard falls over the cake part.

YIELD: 6–8 CUPS

THE JUNIOR LEAGUE OF THE LEHIGH VALLEY, PENNSYLVANIA

. . . .

Macaroon Glacé Parisienne

1 pint vanilla ice cream, softened
1 pint raspberry ice, softened
1 cup heavy cream, whipped
1 2-pint box whole strawberries
2 cups crushed macaroons
½ cup chopped blanched almonds
½ cup Grand Marnier

Mix together ice cream and raspberry ice. Add whipped cream and stir well. Add strawberries, crushed macaroons, and almonds. Mix well and add Grand Marnier. Freeze again.

Remove to refrigerator 30 minutes before serving.

YIELD: 12 SERVINGS

Entirely Entertaining
THE JUNIOR LEAGUE OF MONTCLAIR-NEWARK, NEW JERSEY

. . . .

Maple Mousse

Each spring thousands of trees in the Erie area are tapped and the sap is made into rich and wonderful maple syrup. Young children on school trips can hardly wait for this annual field trip.

1 envelope unflavored gelatin
¼ cup cold water
1 cup maple syrup
½ cup milk
3 egg yolks, lightly beaten
¼ teaspoon salt
½ cup boiling water
3 egg whites, stiffly beaten
½ teaspoon vanilla

Soften gelatin in cold water. In top of a double boiler, combine the maple syrup, milk, egg yolks, and salt. Dissolve gelatin in boiling water and add to maple mixture. Cook over just simmering water until mixture thickens slightly. Stir constantly and keep water from boiling or the egg yolks will curdle.

Remove maple mixture from heat and cool. When cool, fold in the beaten egg whites and vanilla. Turn into a 4-cup mold. Chill until firm. Serve with whipped cream.

YIELD: 6 SERVINGS

THE JUNIOR LEAGUE OF ERIE, PENNSYLVANIA

Mandarin Orange Bread Pudding

½ cup butter
1 cup sugar
4 eggs
1 11-ounce can Mandarin oranges, drained
1 13-ounce can crushed pineapple, drained
6 slices bread, cubed

Cream butter and sugar. Add eggs, one at a time, mixing well. Add remaining ingredients and mix. Place in greased 2-quart casserole and bake, uncovered, at 350° for 50–60 minutes.

YIELD: 6 SERVINGS

THE JUNIOR LEAGUE OF WILMINGTON, DELAWARE

Baked Peach Tapioca

¼ cup minute tapioca
⅛ teaspoon salt
¼ cup sugar + 1 tablespoon
2 cups milk
2 egg yolks, lightly beaten
5 or more fresh peaches
2 egg whites
¼ cup sugar + 1 tablespoon
Whipped cream

Mix tapioca, salt, ¼ cup sugar, milk, and egg yolks in saucepan. Let stand about 5 minutes while you peel, pit, and slice the peaches into a greased 2-quart baking dish. Sprinkle 1 tablespoon sugar on the peaches.

Cook tapioca mixture over medium heat, stirring constantly, for 8–10 minutes, or until thickened. Beat egg whites until stiff, then beat in ¼ cup sugar. Gradually fold into the tapioca mixture.

Pile tapioca lightly on top of peaches and sprinkle with 1 tablespoon sugar. Bake at 350° for 30 minutes, then at 300° for 15 minutes, or until golden brown. Serve with whipped cream.

YIELD: 6 SERVINGS

THE JUNIOR LEAGUE OF NEW BRITAIN, CONNECTICUT

Pear Roly Poly with Spicy Sauce

1½ cups flour
½ teaspoon salt
¼ cup butter
1 egg
4 tablespoons water
2 tablespoons melted butter
½ cup sugar
2 tablespoons flour
½ teaspoon cinnamon
½ teaspoon nutmeg
3 large pears, peeled, cored, and thinly sliced
2 tablespoons butter

In bowl, mix flour and salt. Cut the ¼ cup butter into flour with fork until mixture is crumbly. Beat egg, add water, and stir into flour mixture until soft dough forms. Roll dough out on floured board to 15 x 12-inch rectangle. Brush dough with melted butter.

Mix sugar, flour, cinnamon, and nutmeg and sprinkle half over melted butter. Arrange sliced pears over sugar mixture and sprinkle remaining sugar over top. Dot with the 2 tablespoons butter.

Starting at narrow end, roll up jelly-roll fashion, sealing edges and ends of roll. Place on greased cookie sheet and bake in 350° oven for 30 minutes. Brush top with some of sugar mixture that bakes out of the roll. Continue baking 15 minutes longer.

Serve warm with Spicy Sauce.

Recipe continues . . .

SPICY SAUCE:
1 large pear, peeled, cored, and diced
1 cup water
½ cup sugar
2 teaspoons cornstarch
¼ teaspoon cinnamon
¼ teaspoon nutmeg
1 teaspoon lemon juice
3 tablespoons butter

Combine pear and water and cook over moderate heat for 10 minutes. Mix sugar, cornstarch, and spices and stir into pear mixture. Cook over low heat for 5 minutes, or until thickened and clear. Add lemon juice and butter and stir until butter is melted.

Slice pear roll and pour sauce over.

YIELD: 6 SERVINGS

THE JUNIOR LEAGUE OF POUGHKEEPSIE, NEW YORK

Pots de Crème

1 6-ounce package semisweet chocolate pieces
1 egg
2 tablespoons sugar
1 teaspoon vanilla
Pinch salt
¾ cup scalded milk
Whipped cream

Put first five ingredients in blender. Add scalded milk. Cover and blend 1 minute on low speed.

Pour into ramekins. Chill several hours. Top with whipped cream if desired.

YIELD: **4** SERVINGS

THE JUNIOR LEAGUE OF HARRISBURG, PENNSYLVANIA

Delaware Rice Pudding

5 cups water
¼ teaspoon salt
¾ cup rice
¾ cup sugar
1 13-ounce can evaporated milk
3 eggs, beaten
½–1 cup raisins
1 tablespoon vanilla
Cinnamon

Bring water and salt to a boil. Add rice and simmer until rice is nearly dry. Add sugar and evaporated milk. Bring to boil again. Add eggs, stirring constantly. Fold in raisins. Cool. Add vanilla and sprinkle cinnamon on top.

YIELD: **6–8** SERVINGS

THE JUNIOR LEAGUE OF WILMINGTON, DELAWARE

Creamy Connecticut Rice Pudding

½ cup rice
1 cup water, lightly salted
1 quart whole milk
4 tablespoons butter
3 eggs
½ cup sugar
½ cup raisins
½ teaspoon vanilla
Cinnamon sugar or cinnamon

Pour rice slowly into rapidly boiling water in a large pot. Cover tightly and cook 7 minutes. Add the milk and butter. Stir and bring to a boil. Cover and cook over low heat for 1 hour (no stirring necessary).

Meanwhile, beat eggs. Add sugar, raisins, and vanilla. Pour the mixture slowly into cooked rice, stirring, until it begins to thicken, usually 1–2 minutes.

Serve hot, warm, or cold with cinnamon or cinnamon sugar sprinkled evenly on top.

YIELD: 4–6 SERVINGS

THE JUNIOR LEAGUE OF NEW BRITAIN, CONNECTICUT

. . . .

Sea Moss Farina

*¼ cup dry sea moss**
1 quart milk
¼ cup honey
1 teaspoon vanilla
Any canned or fresh fruit for topping

Rinse sea moss to clean it. Soak in top of double saucepan with milk for a few minutes, then cook over boiling water for 20 minutes. Do not stir. Remove from heat. Strain milk off the moss.

*Gather Irish moss at next trip to beach and dry it out, or buy agar-agar at health food store.

Into the strained milk stir honey and vanilla. Pour into individual sherbet compotes and let set; chill. Top with canned fruit or fresh strawberries.

YIELD: **4** SERVINGS

THE JUNIOR LEAGUE OF BANGOR, MAINE

. . . .

Zuccotto

Zuccotto is a dome-shaped Florentine speciality inspired by the cupola of Florence's Duomo. The Italian word "zucco" means pumpkin, and this dessert, before it is cut, looks like a pumpkin.

> *1 10–12-ounce rectangular pound cake*
> *¼ cup cognac*
> *¼ cup Cointreau*
> *¼ cup maraschino liqueur (can*
> *substitute with another liqueur)*
> *6 ounces semisweet chocolate pieces*
> *2 cups heavy cream*
> *¾ cup confectioners' sugar*
> *4 ounces almonds, shelled,*
> *peeled, and chopped*

Line a 1½-quart round-bottomed bowl with plastic wrap, allowing wrap to extend over edges of bowl. Before slicing the pound cake, take a 2-inch piece off the end and reserve. Then cut the cake into lengthwise slices, each ¼ inch thick. Cut each slice on the diagonal, making 2 elongated triangles of each slice. There will be a dark crust on one edge of each triangle.

Combine cordials in a shallow flat dish. Very carefully so as not to

Recipe continues . . .

break cake, moisten each triangle one at a time, placing each against the inside of the lined bowl, the pointed end at the bottom center, until the inside of the bowl is completely lined. Where one side of a triangle has crust on it, have it meet the crustless side of the next section to it. (When the dessert is unmolded, the lines of crust should form the indented ribs of a pumpkin.)

Coarsely chop half the chocolate pieces. Then whip the heavy cream with the sugar until stiff and mix into it the almonds and chopped chocolate. Divide this mixture into two equal parts; set aside half; spoon other half into lined bowl, spreading it evenly over the entire surface. This should leave a still unfilled cavity in the center. Melt remaining chocolate; fold chocolate into the remaining whipped cream. Spoon it into the empty cavity and smooth off the top. Patch the bottom with remaining moistened slices of pound cake. Cover with plastic wrap and refrigerate overnight.

YIELD: 8 SERVINGS

From Our House
THE JUNIOR LEAGUE OF HARTFORD, CONNECTICUT

Easiest Pie Crust in History

1 cup shortening
½ cup boiling water
3 cups sifted all-purpose flour
2 teaspoons salt

Beat shortening and boiling water with a fork until shortening is dissolved. Mix flour and salt and stir into liquid. Roll into a ball and refrigerate for at least 15 minutes.

Roll out between sheets of wax paper.

For precooked crusts, bake at 400° for 15–20 minutes, or until golden brown.

YIELD: 3 8-INCH CRUSTS OR 1 12-INCH CRUST

THE JUNIOR LEAGUE OF GREATER BRIDGEPORT, CONNECTICUT

Banana Eclair

PASTRY:
½ cup water
¼ cup butter
¼ teaspoon salt
½ cup flour
2 eggs

FILLING:
2 cups heavy cream
2 tablespoons sugar
2 large ripe bananas, mashed
¼ cup crème de cacao

ICING:
1 cup confectioners' sugar
1/3 cup cocoa
1 tablespoon melted butter
1 teaspoon vanilla
3–4 tablespoons boiling water

Bring water, butter, and salt to boil in saucepan over moderate heat. Add flour all at once, stirring vigorously with spoon until dough leaves sides of pan and forms a ball. Remove from heat and beat in eggs one at a time until dough is stiff and glossy. Set one-third of dough aside.

Recipe continues . . .

On a greased baking sheet, form remaining dough into one oblong 2 inches wide. Spoon reserved dough in mounds along top of oblong. Bake in a 400° oven for 30 minutes.

With a sharp knife, make slits along sides of eclair, 2 inches apart, to let steam escape. Return to oven and bake 5–10 minutes longer. Remove to rack, carefully slice off top, and remove any soft dough left inside. Cool completely.

To make filling: Whip cream until soft peaks form; gradually add sugar and whip until stiff. Fold in mashed bananas and crème de cacao. Fill eclair and replace top.

To make icing: Combine confectioners' sugar, cocoa, melted butter, and vanilla. Stir in enough boiling water to make a thin glaze. Pour over eclair; chill at least 1 hour. Slice crosswise to serve.

YIELD: 8–10 SERVINGS

From Our House
THE JUNIOR LEAGUE OF HARTFORD, CONNECTICUT

Chess Pie

1 cup sugar
½ cup brown sugar
2 tablespoons flour
1 cup chopped walnuts
2/3 cup seeded raisins
3 eggs
2/3 cup milk
2 tablespoons softened butter
1 9-inch pastry-lined pie plate

Combine dry ingredients with walnuts and raisins. Combine eggs, milk, and butter and blend with dry ingredients. Pour into prepared pie plate and bake at 275° for 1¾ hours, or until firm.

YIELD: 1 9-INCH PIE

THE JUNIOR LEAGUE OF THE LEHIGH VALLEY, PENNSYLVANIA

Cranberry Pie

2 cups fresh cranberries
1½ cups sugar
½ cup chopped walnuts
2 eggs
1 cup flour
½ cup melted butter

Spread cranberries over bottom of a greased 10-inch pie pan. Sprinkle with ½ cup of the sugar and the nuts.

Beat eggs, add remaining sugar gradually, and beat until mixed. Add flour and melted butter; mix well.

Pour batter over cranberries. Bake at 350° for 1 hour. Best served warm with ice cream.

Pie may also be dusted with sugar and lemon rind before baking, if desired.

YIELD: 10–12 SERVINGS

THE JUNIOR LEAGUE OF MONMOUTH COUNTY, NEW JERSEY

Concord Grape Pie

Erie County abounds in grape vineyards. During fall's harvesting season the air is sweet with their aroma. This recipe uses the grape juice variety for its filling.

> 3½ cups Concord grapes, picked from stems
> 1½ cups sugar
> 1 cup flour
> ⅛ teaspoon salt
> 1 tablespoon lemon juice
> 2 tablespoons melted butter
> 1 9-inch unbaked pastry shell
> 1/3 cup softened butter

Wash grapes. Slip skins and set aside for use later. Cook pulp until soft over low heat. Press pulp through sieve to remove seeds.

Combine 1 cup sugar, ¼ cup flour, and salt. Add grape skins. Add lemon juice, butter, and grape pulp. Pour into pie shell.

Make crumb topping with remaining ½ cup sugar, flour, and butter. Sprinkle over pie. Bake in preheated 450° oven for 10 minutes. Reduce heat to 350° and continue to bake for 25 minutes. Cool to room temperature before serving.

YIELD: 8 SERVINGS

THE JUNIOR LEAGUE OF ERIE, PENNSYLVANIA

Frozen Lemon Pie

*1/4 cup fine graham cracker or
vanilla wafer crumbs
3 egg whites
1/2 cup sugar
3 egg yolks
1 cup heavy cream
2-3 teaspoons grated lemon rind
1/4-1/3 cup lemon juice*

Butter 9-inch pie plate and sprinkle with crumbs.

Beat egg whites until frothy. Gradually add sugar. Beat until stiff and glossy.

In a separate bowl, beat yolks until thick and lemon-colored. Fold yolks into egg white mixture.

Mix and beat cream until stiff. Add lemon rind and lemon juice. Add whipped cream mixture to egg mixture and blend lightly. Pour into pie plate. If desired, sprinkle top with additional crumbs. Freeze. Remove from freezer a couple of hours before serving.

YIELD: 8 SERVINGS

THE JUNIOR LEAGUE OF KINGSTON, NEW YORK

. . . .

Sfingi (Ricotta Puffs)

This is traditional pastry from Italy

CHEESE FILLING:
*1 pound ricotta cheese
1/3 cup confectioners' sugar
2 tablespoons grated orange peel
2 tablespoons chopped semisweet chocolate
1/4 teaspoon cinnamon*

Recipe continues . . .

PASTRY:

1 cup water
1 tablespoon butter
¼ teaspoon salt
1 cup all-purpose flour
4 eggs
1 teaspoon vanilla
1 quart oil for frying
Confectioners' sugar

To make filling: Beat cheese until smooth. Mix in sugar, orange peel, chocolate, and cinnamon. Refrigerate.

For the pastry: Combine water, butter, and salt in medium saucepan and heat until butter melts. Remove from heat. Stir in flour all at once. Return pot to range. Cook over medium heat, stirring constantly, until mixture leaves sides of pan and forms a ball in center. Cool.

Empty dough into medium bowl. Add eggs, one at a time, beating for 1 minute after each addition. Stir in vanilla.

Heat oil in skillet to 365°. Slip batter from tablespoon into hot oil and fry until golden. Do not crowd, since they will turn by themselves as they cook. Remove and drain.

When ready to serve, split puffs and spoon in cheese filling. Dust with confectioners' sugar.

YIELD: 1 DOZEN PUFFS

Show House Recipes
THE JUNIOR LEAGUE OF BINGHAMTON, NEW YORK

Shoo Fly Pie

2 cups flour
1 cup granulated sugar
1 teaspoon baking powder
¼ pound butter
½ cup brown label molasses
½ cup green label molasses
1 teaspoon baking soda
1 cup boiling water
Pinch salt
1 egg, beaten
2 8-inch pastry-lined pie plates

Sift together flour, sugar, and baking powder. Add butter and mix until crumbs are formed.

In a separate bowl, mix molasses, baking soda, and water. Stir in salt, egg, and 2 cups of the crumbs. Pour into prepared pie pans and sprinkle with remaining crumbs. Bake at 375° for 45 minutes.

YIELD: 2 8-INCH PIES

THE JUNIOR LEAGUE OF THE LEHIGH VALLEY, PENNSYLVANIA

Fresh Squash Pie

2 eggs, lightly beaten
1/2 cup sugar
1/4 cup brown sugar
1 tablespoon molasses
1 tablespoon light corn syrup
1 cup scalded milk, mixed with
1 tablespoon butter
2 cups freshly cooked and mashed squash
1/2 teaspoon salt
1/8 teaspoon ginger
1/4 teaspoon mace
1/8 teaspoon allspice
1/2 teaspoon cinnamon
1 9-inch unbaked pastry shell

Mix together eggs, sugars, molasses, corn syrup, and milk with butter. Add squash and spices. Blend thoroughly.

Pour into unbaked pie shell. Bake 10 minutes in preheated 400° oven. Lower heat to 350° and continue baking for 40 minutes, or until knife inserted into center of pie filling comes out clean.

YIELD: 6–8 SERVINGS

THE JUNIOR LEAGUE OF SCHENECTADY, NEW YORK

Fresh Strawberry Pie

2 pints strawberries
3 tablespoons cornstarch
1 cup sugar
1 cup water
Juice of ½ lemon
1 9-inch baked pastry shell
Whipped cream
A few large strawberries for garnish

Slice strawberries. Put into a saucepan half the strawberries, the cornstarch, sugar, water, and lemon juice. Cook and stir until berries are cooked and mixture is thick. Cool.

When cool, stir in remaining uncooked strawberries. Pour into the baked pastry shell. Chill until firm. Serve with whipped cream and garnish with fresh whole strawberries.

VARIATION:

This pie may be made by substituting blueberries for the strawberries.

YIELD: 1 9-INCH PIE

Show House Recipes
THE JUNIOR LEAGUE OF BINGHAMTON, NEW YORK

Altogether Cake and Frosting

1 8-ounce package cream cheese
½ cup shortening
1 teaspoon vanilla
6 cups confectioners' sugar
1/3 cup warm milk
2/3 cup cocoa
1 teaspoon instant coffee
¼ cup melted shortening
3 eggs, beaten
¾ cup milk
2¼ cups flour
3 teaspoons baking powder
1 teaspoon salt

Combine first seven ingredients and mix well. Divide mixture in half, reserving one half for frosting. To remaining half beat in the shortening, eggs, and milk alternately with the dry ingredients.

Grease and flour two layer cake pans and pour in cake mixture, dividing evenly. Bake at 350° for 30–35 minutes. Frost when cool with reserved frosting.

YIELD: 2 8-INCH LAYER CAKES

Recipes by Request
THE JUNIOR LEAGUE OF GREATER WATERBURY, CONNECTICUT

German Blueberry Cake

1½ cups sifted all-purpose flour
1 cup sugar
Dash salt
½ cup soft butter
4 cups blueberries
1 tablespoon lemon juice
3 tablespoons quick-cooking tapioca
¼ teaspoon salt
⅛ teaspoon cinnamon

Combine flour, ½ cup sugar, dash salt, and butter. Mix with pastry blender or fork until crumbs are formed. Measure ¾ cup and set aside.

Press remaining crumbs over bottom and about ¾ inch up the sides of a 9-inch spring-form pan.

Combine blueberries, lemon juice, remaining ½ cup sugar, tapioca, salt, and cinnamon. Let stand for 15 minutes. Spoon the blueberry mixture into the crumb-lined pan. Bake at 425° for 20 minutes. Then sprinkle with the ¾ cup reserved crumbs. Bake 20–25 minutes longer, or until crumbs are golden brown.

Serve warm or cold with whipped cream.

YIELD: 8–10 SERVINGS

THE JUNIOR LEAGUE OF POUGHKEEPSIE, NEW YORK

Best Fruit Cake

1 pound pitted dates
1 cup drained maraschino cherries
3 cups whole walnuts
³/₄ cup flour
³/₄ cup sugar
¹/₂ teaspoon baking powder
¹/₂ teaspoon salt
3 eggs
1 teaspoon vanilla

Put fruit and nuts in bowl. Sift dry ingredients, resift over fruit, and mix with hands. Beat eggs until foamy, fold in vanilla, and stir into fruit mixture. Spoon into greased loaf pan and bake in 300° oven for 1½ hours.

YIELD: 1 LOAF

Recipes by Request
THE JUNIOR LEAGUE OF GREATER WATERBURY, CONNECTICUT

. . . .

New England Apple-Cranberry Cake

1¹/₄ cups sugar
1 egg
1/3 cup oil
1 cup flour
¹/₂ teaspooon salt
1 teaspoon baking soda
1 teaspoon cinnamon
¹/₄ teaspoon nutmeg
¹/₂ cup coarsely cut cranberries
2 cups shredded apples
1 cup chopped walnuts

Cream together by hand sugar and egg. Add oil. Add all at once flour, salt, soda, cinnamon, and nutmeg. Mix by hand. The mixture will be dry and stiff.

Stir in cranberries, apples, and walnuts. Bake at 350° for 45 minutes in oiled 8 x 8-inch pan, or 1¼ hours in oiled bundt pan.

This is best when served warm with ice cream or whipped cream.

YIELD: 1 SQUARE OR 1 BUNDT CAKE

THE JUNIOR LEAGUE OF BANGOR, MAINE

Pecan Roll

4 eggs, separated
1 cup sifted confectioners' sugar
2 cups ground pecans
1 cup heavy cream
3 teaspoons granulated sugar
2 teaspoons unsweetened cocoa
½ teaspoon vanilla
Additional confectioners' sugar
Pecan halves for garnish

Beat egg yolks and confectioners' sugar together for about 5 minutes, or until thick and pale in color. In a separate bowl, beat egg whites until stiff but not dry. Fold beaten yolk mixture and pecans into whites.

Oil a 15 x 10 x 1-inch pan and line with wax paper; oil paper. Spread batter evenly into pan. Bake at 350° for 15 minutes. Remove and roll up hot cake, paper and all. Cool thoroughly.

To make filling: Combine cream, sugar, cocoa, and vanilla. Beat until soft peaks form. Unroll cake, removing paper, and spread with the chocolate whipped cream. Reroll.

Recipe continues . . .

Chill until serving time. Sprinkle with additional confectioners' sugar and garnish with pecan halves.

YIELD: 10–12 SERVINGS

Greenwich Recommends
THE JUNIOR LEAGUE OF GREENWICH, CONNECTICUT

. . . .

Pumpkin Cake Roll

3 eggs
1 cup sugar
2/3 cup mashed pumpkin
1 teaspoon lemon juice
¾ cup flour
1 teaspoon baking powder
2 teaspoons cinnamon
1 teaspoon ginger
½ teaspoon nutmeg
½ teaspoon salt
1 cup chopped walnuts
Confectioners' sugar

Beat eggs for 5 minutes. Add sugar, pumpkin, and lemon juice. Sift together flour, baking powder, spices, and salt and stir into pumpkin mixture. Add walnuts.

Pour into greased and floured jelly-roll pan (12 x 8 x 1-inch). Bake at 375° for 12–15 minutes. Cool slightly. Turn out onto linen towel. Sprinkle with confectioners' sugar. Gently roll lengthwise and cool seam side down.

When cool, gently unroll. Spread with one of the following fillings. Reroll and gently sift confectioners' sugar over top. Refrigerate.

FILLING #1:

1 cup confectioners' sugar
2 3-ounce packages cream cheese
1 teaspoon vanilla

Cream together ingredients and spread over cooled cake.

FILLING #2:

1 3-ounce package cream cheese
1 cup cool whipped cream
4 tablespoons margarine or butter
1 teaspoon vanilla

Cream together ingredients and spread over cooled cake.

YIELD: 10–12 SERVINGS

THE JUNIOR LEAGUE OF SCHENECTADY, NEW YORK

. . . .

Shoo Fly Cake

4 cups flour
1 pound brown sugar
1 cup butter
2 cups boiling water
1 cup molasses
2 teaspoons baking soda
Pinch salt

Combine flour, sugar, and butter and blend to fine crumbs. Reserve 1½ cups of the crumbs for topping.

Mix together water, molasses, and soda. Add to remaining crumbs. Mix well. Batter will be rather thin. Pour into a well-greased and floured 9 x 13-inch pan.

Recipe continues . . .

Sprinkle the 1½ cups crumb mixture on top. Bake at 350° for 45 minutes.

YIELD: 12–16 SERVINGS

THE JUNIOR LEAGUE OF LANCASTER, PENNSYLVANIA

Brandy Snaps

¼ cup light corn syrup
¼ cup molasses
½ cup butter
1 cup sifted flour
2/3 cup granulated sugar
1 teaspoon ground ginger
2 teaspoons brandy

Preheat oven to 300°.

In a saucepan, heat the syrup and molasses until boiling. Remove from heat and add the butter. Sift together flour, sugar, and ginger. Stir this mixture into the molasses mixture. Mix well and add the brandy.

Drop by the ½ teaspoon, 3 inches apart, on an inverted cookie sheet. Bake 10 minutes and remove from the oven. Loosen one cookie at a time and roll each over the handle of a wooden spoon. Slip off carefully. If the cookies get too hard, they can be softened again by returning to the oven for a few minutes.

YIELD: ABOUT 2 DOZEN COOKIES

THE JUNIOR LEAGUE OF YORK, PENNSYLVANIA

Butter Crescents

½ cup soft butter
3 tablespoons confectioners' sugar
1 cup all-purpose flour
½ cup finely ground English walnuts
⅛ teaspoon vanilla
Additional confectioners' sugar

Cream by hand the butter, 3 tablespoons confectioners' sugar, flour, nuts, and vanilla until blended. Form into a ball and chill for 1–2 hours, or until firm.

Remove dough from refrigerator. Pinch off about 1 rounded teaspoon of the dough at a time. Roll between hands until 2 inches long and about the thickness of a little finger. Bend into the shape of a crescent and place on a well-greased cookie sheet. Bake at 375° for 10–15 minutes. Check crescents after 10 minutes. They should be slightly golden, not brown.

Let cool a few minutes before removing from cookie sheet—they break easily when hot. Cool on wire racks. When still slightly warm, roll lightly in confectioners' sugar. Store in tightly closed container.

YIELD: 50–60 2-INCH COOKIES

THE JUNIOR LEAGUE OF THE LEHIGH VALLEY, PENNSYLVANIA

. . . .

Dessert Baskets

¾ cup quick-cooking oatmeal
½ cup sugar
1/3 cup flour
¼ teaspoon baking powder
6 tablespoons melted butter
2 tablespoons milk
2 tablespoons light corn syrup

Recipe continues . . .

Preheat oven to 375°.

Blend all ingredients. Grease cookie sheet (a non-stick surface is preferred). Drop 1 scant tablespoon for each basket on cookie sheet and spread into a 3½-inch circle (four at a time fit well on cookie sheet). Bake approximately 6 minutes, or until brown. Watch carefully as they burn easily. Cool for about 1 minute.

When able to lift with a spatula, invert over upside-down round glasses or other suitable mold. Shape quickly with hands. Cool and store in airtight container.

These are crunchy and delicious, but do not make them on a humid day. Serve filled with vanilla ice cream and Nesselrode topping.

YIELD: 12 BASKETS

THE JUNIOR LEAGUE OF MORRISTOWN, NEW JERSEY

Harvard Squares

Named for the crimson and white colors of Harvard.

½ pound butter (2 sticks)
1 cup sugar
2 eggs, well beaten
2 cups sifted flour
1 cup chopped walnuts
¾ cup raspberry preserves
Confectioners' sugar

Cream butter and sugar; beat in eggs. Add flour and walnuts and stir well.

Grease an 8 x 8-inch pan and spread half the dough in it. This is best done by scattering half the mixture over the bottom and patting it down. Spread preserves over this to within ½-inch of the edge; cover with remaining dough. Bake at 325° for 1 hour. Cool and sprinkle with confectioners' sugar while still in the pan. Cut into squares.

YIELD: 16 2-INCH SQUARES

THE JUNIOR LEAGUE OF MONMOUTH COUNTY, NEW JERSEY

·   ·   ·   ·   ·   ·   ·   ·   ·   ·   ·   ·   ·   ·   ·   ·   ·   ·

Holiday Roll-Ups

³/₄ cup shortening
2 tablespoons sugar
1 egg, beaten
2½ cups sifted flour
1 teaspoon baking powder
¼ teaspoon salt
¼ cup water
1 12-ounce jar raspberry preserves
2 cups chopped walnuts
2 egg whites, beaten
2 cups sugar

Cream shortening with sugar until smooth. Add the egg. Mix together until well blended.

In a separate bowl, sift together the flour, baking powder, and salt, then add slowly to the creamed shortening mixture. Add water and work dough as for pie dough. Divide dough in half.

Roll out one half at a time into a rectangle on lightly floured board and spread with a thin layer of raspberry preserves. Sprinkle with chopped walnuts. Using a knife edge, carefully lift one edge of the dough and fold inward, then continue to roll into a long roll. Repeat procedure with other half of dough. Bake on cookie sheet in 350° oven for about 1 hour.

Recipe continues . . .

Let cool, then cut at an angle crosswise. Brush pieces with beaten egg white, and coat all sides with granulated sugar.

YIELD: 2½ DOZEN

THE JUNIOR LEAGUE OF TROY, NEW YORK

. . . .

Old-Fashioned Ice Box Cookies

2/3 cup butter
1 cup brown sugar
1 egg
1¾ cups flour
½ teaspoon salt
½ teaspoon cream of tartar
½ teaspoon baking soda
½ cup finely chopped nuts
1 teaspoon vanilla

Cream together the butter and brown sugar. Add the egg and beat well. Add the flour, salt, cream of tartar, baking soda, and nuts. Stir in the vanilla.

Roll the dough in foil and chill overnight. It may be frozen at this point. When ready to bake, slice thinly. Bake on a greased cookie sheet for 5–6 minutes at 350° until slightly brown.

YIELD: ABOUT 4 DOZEN COOKIES

THE JUNIOR LEAGUE OF YORK, PENNSYLVANIA

. . . .

Beverages

OR YOUR SAFETY | POUR VOTRE SECURITE

BEACH BALLS | BALLONS DE PLAGE
FLOATS | FLOTTEURS
ALCOHOLIC DRINKS | BOISSONS
BICYCLES | BICYCLETTES
MOTORCYCLES | MOTOCYCLETTES

RE PROHIBITED | SONT DEFENDUS
N THE BEACH | SUR LA PLAGE

Jefferson's Apple Toddy

Thomas Jefferson often served this punch at Monticello, and continued the tradition in the White House.

6 fresh apples
1 quart boiling water
1½ cups sugar
1 cup brandy
1 cup dark rum
1 cup dry sherry
1 cup Madeira
¼ cup anisette liqueur
¼ cup peach brandy
¼ cup orange liqueur
Dried or fresh apple rings
Nutmeg

Preheat oven to 350°. Bake apples for 50 minutes. Pour boiling water over apples; let stand for 20 minutes. Put apples and liquid through a sieve to remove skins and seeds. (*Or* substitute 1 quart apple cider for baked apples and water.)

Combine apples, liquid, sugar, brandy, rum, sherry, Madeira, anisette, peach brandy, and orange liqueur. Chill overnight. Strain mixture into punch bowl. Garnish with apple rings and nutmeg.

YIELD: 2¼ QUARTS OR 12 6-OUNCE SERVINGS

THE JUNIOR LEAGUE OF SUMMIT, NEW JERSEY

Chatham Artillery Punch

12 cups Catawba wine
1 quart light rum
2 cups gin
2 cups cognac
4 ounces Benedictine
3 cups rye
12 cups strong tea
1¼ pounds brown sugar
Juice of 9 oranges
Juice of 9 lemons
1 small bottle maraschino cherries
6 bottles champagne

Combine first eleven ingredients and chill at least 24 hours. Just before serving, add the champagne.

YIELD: **100** SERVINGS

Before and After Thoughts
THE JUNIOR LEAGUE OF PITTSBURGH, PENNSYLVANIA

. . . .

Festival of Trees Hot Cider

1 gallon cider
¼ teaspoon nutmeg
½ cup brown sugar
4 sticks cinnamon
12 whole cloves
12 whole allspice

Recipe continues . . .

Heat cider, nutmeg, and sugar. Tie cinnamon, cloves, and allspice in a cheesecloth bag. Add bag to cider mixture and simmer for 30 minutes, uncovered. Do not boil.

Pour into a bowl and keep hot on a hot tray.

YIELD: 24 SERVINGS

Greenwich Recommends
THE JUNIOR LEAGUE OF GREENWICH, CONNECTICUT

.　.　.　.　.　.　.　.　.　.　.　.　.　.

Abigail Adams's Champagne Punch

Tea is an unusual addition to this refreshing punch popular for women's gatherings in the 1700s.

1½ cups sugar
1 cup strong black tea
1¾ cups orange juice
Rind of 2 lemons, thinly sliced
½ cup lemon juice
1 cup light or dark rum
1 fifth chilled champagne (26 ounces)
Fresh orange slices and mint sprigs for garnish

Dissolve sugar in tea. Add orange juice, lemon juice and rind, and rum. Chill.

Just before serving, pour rum mixture and champagne over ice in a punch bowl. Garnish with fresh orange slices and mint sprigs.

YIELD: 2 QUARTS OR 16 4-OUNCE DRINKS

THE JUNIOR LEAGUE OF SUMMIT, NEW JERSEY

.　.　.　.　.　.　.　.　.　.　.　.　.　.

Cold Duck Punch

2 bottles Cold Duck
2 cups gin
8 ounces club soda
3/4 cup lemon juice
1/3 cup sugar
1 2-pound block dry ice

Have Cold Duck chilled. Add gin, soda, lemon juice, and sugar, then dry ice.

YIELD: 24 SERVINGS

Before and After Thoughts
THE JUNIOR LEAGUE OF PITTSBURGH, PENNSYLVANIA

Cranberry Daiquiris

Follow directions on a can of frozen daiquiri mix. Fill blender with crushed ice, prepared daiquiri mixture, and approximately 3 tablespoons jellied cranberry sauce. Blend well. Serve in chilled champagne glasses.

YIELD: 6 FROZEN DAIQUIRIS

Entirely Entertaining
THE JUNIOR LEAGUE OF MONTCLAIR-NEWARK, NEW JERSEY

Baltimore Eggnog

1 dozen fresh eggs
12 tablespoons sugar
1 quart milk
1 pint best bourbon
1 pint heavy-bodied rum
1 quart heavy cream
¾ cup peach cordial
Grated nutmeg

Separate the eggs; beat the yolks and add them to the sugar. Gradually work in half the milk. Still stirring, add the bourbon and the rum. Let stand for about 15 minutes, then add the other half of the milk, all of the cream, and all of the peach cordial.

Beat the whites of the eggs until stiff, then fold into the mixture. Sprinkle with nutmeg.

YIELD: 1 GALLON

Before and After Thoughts
THE JUNIOR LEAGUE OF PITTSBURGH, PENNSYLVANIA

Jack Cooper's Eggnog

6 eggs, separated
¾ cup sugar
1 pint heavy cream
1 pint milk
1 pint whiskey
1 ounce rum

Beat egg yolks with ½ cup sugar until thick and lemony. Beat egg whites, gradually add ¼ cup sugar, and continue beating until very stiff. Mix yolks and whites. Stir in cream, milk, whiskey, and rum. Refrigerate until cold.

YIELD: 10–12 SERVINGS

THE JUNIOR LEAGUE OF ALBANY, NEW YORK

Muzzy's Fuzz

Inspired by a stiff North Easter and fresh peaches on the Jersey shore.

1 quart Southern Comfort
1 quart fresh peaches, sliced and
juiced in blender
½ cup lemon juice
½ cup honey

Mix one-third of each ingredient together in blender. Combine all in jug. Pour over ice cubes.

YIELD: 2 QUARTS

The Melting Pot
THE JUNIOR LEAGUE OF THE CENTRAL DELAWARE VALLEY, NEW JERSEY

Kahlúa (Coffee-Flavored Liqueur)

1 quart water
3 cups sugar
10 teaspoons rich instant coffee
4 teaspoons vanilla
1 fifth vodka

Combine water, sugar, and coffee and simmer for 1 hour, stirring occasionally. Let cool. Add vanilla and vodka.

YIELD: 1½ QUARTS

Something Special
THE JUNIOR LEAGUE OF YORK, PENNSYLVANIA

. . . .

The President's Punch

2 quarts ginger ale
1 quart pink champagne
1 quart rosé wine
1 11-ounce can Mandarin oranges
1 pint fresh strawberries or
1 10-ounce package frozen berries

In advance, freeze one quart ginger ale into ice cubes.

In punch bowl, pour 1 quart pink champagne, 1 quart wine, and 1 quart ginger ale. Add frozen ginger ale cubes, Mandarin oranges, and strawberries.

YIELD: 32 SERVINGS

THE JUNIOR LEAGUE OF SYRACUSE, NEW YORK

. . . .

Hot Buttered Rum

1 pound dark brown sugar
½ pound butter, softened
1 teaspoon nutmeg
1 teaspoon cinnamon
1 pint vanilla ice cream

To make base, cream sugar and butter; add remaining ingredients and beat until smooth. Spoon into freezer container and store in freezer.

To make hot buttered rum as needed, spoon 2–3 heaping tablespoons of base in a large mug and add boiling water and 1½ ounces dark rum. Stir well and serve.

YIELD: **20–25** SERVINGS

THE JUNIOR LEAGUE OF FALL RIVER, MASSACHUSETTS

. . . .

Frozen Strawberry Daiquiri

1 6-ounce can frozen lemonade concentrate
6 ounces water
1 10-ounce package frozen strawberries
6 ounces light rum
8–10 ice cubes

Put all ingredients into blender except ice cubes. Blend together and add cubes 2 or 3 at a time until all cubes are used and mixture is frozen to a mush.

YIELD: **6** SERVINGS

THE JUNIOR LEAGUE OF WILKES-BARRE, PENNSYLVANIA

. . . .

Whisper

1 pint vanilla ice cream
1 ounce brandy
1 ounce crème de cacao
2 ounces black coffee

Mix all ingredients in a blender and refrigerate. Blend quickly before pouring into cocktail glasses.

YIELD: 4 DRINKS

THE JUNIOR LEAGUE OF ROCHESTER, NEW YORK

. . . .

Mulled Wine

2 cups water
1 cup sugar
4 cloves
4 sticks cinnamon
2 lemons, thinly sliced
1 bottle red wine
1 sherry glass brandy

Boil water, sugar, and spices for 5 minutes. Add lemons and let stand for 10 minutes. Add wine and brandy and heat but do not boil.
    Serve immediately.

YIELD: 12 SERVINGS

THE JUNIOR LEAGUE OF SPRINGFIELD, MASSACHUSETTS

. . . .

Condiments

Blackberry and Rhubarb Jam

1 quart blackberries
½ cup water
4 cups diced rhubarb
2 cups sugar
2 cups corn syrup

Pick over berries and cook slowly with water for 10 minutes. Rub through a sieve to remove seeds. Combine all ingredients and cook 20–25 minutes, stirring frequently to prevent sticking. Pour into hot, sterilized glasses and seal with paraffin.

YIELD: 5 GLASSES

THE JUNIOR LEAGUE OF STAMFORD-NORWALK, CONNECTICUT

. . . .

Grandmother's Bread and Butter Pickles

8 cups thinly sliced small cucumber
2 cups thinly sliced onion
1½ tablespoons pickling salt
6 green peppers, sliced into thin strips
2 teaspoons celery seed
1 stick cinnamon
3 cups sugar
2 cups vinegar

In a preserving kettle or enamel pot, combine cucumber, onion, and pickling salt. Let stand 1 hour, then drain.

Add remaining ingredients, bring to a boil, and boil for 20 minutes. Pack in sterilized jars.

YIELD: 8–10 PINTS

THE JUNIOR LEAGUE OF GREATER BRIDGEPORT, CONNECTICUT

. . . .

Cranberry Chutney

1 cup water
4 cups fresh cranberries
1 cup raisins
2 cups sugar
½ teaspoon ginger
½ teaspoon cinnamon
¼ teaspoon allspice
¼ teaspoon salt
1 8-ounce can pineapple,
chopped and drained

Combine water, cranberries, raisins, sugar, spices, and salt in a large saucepan. Mix well and cook over medium heat until the cranberries pop and the mixture begins to thicken, about 20 minutes. Stir in the drained pineapple. Continue cooking for an additional 20 minutes, or until the sauce has reached the desired consistency.

Cool and store in the refrigerator for up to two weeks. Delicious with fish or poultry.

YIELD: 5 CUPS

Presenting Boston . . . A Cookbook
THE JUNIOR LEAGUE OF BOSTON, MASSACHUSETTS

Autumn Harvest Chutney

3 cups peeled, seeded, diced tomato
2 cups diced fresh pears
1 cup peeled, chopped apple
½ cup raisins
1 cup halved green grapes
1 green pepper, chopped
2 medium onions, chopped
1 cup brown sugar
¾ cup white vinegar
½ teaspoon ginger
½ teaspoon dry mustard
⅛ teaspoon cayenne

Combine all ingredients. Bring to a boil and cook for 1 hour, or until mixture thickens.

Pack in sterilized jars and process in hot water bath for 10 minutes. Store in a cool, dark area.

YIELD: 6 HALF-PINT JARS

THE JUNIOR LEAGUE OF GREATER UTICA, NEW YORK

· · · · · · · · · · · · · · · · · ·

Curried Fruit

2 28-ounce cans mixed fruit chunks
1 cup dried apricots, soaked 1–2 hours
2 oranges, peeled, seeded, and thinly sliced
1 8-ounce can pear halves
1 9-ounce package frozen dark sweet cherries
1/3 cup butter
1 tablespoon curry powder
2/3 cup brown sugar

Drain fruit and arrange in shallow casserole. Melt butter with curry powder and pour over fruit. Sprinkle with brown sugar. Bake uncovered in 325° oven for 45 minutes.

Remove from oven and let stand for at least 2 hours for flavors to blend. Reheat for 15 minutes before serving. Excellent with ham or pork.

YIELD: 6 SERVINGS

THE JUNIOR LEAGUE OF WILMINGTON, DELAWARE

· · · · · · · · · · · · · · · · · · ·

Green Tomato Relish

3-4 pounds green tomatoes
6 large onions
12-18 peppers
3½ cups vinegar
6 cups sugar
2 tablespoons pickling spice
2 tablespoons cloves
1 tablespoon broken stick cinnamon
2 tablespoons mustard seeds
1 tablespoon celery seeds

Grind tomatoes, onions, and peppers and drain. Combine in preserving kettle and cook for 15 minutes. Add vinegar, sugar, the pickling spice and cloves tied in a cloth bag, and other spices. Boil 15 minutes more. Cool. Remove spice bag.

Bottle in clean quart or pint jars.

YIELD: 8 QUARTS

THE JUNIOR LEAGUE OF ROCHESTER, NEW YORK

· · · · · · · · · · · · · · · · · · ·

Green Tomato and Cabbage Relish

2 pounds onions
1 pound green peppers
5 pounds green tomatoes
3½ pounds cabbage
5 cups sugar
2 tablespoons white mustard seeds
2 tablespoons celery seeds
2 tablespoons salt
2 quarts vinegar

Peel onions and seed green peppers. Put all vegetables through food chopper using medium blade. Combine all ingredients. Cook until vegetables are tender and sauce is slightly thickened, about 20 minutes, stirring occasionally. Pour boiling hot into hot, sterilized containers. Seal.

YIELD: 10–12 PINTS

THE JUNIOR LEAGUE OF WILMINGTON, DELAWARE

. . . .

Hudson Valley Pickles

4 quarts sliced cucumber
6 medium onions, sliced
2 green peppers, seeded and
chopped or sliced
3 cloves garlic, sliced
½ cup sliced carrot
1 cup cucumber blossoms
½ cup salt
4½ cups sugar
2¾ cups vinegar
2¼ teaspoons celery seeds
2 teaspoons pickling spices

Combine vegetables in a large bowl and sprinkle with the salt. Cover with 2–3 trays of ice cubes, cover, and let stand 3 hours. Drain.

In large preserving kettle, combine sugar, vinegar, celery seeds, and spices. Bring to a boil. Add vegetables; bring to a boil again. Pack in hot jars.

YIELD: 7–8 PINTS

THE JUNIOR LEAGUE OF TROY, NEW YORK

Jezebel Sauce

This is hot stuff! Excellent with ham, roast pork, cold meats.

1 12-ounce jar apple jelly
1 12-ounce jar pineapple preserves
1 5-ounce bottle horseradish
1 1½-ounce can dry mustard

Blend all ingredients thoroughly. Refrigerate. Serve as a meat accompaniment.

Keeps 6–8 weeks in refrigerator. Also great to package in half-pint jars and give as gifts.

YIELD: ABOUT 3 CUPS

From Our House
THE JUNIOR LEAGUE OF HARTFORD, CONNECTICUT

Sweet Hot Mustard

¾ cup dry mustard
¾ cup white sugar
1 tablespoon flour
1 teaspoon salt
2 eggs, beaten
1 cup evaporated milk or light cream
¾ cup white vinegar

Mix dry ingredients. Slowly add beaten eggs and milk. Slowly add vinegar. Cook over medium heat until thickened.
Store in tightly covered jar in refrigerator.

YIELD: 2½ CUPS

THE JUNIOR LEAGUE OF HAMILTON-BURLINGTON, ONTARIO

. . . .

Raisin Sauce

1 cup raisins
1 cup brown sugar
1 tablespoon cider vinegar
1 tablespoon flour
½ cup water or ¼ cup dry
sherry and ¼ cup water
Dash salt
⅛ teaspoon vanilla (optional)
2 tablespoons butter

Into a 3-cup heavy saucepan, put raisins and brown sugar. Mix vinegar, flour, and liquid and add to pan. Cook over medium heat, stirring constantly, until sauce begins to thicken. Add salt and vanilla and cook for 1 minute. Remove from heat and stir in butter. Serve hot.

This sauce keeps a week or so in the refrigerator. It can also be frozen and reheated months later. Great with baked ham.

YIELD: ABOUT 2 CUPS

THE JUNIOR LEAGUE OF THE LEHIGH VALLEY, PENNSYLVANIA

Red Pepper Jam

1 dozen sweet red peppers
1 tablespoon salt
1 pint white vinegar
3 cups sugar

Seed peppers and grind in a blender, food processor, or meat grinder. Mix with salt and let stand for 3 hours. Drain well.

Empty peppers into large pot and add vinegar. Simmer for 1–2 hours, or until the consistency of jam. Pour into small jars (baby food jars are ideal) and seal with paraffin.

Do not double this recipe.

Pour red pepper jam over cream cheese for a great appetizer. Serve with crackers.

YIELD: 7–8 SMALL JARS

THE JUNIOR LEAGUE OF BUFFALO, NEW YORK

North Country Chili Sauce

13 pounds tomatoes
1 pound celery, chopped
4 cups chopped onion
4 green peppers, chopped
½ tablespoon ground cloves
1 tablespoon dry mustard
2 sticks cinnamon
2 pounds brown sugar
¼ cup pickling salt
1 quart cider vinegar

Scald tomatoes; peel. Cook in large kettle over medium heat for 15 minutes; drain off two-thirds of the juice. Combine remaining vegetables, add to tomatoes, and simmer for 1½ hours.

Tie spices in cheesecloth bag. Add spices and vinegar to vegetable mixture and continue to cook 1½ hours longer. Remove spices; ladle mixture into hot sterilized jars. Seal; leaving ½-inch headspace. Process in hot water bath for 5 minutes.

YIELD: 6 PINTS

THE JUNIOR LEAGUE OF GREATER UTICA, NEW YORK

· · · · · · · · · · · · · · · · · · ·

Hot Tomato Chili Sauce

15 very ripe, medium tomatoes
6 hot red peppers
7 small onions
1½ cups white vinegar
2 cups granulated sugar
2 teaspoons salt

Wash, peel, and cut the tomatoes into quarters. Discard seeds from the peppers and chop peppers finely. Cut the onions finely. Boil all ingredients together for 3–5 hours, or until sauce is thick. Pour into jars and seal.

YIELD: 8–10 12-OUNCE JARS

THE JUNIOR LEAGUE OF HAMILTON-BURLINGTON, ONTARIO

· · · · · · · · · · · · · · · · · · ·

Tomato Marmalade

Double, triple, or quadruple this recipe to use excess garden tomatoes. Serve with cream cheese or cold meats.

Garden ripe tomatoes
3 lemons, seeded and chopped in
blender or food processor
1 large orange, seeded and chopped in
blender or food processor
6 cups sugar
1 cup sweet sherry

Squeeze excess moisture and seeds from tomatoes and chop enough to measure 6 cups. Put into a large pan with all remaining ingredients. Let stand 8 hours or overnight at room temperature.

Bring mixture to a boil and cook over medium heat for about 1¼ hours, or until thickened, stirring frequently to prevent burning on the bottom. Pour into sterilized jars and seal.

YIELD: 8 CUPS

From Our House
THE JUNIOR LEAGUE OF HARTFORD, CONNECTICUT

· · · · · · · · · · · · · · · ·

Two-Pound Pickles

2 pounds red or green tomatoes
2 pounds onions
1 sweet red pepper
2 pounds MacIntosh apples
2 pounds brown sugar
1½ tablespoons salt
1 pint cider vinegar
Small cheesecloth bag of whole spices

Chop vegetables and apples finely and mix together in preserving kettle with remaining ingredients. Boil for 1½ hours, or until thick. Remove cheesecloth bag. Pour into sterilized jars and seal.

YIELD: APPROXIMATELY 8 8-OUNCE JARS

THE JUNIOR LEAGUE OF HAMILTON-BURLINGTON, ONTARIO

• • • • • • • • • • • • • • • • • • • •

Pickled Watermelon Rind

Rind of ½ large watermelon
2 cups vinegar
6 cups sugar
2 teaspoons whole cloves
4 cinnamon sticks

Cut watermelon rind into bite-size pieces and cook in water to cover until barely tender. Drain.

Boil vinegar and sugar until clear. Tie spices in a cheesecloth bag and add to boiling syrup. Add drained watermelon rind to syrup and cool overnight.

Next day heat rind in syrup and cool overnight. Repeat for 2–3 days, or until rind is glossy and transparent. Discard spice bag, pack in sterilized jars and seal.

YIELD: APPROXIMATELY 10 PINTS

THE JUNIOR LEAGUE OF HARRISBURG, PENNSYLVANIA

Order Information

Many of the recipes for *The Eastern Junior League Cookbook* have been selected from the cookbooks published by the individual Junior Leagues. To obtain a particular League's own book of recipes, send a check or money order plus a complete return address to the appropriate address listed below. (Price of all cookbooks subject to change.)
All proceeds from the sale of cookbooks will be used for charitable purposes.

Show House Recipes
The Junior League of Binghamton
435 Main Street, Room 219
Johnson City, New York 13790
Price per copy: $7.00
Postage per copy: $1.00
Make checks payable to: *Show House Recipes*

Presenting Boston . . . A Cookbook
The Junior League of Boston, Inc.
117 Newbury Street
Boston, Massachusetts 02116
Price per copy: $7.95
Postage per copy: $1.25
Massachusetts residents add 40¢ sales tax per copy.
Make checks payable to: *Presenting Boston . . .*

The Melting Pot, published by the Junior League of the Central Delaware Valley, is out of print and not available for sale.

New York Entertains
Published by Doubleday & Company, Inc.
Available at bookstores or from:
The Junior League of the City of New York
130 East 80th Street
New York, New York 10021
Price per copy: $10.00
Postage per copy: $1.65
Make checks payable to: Junior League of the City of New York

Simply Superb
The Junior League of Elizabeth-Plainfield
110 Walnut Avenue
Cranford, New Jersey 07016
Price per copy: $6.95
Postage per copy: $1.25
New Jersey residents add 35¢ sales tax per copy
Make checks payable to: *Simply Superb*

Cooks Book
The Junior League of Greater New Haven, Inc.
Junior League` Shop, Inc.
258 Church Street
New Haven, Connecticut 06510
Price per copy: $4.95
Postage per copy: 85¢
Connecticut residents add 7% sales tax per copy.
Make checks payable to: Junior League Shop, Inc.

Recipes by Request
The Junior League of Greater Waterbury, Inc.
Box 1962
Waterbury, Connecticut 06708
Price per copy: $3.00
Postage per copy: $1.00
Make checks payable to: Junior League of Greater Waterbury, Inc.

Greenwich Recommends
Junior League of Greenwich, Inc.
Mead House
48 Maple Avenue
Greenwich, Connecticut 06830
Price per copy: $5.50
Postage per copy: 65¢
Connecticut residents add 39¢ tax per book.
Make checks payable to: The Junior League of Greenwich, Inc.

From Our House, published by The Junior League of Hartford, Inc., is out of
print and not available for sale.

Culinary Creations
The Junior League of Kingston, N.Y., Inc.
U.P.O. Box 3464
Kingston, New York 12401
Price per copy: $4.00
Postage per copy: 47¢
New York residents add 28¢ sales tax per copy.
Make checks payable to: The Junior League of Kingston

Entirely Entertaining
The Junior League of Montclair-Newark, Inc.
P.O. Box 814
Upper Montclair, New Jersey 07043
Price per copy: $5.95

Postage per copy: $1.00
New Jersey residents add 30¢ sales tax per copy.
Make checks payable to: *Entirely Entertaining*

The Everyday Gourmet
Junior League of Northern Westchester
Box 333, Depot Plaza
Bedford Hills, New York 10507
Price per copy: $8.50
Postage per copy: $1.00
New York residents add 5% sales tax per copy.
Make checks payable to: *The Everyday Gourmet*

Bicentennial Cookbook: Revolutionary Settings Varied Parties
Published by Chilton Book Company
Available at bookstores or from:
The Junior League of Philadelphia
Free Quaker Meeting House
Fifth and Arch Streets
Philadelphia, Pennsylvania 19106
Price per copy: $7.95
Postage per copy: $1.25
Pennsylvania residents add 48¢ sales tax per copy.
Make checks payable to: The Junior League of Philadelphia

Before and After Thoughts, published by The Junior League of Pittsburgh, Pennsylvania, is out of print and not available for sale.

A Taste of History
The Junior League of Poughkeepsie, Inc.
Room 226, New Tower Building
Vassar Hospital
Reade Place
Poughkeepsie, New York 12601
Price per copy: $3.00
Postage per copy: 50¢
New York residents add 21¢ sales tax per copy.
Make checks payable to: The Junior League of Poughkeepsie, Inc.

Hors D'Oeuvres Cookbook
The Junior League of Reading, Pennsylvania, Inc.
Trent and Belmont Avenues
Wyomissing, Pennsylvania 19610
Price per copy: $4.00
Postage per copy: $1.25
Pennsylvania residents add 24¢ sales tax per copy.
Make checks payable to: The Junior League of Reading, Pennsylvania, Inc.

Applehood & Motherpie, by The Junior League of Rochester, will be available in February, 1981. For more information, write to:
The Junior League of Rochester, Inc.
33 S. Washington Street
Rochester, New York 14608

5 O'Clock Sustainers
Junior League of Scranton
232 Wyoming Avenue
Scranton, Pennsylvania 18503
Price per copy (postpaid): $2.75
Make checks payable to: Junior League of Scranton

Hudson River Hospitality
The Junior League of Westchester-on-Hudson, Inc.
35 South Broadway
Tarrytown, New York 10591
Hudson River Hospitality is in the pre-publication planning stage. Further inquiries may be directed to the above address.

Something Special
The Junior League of York, Pennsylvania
166 West Market Street
York, Pennsylvania 17401
Price per copy: $3.50
Postage per copy: 70¢
Pennsylvania residents add 21¢ sales tax per copy.
Make checks payable to: Cookbook, Junior League of York

Index

Cassoulet, Lentil, 251–252
Cauliflower
    Shrimp Salad, 305–306
    Soup, Chelmsford, 50
Cavatelli with Broccoli, 255
Caviar Eggplant, 20–21
Celery
    Braised, 279
    and Broccoli Salad, 294
Chablis, Swordfish Steaks with, 180
Champagne Punch, Abigail Adams's, 388
Charlotte Russe, Fresh Lemon, 354–355
Chatham Artillery Punch, 387
Cheddar Beer Dip, 15–16
Cheese, 225–236
    Artichokes au Gratin, 271–272
    Berege, 226–227
    Bread, Father Samanski's, 225
    Chicken Chowder, 52
    Featherweight Cottage Cheese Pan-
        cakes, 227
    Fondue, 25
    Frozen Soufflé with Broccoli Sauce,
        233–234
    Laurana's Cottage Cheese Roast, 228
    Little Pancakes Filled with, 229–230
    Mousse, 28–29
    -Mushroom Rolls, 4
    Mushrooms au Gratin, 265
    Pennies, 26
    Pimento Dip, 16
    Puffs, Brooklyn, 26–27
    Puffs, Reading, 27
    Rarebit à la Italienne, 233
    Romanoff, 347–348
    Sesame Straws, 28
    Skyscraper Soufflé with Crabmeat
        Sauce, 235–236
    Strata, 226
    Veal Scallopini with, 108
    -Vegetable Casserole, 232
    Zucchini Puff, 231
    See also names of cheeses
Chelmsford Cauliflower Soup, 50
Cherries Jubilee, 348
Cherry Tomatoes, Zucchini with, 289
Chess Pie, 366–367

Chicken, 130–166
    Apricot, 140
    Baked, in Savory Sauce, 164
    Bianco, 145
    Bisque Normande, 51
    Brandied, 136–137
    Breasts with Brandy, 157
    Breasts with Garlic Cream and
        Onions, 148
    Breasts in Phyllo Pastry, 142–144
    Breasts with Sour Cream, 151
    Breasts in Sour Cream Lemon Sauce,
        152–153
    Breasts Wellington, 156
    Caribbean, 163–164
    Cheese Chowder, 52
    Chinese, 142
    Cold Dodine of, 139
    for Company, Diana's, 160
    and Fruit Salad, 298
    Garlic, 137
    Herbed Breasts, 157–158
    Hot Chinese Salad, 161
    with Lemon and Raisins, 133
    Mandarin Breasts, 150
    Mediterranean, 141
    Momi, 145–146
    Nuggets, 29
    Opulent, 147
    Orange, 153–154, 155
    Oven-Baked Delaware Valley, 162
    Oyster Stifle, 131
    Piccata, 154–155
    Pollo alla Florentine, 159
    and Potatoes, Baked, 136
    Reunion, 149
    Salad, Swedish, 297
    Sauté au Parmesan, 135
    Sour Cream, 158
    Stuffed under Its Skin, 130
    Supreme, 165–166
    in Tarragon Cream Sauce, 132
    Überraschung, 138
    Valley, 134
    Wings, Parmesan, 165
    Wrapped Breasts, 152
Chicken Liver Pâté, 17

Genesee Country Sauerkraut Salad,
296–297
German Blueberry Cake, 375
German Potato Salad, 302–303
Gingerbread, Old-Fashioned Hot Water,
323–324
Glaze, Vinegar, Sautéed Calves' Liver
with, 113–114
Goose, Roast, 171–172
Goulash, Hungarian, 122–123
Gourmet Potatoes, 276
Grains, 251–253, 257–258
Barley Casserole, 253
Lentil Cassoulet, 251–252
Mushroom Almond Rice, 258
Purée of Lentils, 252–253
Rice Pilaf, 257
Rice Savoy, 257–258
See also names of grains
Grand Marnier Mousse, Frozen, 352
Grandma's Raisin Bread, 327
Grandmother's Bread and Butter Pick-
les, 396
Grape Leaves, Stuffed (Dolmas), 98–99
Grape-Nut Shredded Wheat Bread, 321
Grape Pie, 368
Great Lakes Salmon with Crabmeat
Stuffing, 177–178
Great Roast, 74
Green Onion Soup, 65
Greens, Sweet and Sour Sauce for, 314
Green Tomato Relish, 399
with Cabbage, 400
Greenwich Coquilles Saint Jacques,
201–202

Halibut Royale, 178
Ham
and Pork Loaf, Sweet, 122
Puffs, 32
Rolls, Delightful, 2
Haricots Verts, 263
Harvard Squares, 382–383
Hash, Yankee Red Flannel, 91
Hearty Minestrone Soup, 61
Herb Basted Rack of Lamb, 96–97
Herbed Chicken Breasts, 157–158

Herbed Clam Sauce, Linguine with, 246
Herbed Shrimp Scampi, 214
Herbed Spinach Bake, 280
Hodge Podge Vegetables, 264
Holiday Roll-Ups, 383–384
Hollandaise Mustard, Beignets Soufflés
aux Fromages with, 24–25
Homemade Noodles, 238
Honey Bread, 318
Whole Wheat, 319
Hot Buttered Rum, 393
Hot Chinese Chicken Salad, 161
Hot Cider, Festival of Trees, 387–388
Hot Clam Cracker Spread, 18
Hot Crab, 19
Hot Dogs, Bourbon, 2–3
Hot Spinach Salad, 307
Hot Tomato Chili Sauce, 404–405
Hudson Valley Pickles, 400–401
Hungarian Goulash, 122–123

Iced Blueberry Brûlée, 346
Imperial Crab, 193
Inlet Bluefish, 174

Jack Cooper's Eggnog, 390–391
Jam
Blackberry and Rhubarb, 396
Red Pepper, 403
Jayhawk Noodles, 242
Jefferson's Apple Toddy, 386
Jezebel Sauce, 401
Joanne's Lamb Curry, 100–101
Juicy Meat Loaf, 90

Kahlúa (Coffee-Flavored Liqueur), 392
Kielbasa, Black Bean Soup with, 40
Kuchen, Country Apple, 342

Lamb, 94–101
Agneau à la Moutarde, 96
Chasseur, 95
Curry, 97–98
Dolmas (Stuffed Grape Leaves), 98–99
Herb Basted Rack of, 96–97
Joanne's Curry, 100–101
Korma Curry, 92

Wine
 Mulled, 394
 and Mushrooms en Casserole, 269
 Scallops in, 200–201
Winter Beef Vegetable Soup, 42
Wrapped Chicken Breasts, 152

Yankee Red Flannel Hash, 91
Yugoslavian Barbecue, 82–83
Yugoslavian Vegetable Casserole,
 287–288

Zesty Zucchini, 291
Zucchini, 286–291
 Boats, 288

 with Cherry Tomatoes, 289
 in Cream, 289–290
 Cream Soup, 70–71
 Fritters, 290
 and Lamb Casserole, 99–100
 and Potato Soup, Curried, 72
 Puff, 231
 with Sour Cream and Dill, 291
 Sour Cream Soup, 71
 Tomato Salad, 313
 -Tomato Scallop, 286
 Tourlou Tava, 286–287
 Yugoslavian Vegetable Casserole,
 287–288
 Zesty, 291
Zuccotto, 363–364